AF607889

COGNITIVE DISABILITY AESTHETICS

Visual Culture, Disability Representations, and the (In)Visibility of Cognitive Difference

COGNITIVE DISABILITY AESTHETICS

Visual Culture, Disability Representations, and the (In)Visibility of Cognitive Difference

BENJAMIN FRASER

UNIVERSITY OF TORONTO PRESS
Toronto Buffalo London

Toronto Buffalo London
utorontopress.com

ISBN 978-1-4875-0233-1

Toronto Iberic

Library and Archives Canada Cataloguing in Publication

Fraser, Benjamin, author
Cognitive disability aesthetics : visual culture, disability representations, and the (in)visibility of cognitive difference / Benjamin Fraser.

(Toronto Iberic ; 32)
Includes bibliographical references and index.
ISBN 978-1-4875-0233-1 (cloth)

1. Disability studies. 2. Aesthetics. 3. Cognition disorders – Social aspects – Spain. 4. Popular culture – Spain. 5. Arts – Spain. I. Title. II. Series: Toronto Iberic ; 32

HV1568.2.F73 2018 704.9'496168 C2017-906090-2

This book has been published with the assistance of the Thomas Harriot College of Arts and Sciences at East Carolina University.

University of Toronto Press acknowledges the financial assistance to its publishing program of the Canada Council for the Arts and the Ontario Arts Council, an agency of the Government of Ontario.

Canada Council for the Arts   Conseil des Arts du Canada

Funded by the Government of Canada   Financé par le gouvernement du Canada

For Ben, Abby, and Judd

Contents

Preface

Three book-length publications are arguably the foundational contributions to the study of physical disability representations in the aesthetic realm: Martin Norden's *Cinema of Isolation: A History of Physical Disabilities in the Movies* (1994), which traces the centrality of disabled characters in one hundred years of American film; David Mitchell and Sharon Snyder's innovative and foundational *Narrative Prosthesis: Disability and the Dependencies of Discourse* (2000), which privileges the nuances of literary disability representation; and Tobin Siebers's *Disability Aesthetics* (2010), which brought a similarly innovative thesis to bear on visual art forms, prioritizing painting and sculpture. Norden writes that "the history of physical disability images in the movies has mostly been a history of distortion in the name of maintaining an ableist society" (1994: 314). Mitchell and Snyder's book "argues that images of disabled people abound in history" (2000: 52) and that "once a reader begins to seek out representations of disability in our literatures, it is difficult to avoid their proliferation in texts with which one believed oneself to be utterly familiar" (2000: 52). Siebers's argument asserts that in painting and sculpture, the presence of disability is the element that has allowed "the beauty of an artwork to endure over time" (2010: 5). The representation of disability is, each text argues in its own way, thus central to the aesthetic histories of these directions in human cultural production. Often under-acknowledged as such in both literary and visual art, physical disability has long been clothed in the normative trappings of an able-bodied society and mobilized to suit a range of symbolic, metaphorical, and perhaps even purportedly transcendent artistic purposes.

This direction in disability studies research has proven essential to an interdisciplinary field that is at once an academic and a political project (Davis 1997: 1). In launching a powerful critique of what Rosemarie Garland-Thomson (1997) termed the normate, it has extended the force of disability rights movements into aesthetic arenas where systems of social power and their consequences for bodily difference can be rendered visible, dissected, and critiqued – with implications for the extra-textual world, of course. In prioritizing aesthetics and cultural production, disability studies research has not only called attention to the value of textual analysis and humanistic work more generally, but also reasserted the materiality of culture and highlighted the imbrication of thought and action. Nonetheless, to the extent that such high-profile previous studies have privileged physical over cognitive disabilities, these invaluable contributions have left part of the picture unclear. To date, and speaking broadly, a certain invocation of the visible world has driven the study of both literary and visual representations of disability. That is, the concept of the visible in existing disability studies research is largely synonymous with the physical in a simple sense. The critique of able-bodied bias in film, literature, and visual art has tended to centre on the way in which the physical or material body – again, in a sense that largely marginalizes the cognitive – has been mobilized for another purpose. A visible trait, a mark, a scar, a missing limb, a deformity, a limp, a physical impairment … in ableist cultural production, historically speaking, these are taken to be signs of evil, of corruption, of moral decline, and so on. Or, on the other hand, the exceptional body is problematically taken to be a vehicle to salvation or redemption in a process that symbolically others the extraordinary body in order to reaffirm the centrality of myths associated with able-bodied norms.

It is important to note that to date, in scholarship exploring the aesthetic realm, the physically disabled body in literature has been seen as a form or shape relating to a symbolic experience. Mitchell and Snyder write of disability in a range of specific works in which "the meaning of the relationship between having a physical disability and the nature of a character's identity come under scrutiny. Disability recurs in these works as a potent force that challenges cultural ideals of the 'normal' or 'whole' body" (2000: 50). The books and essay-length studies that have directed similar insights towards specific instances of Anglophone literary and cultural production are too numerous to mention here. This research is important in its own right. It is equally important, however, to recognize that the social and political need for such academic work centred on the physical – and also its power and potential – stems from the need to respond to a very specific form of bodily oppression, one that is more visible in society than that involving embodied cognitive disability. The point is to understand the power and potential of this research on physically oriented disability while recognizing that it is an academic and political reaction to very specific social circumstances – and not necessarily an attempt to address all constructions of disability that obtain in society. That is, in seeking to combat able-bodied society's highly visible and historical marginalization and oppression of physical disability in particular, this strain of disability studies has largely focused on the appearance of physical disability throughout social history and in the aesthetic realm. The interplay between inner reality and outward appearance has been a key part of physical disability representations – as Norden, Mitchell and Snyder, and Siebers illustrate with reference to work by numerous authors and critics – and thus it makes sense that analysis of this particular interplay would be so essential to the social and political critique launched by disability studies in the period I refer to as the first wave of disability studies in the humanities.

Readers of this book may find it to be provocative on many counts. In identifying the need to pay more attention to cognitive disabilities as the defining characteristic of a second wave of disability studies, I join a growing group of scholars who in one way or another have called for a move beyond the physical orientation of much disability studies research. In addition, some readers may conclude that in underscoring the material reality of cognitive impairment as I do here – in seeing cognitive impairment not solely as a cultural construction but also as a material experience connected with biological or developmental factors – I sacrifice the strong constructivist tradition of disability studies. Moreover, my suggestion that an acknowledgment of the material reality of severe cognitive impairments can connect the social model of disability so strongly embraced in the humanities with the medical, clinical, and health sciences, may seem a betrayal to some. From the outset, I admit a friction and even a sharp divergence between the goals of a social model of disability and a medical model of disability. I nonetheless assert that a clean break between social and medical paradigms is neither possible nor entirely desirable when approaching the topic of cognitive disability, in particular regarding those experiences of cognitive disability that tend to be considered severe.

As I am myself a cognitively abled scholar, this perspective may invite certain criticisms. Anticipating those criticisms, let me say that I can imagine a society in which it is not necessary for some to speak on behalf of those with severe cognitive disabilities, but that such a society is not the one in which we find ourselves. In this society there are populations who experience severe cognitive impairment and who are not able to communicate their needs in the way required by normative ableist power structures. While some members of these populations may have advocates and allies at the small scale, or at the larger scale in disability movements, there are many who do not. It is important to recognize that disability scholars in the humanities have not traditionally explored the social realities or cultural representations relevant to those with cognitive disabilities. Neither have they explored the distinct needs these populations may have related to severe cognitive impairments. My hope is that these provocations do not prove too much of an obstacle for readers. I believe that considering these issues through their appearance in social and cultural disability representations is necessary if we are to expand the scope and impact of disability studies in the humanities.

It is important in this preface to take a moment to disclose my interest in and connection to disability studies. In the twenty-first century, the push to bring academic disability work in line with practices from the disability rights movement has evoked much discussion. An article in *Disability Studies Quarterly* (33[2], 2013) by Corbett Joan O'Toole, former president of the Society of Disability Studies (SDS), explores how practices of disclosure have differed across community and scholarly contexts, stating that "not to locate oneself is considered impolite – as if one's relationship to disability is unimportant. Within disability communities, acknowledging one's relationship provides valuable information to others in similar situations. It also shapes how people receive the presenter's information."[1] O'Toole explores how scholars reacted adversely when they were invited to promote a culture of disclosure in the context of the SDS conference, and she warns that non-disclosure ends by affirming the marginalizing structures of ableism. Here I will take the opportunity to state that I am not disabled. I do so for two reasons: as a response to O'Toole's call; and because this allows me to suggest that our perspective on impairment discourse delimits which material experiences of disability fall under the purview of the humanities and which are ceded to the health and medical sciences.

My current interest in disability studies can be traced to two sets of circumstances that, taken together, reveal what I consider to be a productive ambivalence about the role of impairment in disability studies. First, I became interested in American Sign Language (ASL) and Deaf culture while completing an undergraduate double-major in cultural anthropology and Spanish as a BA student at the University of Virginia. I pursued this interest post-graduation as a non-degree-seeking student at Virginia, and then again, more intensively, during my MA and PhD work in Hispanic Language and Literature at the University of Arizona. During my time at Arizona, I took graduate courses that were conducted in ASL outside of my major area, with Dr Samuel Supalla, and – with the help of the Department of Spanish and Portuguese graduate director, who was a knowledgeable linguist – applied those classes as proof of the additional language proficiency required by my PhD program. I was also fortunate to work as a graduate assistant on a grant studying language acquisition in a comparative Spanish–ASL–English educational context. This all led to my first book publication, which was not my dissertation in the field of Spanish Language and Literature (later published as Fraser 2010c), but rather an edited and translated anthology of documents titled *Deaf History and Culture in Spain* (Gallaudet University Press, 2009). I conducted research for the book in Madrid with access to the archives of the Confederación Nacional de Sordos de España (Spanish National Confederation of the Deaf; CNSE) and also those housed in the Biblioteca Nacional de España (Spanish National Library). My intent was for the introduction and contents to reflect the values of the strong Deaf culture that existed in the United States and that I had come to know through coursework but also through Dr Supalla, other instructors of ASL, and culturally Deaf people (including children of Deaf adults or CODA) I met while in Tucson. This was a culture that differentiated between lower-case-d deafness, understood as an impairment, and capital-D Deafness, understood as a minority identity grounded in a shared visual language and cultural identity. On account of my exposure to ASL and Deaf culture, I did not think to apply a disability studies framework to this interest. Influenced by the values of a strong Deaf culture, I tended to separate a culturally Deaf identity from the issue of impairment entirely. I would say that I adopted the point of view that approached lower-case-d deafness through a hearing-centred paradigm emphasizing impairment and that approached capital-D Deafness through the paradigm of a minority culture possessing a distinct political identity.

Second, my previous books *Disability Studies and Spanish Culture: Films, Novels, the Comic and the Public Exhibition* (Liverpool University Press, 2013) and *Cultures of Representation: Disability in World Cinema Contexts* (Wallflower/Columbia University Press, 2016) centred largely but not exclusively on cognitive disability because my brother in-law is a person with Down syndrome, intellectual disability, and epilepsy. He attends an adult day program, loves dancing, colouring, coffee, and flirting, and takes medications that are crucial to his well-being. He is healthy and able-bodied, quite strong when he wants to be, and capable of quick fine-motor movements that have earned him a playful reputation. He is minimally non-verbal, and because his intellectual disability is considered severe, it is difficult for him to communicate his needs to others. He also requires assistance with basic everyday tasks. It is because of my brother in-law's experiences that my previous work in the field has tended to focus on intellectual and developmental disabilities (IDD). In publishing articles and book chapters on IDD/Down syndrome representations in particular I have found there to be disconnects between the strong social model of disability studies, to which I have aspired in my scholarship, and its application to the realities faced by people with severe intellectual disabilities. As presented in the Spanish-made documentary film *¿Qué tienes debajo del sombrero?* (What's Under Your Hat; 2006), the case of renowned American fibre artist Judith Scott (who was deaf and had Down syndrome) also suggested to me that it was more difficult to apply the strong social model to severe cognitive disabilities. This does nothing to mitigate one of the disability movement's slogans "*Nothing About Us Without Us*" – italicized here because it is also the title of James Charlton's important book; nor the spirit of the volume by Paul Williams and Bonnie Shoultz titled *We Can Speak For Ourselves: Self-Advocacy by Mentally Handicapped People*. Put simply, however, the more I engaged in disability studies research the more I became convinced that those who cannot communicate their mind to others in concise, precise, or socially conventional ways due to issues of cognition – those like my brother in-law – were often being left out of the discourse of disability studies research and of scholarship in the humanities in particular. Accordingly, I am acutely aware of how infrequently humanities research speaks to my brother-in-law's life experience and needs. For this reason, when I look at the landscape of disability studies I see a field that might be more comfortable with discussing impairment and – perhaps more notably – a field that might become more interested in cognition. In this context, I will not adopt the point of view that fully separates impairment from cognitive disability – the latter understood as a label for a political identity or even a cultural minority identity – for such a view in practice excludes my brother in-law from consideration.

The two contexts I have related above have more in common than I fully realized. In point of fact, impairment is an important but complicated issue for both deaf/Deaf studies and disability studies, although historically it has been easy and perhaps even appropriate to ignore it (see Burch and Kafer 2010; Scully 2014). The risk in both cases has been to see impairment in terms that essentialize disability in a specific body, thus reaffirming the values of an ableist society and its marking of the non-normate. In deaf/Deaf studies, it is easy to see there is a connection between the discourse of bodily impairment and certain bodily modification procedures. The case of the cochlear implant is the clearest and perhaps the most significant example of the ills of such impairment discourse, and it may be easy for readers to see why the medical paradigm that at present disproportionately informs such impairment discourse is widely held to be suspect. The wider capital-D Deaf community takes cochlear implants to be dismissive of ASL's status as a natural language, harmful and invasive both physically and psychologically, and to be the final act of a hearing society's colonization of the individual body (see Lane 1993). Similarly, an overindulgence in impairment discourse related to experiences of cognitive disability may suggest to some that cognitive difference needs to be "corrected" in the individual by encouraging the use of prenatal testing, surgeries, debilitating dependence on pharmaceuticals, or other invasive measures and colonializing attitudes. In both contexts, however, the practice of avoiding impairment discourse in humanities analysis produces an exclusion – and is in fact only made possible by way of that exclusion. That is, it may be easier to ignore the issue of impairment and advocate for a strong capital-D Deaf position when one excludes hard-of-hearing populations from consideration. Similarly, it may be easier to ignore the issue of impairment and focus on the disabling condition of the physical and social environment when one excludes cognitively disabled populations with severe impairments from consideration.

If we are able to sustain an encounter between the strong social constructivist model of disability and the medical, clinical, and psychosocial needs of populations with severe cognitive disabilities, I believe that the tenets of the social model of disability may in the end positively impact the way disability is discussed in the health and medical sciences. I take the position that in largely ignoring the nuances of severe cognitive disabilities, humanities scholars have ceded discursive control over cognitive difference to the medical and clinical fields. Bridging this epistemological gap requires a different way of thinking than has prevailed until now in the field of disability studies in the humanities. I do not believe that it will require a sacrifice. Some will undoubtedly disagree. As evident in the early portions of this book, however, I find encouragement in recent work by David T. Mitchell with Sharon L. Snyder (2015) and Lennard J. Davis (2013), as well as an earlier essay by Mark Jeffreys (2002), all of which push disability scholars to reconsider the material experience, if not also the material reality, of impairment.

This book also seeks to bridge another gap – that is, the distance that persists between Anglophone disability studies, on one hand, and disability studies in the Hispanic world, on the other. Although there has been much talk in recent years about the need to globalize disability studies, insufficient attention has been given to attempts by scholars in language and literature departments other than English to engage and influence the wider interdisciplinary field of disability studies. While this was not the case with my previous book on disability representations in Spanish cultural production – published in the Representations series by Liverpool University Press alongside titles focusing on the Anglophone world – my experience has been that academic publishers in general, unfairly I think, tend to see book projects focused on the Hispanic world as a niche market of their own. This viewpoint encourages some to pass on publishing opportunities even when those books connect with interdisciplinary fields. This may be changing as productive developments in Hispanic studies have seen a rapidly increasing spate of book-length texts explicitly engaging disability studies perspectives. The publication of monographs, edited volumes, and special sections by Susan Antebi (2009), Encarnación Juárez Almendros (2013), Matthew Marr (2013), Julie Avril Minich (2014), and Susan Antebi and Beth Jörgensen (2016), has been particularly inspiring for me in this regard.

My hope in the present book project is that readers from all fields will connect with the historical literature review and the theoretical chapters in Part I of this book, and that they will continue through the chapters in Part II that focus on Spanish cultural production but speak more broadly to questions important to the wider field. Parts of this work have been based on my previous article-length publications, although in their present form they have been greatly revised and elaborated. Half of chapter 4 includes material from the article "Disability Art, Visibility, and the Right to the City: The Trazos Singulares (Singular Strokes) (2011) Exhibit at Madrid's Nuevos Ministerios Metro Station," published in the *Arizona Journal of Hispanic Cultural Studies* 17 (2013): 245–61. Half of chapter 6 includes material from the article "Battling Voices: Schizophrenia as Social Relation in Abel García Roure's *Una cierta verdad* (A Certain Truth) (2008)," published by *Disability Studies Quarterly* 36, no. 2 (2016), n.pag. (http://dsq-sds.org/article/view/5007). The material republished from these article-length publications has been significantly recast, recontextualized, and further elaborated upon for the current purposes, and I thank those publishers for allowing the appearance in this book of that revised material. I also thank the three anonymous reviewers of this manuscript for their close reading of the text and suggestions for revision, which have led to a more polished final product. Last but not least, I am grateful to the Toronto Iberic series, and to its co-editors Robert Davidson and Frederick A. de Armas, as well as Mark Thompson and the production team at UTP, for valuing this discipline-spanning book project.

COGNITIVE DISABILITY AESTHETICS

Visual Culture, Disability Representations, and the (In)Visibility of Cognitive Difference

Introduction

"While most of the work in the humanities to date has centered upon physical disability as its grounding object of study, one of the major new areas of research in disability studies will need to be that of cognitive disabilities."
"Perhaps it is time to return to the scholarly suppressed topic of impairment."
– David T. Mitchell and Sharon L. Snyder (2000: 39; 2015: 160)

A move is already under way to shift from a first-wave disability studies, focused above all else on the physical body and constructions of able-bodiedness, to what might be called a second-wave disability studies more willing to explore cognition and constructions of able-mindedness. *Cognitive Disability Aesthetics* seeks to outline this shift and underscore its potential – pushing this second wave of disability studies further by documenting the (in)visibility of cognitive disability in the theoretical, historical, and cultural realms. It provides a theoretical context for approaching representations of cognitive disability in humanities texts, and it analyses selected works of visual cultural production from Spain – namely, the documentary film, the graphic novel, and visual art in urban space. As this concise introduction makes clear, this effort necessarily brings readers into contact with certain tensions implicit in the histories of academic disability work and disability movements alike, tensions that are now reasserting themselves productively in disability studies scholarship.

Among the key questions that have not yet been resolved in disability studies are these: Are the insights produced by disability work emphasizing physical disabilities transferrable to work foregrounding cognitive disabilities? Are social models of disability compatible with explorations of impairment and medication? Do theoretical arguments that disability is a universal or a fundamental basis for human experience weaken the political force of disability advocacy and the potency of disability identity politics? Are struggles for inclusion over the short term compatible with a more radical agenda for social change over the long term? How might attending to cognition more explicitly change the tenor of intersectionality theory? Do studies of disability representations in the humanities require the development of different approaches to prose literature, on one hand, and visual media, on the other? Is it fair to expect studies of disability in global contexts – beyond the United States, the United Kingdom, and Canada, for example – to replicate (or, for that matter, to distinguish themselves entirely from) Anglophone disability studies? That is, to what extent should expectations vary according to regional, linguistic, cultural, national and disciplinary contexts?

These interlinked questions are addressed briefly in this introduction but do not figure as explicitly in the chapters that follow. This book does not aim to provide definitive resolution on such matters; instead it is content to chart out new sets of questions. *Cognitive Disability Aesthetics* asks readers to consider how a consistent focus on cognition has the potential to change the way in which disability representations operate and are analysed by research in the humanities. It also prioritizes visual representations as a way of connecting aesthetics with material experiences of cognitive disability. The sections that follow serve as concise snapshots of the key issues that motivate this book. They focus, in turn, on the return of impairment discourse in disability studies, the nuanced role of inclusion under neoliberalism, the impact and potential of intersectionality and approaches from gender, sexuality, and queer studies, and the arguable universality/specificity of disability. The treatments these topics receive are intentionally brief, and as readers will see, it is difficult to untangle each of these matters from the others. Before turning to chapter summaries, a final section asserts the value of humanities scholarship that crosses disciplinary as well as national, linguistic, and cultural borders as part of a global turn in disability studies.

The Return to Impairment

A concise history of disability studies would suggest that in both the academic and political realms the social model of disability has been asserted against the medical model of disability. This has been a powerful way of exploring the social constructedness of disability and thereby wresting discursive control over the experience of disability from ableist power structures. The social model of disability has long been synonymous with a strong suspicion of impairment discourse. After all, to focus on bodily impairment is to risk holding individuals responsible for adapting to a physical and social environment, when the push of disability studies should be to change the entrenched ableism that produces that same physical and social environment in the image of the constructed idea of the normate.

As two recent books have illustrated, there is a persistent ambivalence in the field surrounding the matter of impairment – not only its relationship to social difference but also its links to material experiences of disability. Reading disability studies monographs such as Lennard J. Davis's *The End of Normal: Identity in a Biocultural Era* (2013) and David T. Mitchell and Sharon L. Snyder's *The Biopolitics of Disability: Neoliberalism, Ablenationalism, and Peripheral Embodiment* (2015), one can observe that the notion of impairment is once again reasserting itself as a question to be explored. I focus on the work of Mitchell and Snyder in the earlier portions of this introduction and deal with the comments made by Davis towards its conclusion.

It is necessary to make an observation and an assertion: I observe that impairment has not yet been considered specifically in terms of cognition by scholars in the humanities, and I assert that such consideration can be productive. The truth is that the issue of impairment – be it physical or cognitive – has been systematically neglected in disability studies research. The aura of suspicion surrounding it suggests that to invoke impairment is to obscure the social constructedness of disability. The reasons for this are well documented and familiar to disability studies scholars and disability activists. As Mitchell and Snyder point out directly as they reflect on the history of disability studies, the issue of impairment was distinguished from the issue of barrier removal early on precisely as a way to assert the social nature of disability (2015: 1). As the tradition of humanities work on disability experiences bears out, rather than risk essentializing disability within a body, it was important for academic work and disability movements alike to locate disability in the environment.[1] As disability scholars in the humanities know very well, of course, this push has gained force by focusing on the body as the site where ableist social and political structures become socially visible. This has frequently meant directing attention towards the appearance of bodies in humanities work: their shape, contour, outline, form, and so on. Nevertheless I would state that this primary focus on the shape and appearance of bodies, while playing a significant role that should neither be ignored nor be ceased, has tended to cast aside issues of impairment that might otherwise prove instrumental to a more capacious view of disability.[2]

This issue is important precisely because in opting to focus on the presence and appearance of physical bodies at the expense of a more thorough consideration of impairment, disability studies has cast aside the issue of cognition. Cognitive impairment, in the realm of cognitive disabilities, may not be merely an extension of the issue of bodily impairment, historically understood in relationship to physical disabilities. Returning to discussions of cognitive impairment today – in the context of a robust, decades-long, political and academic commitment to dismantling the structures of ableist society – need not indicate a move away from the strong social model of disability. In ignoring this issue, however, we risk condemning cognitive disability to a condition of both social and academic (in)visibility, and we risk ceding discursive control over experiences of cognitive disability from the humanities to the health and medical sciences. I contend that this is the very situation that one encounters today.

In the absence of a sustained consideration of how issues of cognitive difference impact existing disability studies methods in the humanities, cognitive disabilities are primarily a matter for the health and medical sciences to document, describe, and define.[3] Consider Mitchell and Snyder's assessment that "disability studies as a field of inquiry has broadly come to agreement on issues of impairment. Whether through the assignment of interventions to embodied incapacities and inadequacies writ large, or by the application of 'medical model' diagnoses of pathologized states, impairment is left on the other side of the boundary" (2015: 158). They specifically mention that "this strategic walling off of impairment from scholarly examination in disability studies has been largely accomplished through the excise of medical terminology" (2015: 158). If the humanities are to reclaim the discursive power to document, describe, and define cognitive disability representations within a sociocultural – and not a medicalizing – context, humanities scholars must become more comfortable, at the least, with the topic of impairment.[4] This need not present a challenge to the core principles of disability studies in the humanities, which tend to take "the very meanings of 'disability,' 'impairment' and disabled' as contested terrain," and which see "disability as a site of questions rather than firm definitions" (Kafer 2013: 10, 11). Acknowledging the material realities of cognitive impairment in particular, however, does indeed change the way we interrogate disability as a site of questions: first, because it arguably changes how we approach the definition, limitations, and potential benefits of inclusion in neoliberal frameworks; and second, because it problematizes existing pathways to intersectional coalition building in both the academic and political realms.

Neoliberalism and Inclusion

The material experience of disability cannot be separated from the accumulative strategies of neoliberal capitalism that unfold unevenly across and within national contexts. Robert McRuer puts it quite well in *Crip Theory: Cultural Signs of Queerness and Disability* when he states concisely, "I take neoliberal capitalism to be the dominant economic and cultural system in which, and also against which, embodied and sexual identities have been imagined and composed over the past quarter century" (2006: 2). This approach identifies and also takes a critical stance on the reality that minoritized groups must in practice organize as such in order to engage in rights-based claims to inclusion. The claims of populations that do not organize as defined minoritized and politicized identities are otherwise ignored by a normative constellation of social, economic, cultural, and state influences. Tobin Siebers directly acknowledges the concrete value of such politicized organizational practice when he writes in *Disability Theory* that "disability is not a physical or mental defect but a cultural and minority identity" (2008: 4).[5] As recent work in disability studies has explored, however, gains targeting inclusion that are made through the rights-based claims of minoritized identity groups tend to come at a price.

When groups position themselves for recognition by normative institutions and practices, their disruptive potential can become weakened. Jasbir Puar's exploration of "homonationalism" in *Terrorist Assemblages* (2007) and Mitchell and Snyder's interrogation of "ablenationalism" (2015) both draw attention to the complex way in which capitalist neoliberalism intersects with and can impact or co-opt minoritized identity politics. This occurs, for example, when nation-states require the assimilation of minoritized identities via a rights-based discourse that ultimately reaffirms the normative logic of that economic and cultural neoliberal system.[6] Mitchell and Snyder's critique calls into question "the degree to which neoliberalism holds out a false promise of inclusion" (2015: 62). Equally, the authors "insist that something within the social/minority models of disability is also amiss, and perhaps unwittingly fueling neoliberal strategies of inclusion on a more superficial level than has been acknowledged to date" (2015: 63).[7]

There is no doubt that the potential gains made through inclusion may be continually weakened by neoliberal capitalism, but I believe there are few willing to write them off completely.[8] In the essay "Disability Nationalism in Crip Times," for instance, McRuer comments rather ambivalently on the potential of "identity and state-based appeals (appeals that may, of course, nonetheless remain indispensable – necessary but simply and always insufficient)" (2010: 173). More important, invoking the work of Siebers, he also asks a question that is pertinent, I think, for the consideration of cognitive disabilities: "How does 'the group' grapple with those figures who do not, or cannot, or will never 'constitute themselves as a minority identity'?" (McRuer 2010: 174). While issues of inclusion may have been thoroughly considered and perhaps even set aside by a critical disability studies that historically has been focused on the physical body, I am not convinced that inclusion has been seriously explored as it relates to cognitive disabilities. The need to reach "more meaningful levels of participation by disabled people" (Mitchell and Snyder 2015: 36) is certainly relevant to a wide range of disability experiences, but what participation means for populations with severe intellectual, developmental, and psychiatric disabilities may differ somewhat substantially from what it means for those with physical disabilities. We do indeed need to "ask difficult questions of the minority group model and about the ways that model moves through history and through authoritative institutions" (McRuer and Mollow 2012: 7).

It is crucial to understand that the discourse of inclusion can be limiting in the following sense: it can function as a way for power structures to superficially integrate one or more specific constructions of difference without substantially changing wider patterns of exploitation or disempowerment, which persist largely unchanged (Titchkosky 2011: ix). For example, in their discussion of education Mitchell and Snyder write of "inclusionism as a neoliberal gloss on diversity initiatives that get some disabled students in the door while leaving the vast majority of crip/queer students behind" (2015: 80). Under neoliberalism, there is no doubt that inclusionism systematically enjoys a spectacular presence that works against more substantial efforts at diversity. I would argue, however, that the flaw lies in the way inclusion has been sought and promoted, in the way it has been co-opted by neoliberal designs, rather than in the goal of prioritizing inclusion itself. The fact that disability may be "a limited form of inclusionism within late liberal capitalism" (Mitchell and Snyder 2015: 37) should not suggest the elimination of attempts at inclusion, but rather a two-pronged approach.

The question is whether it is possible to advocate for inclusionism in the short term and also to support a more radical and long-term course for the dismantling of ableist power structures. Some may feel that a short-term perspective risks reifying disability and delaying more radical political change; others may feel that a long-term perspective fails to produce the more tangible results that identity politics can reasonably achieve in the short term. There is no real reason these two perspectives need be taken as polarized, for in truth they might be seen in terms of a short revolution and a long revolution, a near goal and a far goal. I believe that these are complementary rather than divisive efforts. As the above question asked by McRuer (2010: 174) expresses quite plainly, in the end inclusionism is neither sufficient on its own nor incompatible with more radical social change. My response to those who see this as a renunciation of critical disability studies is to state that the field has not dealt systematically either with the issue of severe cognitive impairment or with the question of what inclusion really means for the full range of populations experiencing cognitive disability.

Gender/Sexuality Studies, Queer Studies, Intersectionality

The more disability studies turns towards issues of cognition, the more it may encounter opportunities to re-examine the nature and value of inclusion discourse. Cognition arguably also makes it possible to reinvest in the connections that disability studies already enjoys with gender and sexuality studies, queer studies, and intersectionality theory more generally. Disability can be seen "as an expression of intersectional identity wherein devalued social characteristics compound stigma" (Erevelles and Minear 2013: 354). Moreover, advances in intersectionality theory recognize the mutually constitutive nature of systems of oppression, and present the opportunity for a coalition building whose impact might grow beyond what are sometimes seen as limited gains within more restricted contexts of identity politics. Consider, for example, Mitchell and Snyder's statement that "gender, sexuality and racial liberation movements have all pursued a rights-based rhetoric that opts to normalize differences across populations" and that in this process "civil rights-grounded arguments for social inclusion based on universal human similarities have strategically promoted normatively oriented assimilationist models" (2015: 43). Intersectional perspectives can certainly reinforce solidarity across minoritized identities in order to denounce a common normate as well as an exclusionary structure that constructs not merely disability identities but also the sociopolitical identities of women, LGBTQ, and racialized populations as minoritzed subjects (see Kafer 2013; McRuer 2006; Siebers 2010).

Disability studies as an academic area corresponding to a political commitment owes a great debt to gender/sexuality and queer studies approaches and thus also to the departments in humanities disciplines that have historically served as homes for these programs. It follows in the footsteps of these fields at the same time that it pushes each of them onward. As Rosemarie Garland-Thomson recounts, feminist disability studies itself sought to constitute the female body as the object of humanities critique, reclaiming it from medical analysis (2013: 339). It is precisely this sort of shift carried out by feminist disability scholars that can serve as a model for scholars of cognitive disability experiences. Recent assessments by prominent disability scholars indicate, however, that the current state of queer theory may offer a less robust set of connections. In Mitchell and Snyder's estimation, "a more direct engagement with disability has been slow in coming within queer studies" (2015: 79), and as Anna Mollow and McRuer assert, "the major texts in the much larger field of sexuality studies, including those in queer theory, rarely mention disability" (2012: 3).

Here the work of Alison Kafer deserves particular recognition. Kafer is one of a number of disability scholars who have charted a course for intersectionality, as reflected in the statement that her book *Feminist Queer Crip* is "a fundamentally coalitional text" (2013: 17). While she embraces the potential relevance of crip theory to other academic fields and political struggles in her work, she also points to the way in which it tends to privilege physical disabilities, writing that "this potential flexibility is precisely what excites me about crip theory, but ... this inclusiveness is often more hope than reality. Many expressions of crip pride or crip politics often explicitly address only physical impairments, thereby ignoring or marginalizing the experiences of those with sensory or mental impairments" (2013: 15–16). It is notable that Kafer draws attention to the wider field's avoidance of cognitive impairment and that the scholar routinely mentions "able-bodiedness/

able-mindedness" (e.g., 2013: 20) together as a pair in her intersectional disability studies work.

It is clear that the collective push of intersectionality theory encourages disability studies theorists to seek the common ground from which all might work together to denounce normative ableist paradigms, whether related to physical or cognitive disabilities. If disability theory is able to sustain conversations related to intellectual, developmental, and psychiatric disabilities, this will certainly open new pathways for global inclusion that focus not merely on bodies but on minds.[9] Intersectional work drawing from gender and sexuality studies and queer studies should prove instrumental to this push, given that the focus on corporeal embodiment has always necessarily implied the connection of body and mind (as in Mitchell and Snyder 1997: 13). Making this connection more explicit, however, can open up a discursive space in which to interrogate the notion of cognitive impairment. The opportunity moving forward is to value the investigation of cognitive disability for its potential resonance with the hallmark inquiries of these fields and even to appreciate the productive friction it may demonstrate with respect to overlapping themes of identity politics.

But while physical disabilities have been constituted as political identities in similar terms, cognitive disabilities have not enjoyed the same levels of collective and politicized identity. Extending the comments of Joseph N. Straus in his essay "Autism as Culture," it can be said that populations with cognitive disabilities tend to face two intertwined problems that impact their ability to constitute themselves as a political identity in the way required by neoliberalism and representational democracy. Straus underscores "the problem of narration: the member of the minoritized social group should be able to resist medicalized discourse by speaking for him or herself," as well as "the problem of community: a group of people who have problems with communication and social relatedness may find it difficult to forge a social group, and may thus be difficult to constitute as a self-aware community within a social model of disability" (2013: 462). Consideration of these problems of narration and community suggests that the experience of cognitive disabilities is not easily mapped onto rights-based discourse. This presents an obstacle to minority culture approaches to cognitive disability; it also problematizes some aspects of existing critical theorizations of the neoliberal exploitation of cognitively disabled people. In the end, the question of how cognitive disability experiences map onto intersectional approaches may depend on how far we move towards valuing collaboration across multiple discourses: political, institutional, scholarly, and aesthetic.

The Universality/Specificity of Disability

Intersectional approaches and the notion of coalition building ultimately bring to mind the fundamental idea of moving from minoritized and politicized identities towards a common experience. It is relevant that scholarship has often addressed the degree to which disability is a universal experience. Thus McRuer writes of "the oft-repeated invocation of what we might call the spectral disability yet to come: 'If we live long enough, disability is the one identity we will all inhabit'" (2006: 200; see also Siebers 2008: 71). The kind of thinking expressed through the latter embedded quotation is undoubtedly a commonplace of much disability studies scholarship. Its appearance is particularly conspicuous during those moments when scholars engage in the reporting of fractions and/or percentages – that is, statements that a given percentage of the population is, or at one time will be considered, disabled. There is, however, a much larger debate underlying the character of such discourse. I contend that this debate is of interest not merely because it speaks to the purported universality of disability or how it is that definitions of disability are socially constructed, but moreover because it is a sign that discomfort over the notion of impairment persists. In exploring this argument, we may come to consider the reality of impairment and recognize its relevance to contemporary debates.

The recent interest in biology and culture expressed in the subtitle of Lennard J. Davis's book – *The End of Normal: Identity in a Biocultural Era* – ultimately squares with Mitchell and Snyder's interest in returning to impairment and indicates that a more nuanced disability studies criticism may now be possible in a way it has not been before. As a way of setting up discussion of Davis's comments, I want to make some general observations on the juxtaposition of the presumed universality versus the presumed specificity of disability by thinking through two distinguishable viewpoints.

The first point of view is one that I take to be the canonical view characterizing the strong social model of disability developed over the course of decades in tandem with disability rights movements. This view holds that, as Tanya Titchkosky puts it quite concisely, "one cannot be disabled alone" (2011: 5). Thus disability is not a trait that an individual possesses but rather a way of seeing things that implicates the whole of society. Consider the concise and instructive example she gives in *The Question of Access: Disability, Space, Meaning*: "without mass literacy demands there is no dyslexia; with dyslexia, there arises something other than a person fully at one with literate culture" (Titchkosky 2011: 21). Disability is indeed a social relationship that appears as such only in a society constructed by ableist understandings of the normate (Garland-Thomson 2005). This is the point of view that has been marshalled by an entire tradition of disability studies research in the humanities, to great effect. With good cause, such scholarship has warned against essentializing disability in the individual body. It has staked a claim to the need for substantial social changes, changes that should be implemented over both the short and the long term. It has sought to encourage more people to think more deeply about the social origins of disability – but not necessarily the biological or developmental components of the disability experience, a topic that has been seen as controversial. To wit, Titchkosky writes that "a further issue with individualizing disability is that this perception can act as a barrier to reflection on who and what is considered disabled" (2011: 5). I do not dispute the value of this essential kernel of disability studies. I do wonder, however, whether the supposition that the social model might be wholly incompatible with issues that have formerly been the purview of the health fields leaves much more to be said about the material experience of cognitive impairment.

The second point of view is one that has received at least growing attention – though certainly not growing acceptance – and involves an extension of the motivation behind the strong social model of disability. In this view, disability is said to be universal. The idea is that all human beings are disabled or, at the very least, interdependent. The former point of view has been attributed to Davis despite his insistence it is not a fair charge (Mitchell with Snyder 2015: 164; cf. Davis 2013). The latter view has perhaps been expressed most effectively by scholars such as Eva Feder Kittay. Supporters of the interdependency argument appeal to universality through a call for recognition that all human beings pass through periods when we are "inevitably dependent" (Kittay, Jennings, and Wasunna 2005). Kittay has put the spirit of this appeal – which some readers will consider to be obvious – quite clearly by asking the following rhetorical question: "But who in any complex society is not dependent on others, for the production of our food, for our mobility, for a multitude of tasks that make it possible for each of us to function in our work and daily living?" (2001: 570). The work synthesizing disability, dependence, and care, along with the work on intellectual disability by Licia Carlson (*The Faces of Intellectual Disability*, 2010), with whom Kittay has co-edited *Cognitive Disability and its Challenge to Moral Philosophy* (2010), deserves much wider recognition than it has received to date in disability studies contexts. I do think, however, that to make an argument about disability that is similar to the argument about dependence would be to resort to hyperbole as a way of echoing arguments that disability exists in the social environment, not the individual. If such an argument is not in fact merely hyperbole, then it risks rendering disability a meaningless term. The question of disability certainly raises the question of difference, and even if disability is not universal, difference indeed is. Not all differences are historically, culturally, or socially visible in the same way or to the same degree, however.

When one puts these two points of view in extremely reductive ways, they appear to be markedly similar in the priority they give to society. The first suggests that no individual person is disabled, that we need to recognize that disability is purely the product of an ableist social environment. The second suggests that everyone is disabled (or at least interdependent), that we need to recognize that interdependence is the basis of the human experience. I suggest that thinking through these somewhat crude reductions is helpful because it can explain why some discomfort persists in the field surrounding the issue of impairment. That is, neither point of view explains what can be done to address the social invisibility of different kinds of impairment. Both points of view encourage an all-or-nothing approach to disability that, frankly, is inadequate when considering cognitive difference. Moreover, this approach is inadequate because it fails to address the materiality of severe cognitive disability as experienced in society.

Thinking through these issues by way of the discussions in *The End of Normal* can help outline what I would refer to as a newly emerging third point of view. This third viewpoint is nimble enough to recognize both the social nature of cognitive disability, on one hand, and the material experience of cognitive difference, on the other. It reaffirms both the material and the immaterial conditions of the experience of disability, and it suggests that it is important to see disability in terms of a socially uneven geography. It does not, in my view, indicate that disability is not social in nature. Like other twenty-first-century approaches, Davis's text folds the biological, the material, and the concrete together with the cultural, the immaterial, and the social. This is a nuanced operation, to be sure, but it is important to understand that this is a general premise shared also by Mitchell and Snyder.[10]

The End of Normal strongly embraces a fusion of concerns, which Davis denotes through the notion of the biocultural, a term he employs "to describe the intersection among the cultural, social, political, technological, medical and biological" (2013: 1).[11] Davis wonders "whether diversity can ever encompass disability," over which "the older concept of normal still holds sway" (2013: 6), and interestingly, he imagines diversity by employing terms such as "celebration and choice" (2013: 8) that in effect reflect the discourse of late-capitalist consumerism. He is not unaware of these connotations; his point is that disability reaffirms the notion of diversity as a celebration of choice due to the fact that it is the exception that proves the rule. "Disabled bodies are," he writes, "in the current imaginary, constructed as fixed identities. Outside of the hothouse of disability studies and science studies, impairments are commonly seen as abnormal, medically determined, and certainly not socially constructed" (2013: 7). He further offers an explanation: "This may be because disability is not seen as an identity in the same way as many see race, gender and other embodied identities. And the reason for that is that disability is largely perceived as a medical problem and not a way of life involving choice" (2013: 7). Following from these comments, I read what Davis refers to as "kicking the stone" (2013: 15; also, "kicking the rock") as a call to recognize the limits of social construction discourse. The phrase itself uses a metaphor of physical solidity, material mass, and space to underscore the materiality of disability experience.[12] Here, what seems to ground the argument concerning the "fixed identities" of disability is a notion that disability is material in the simple sense – that disability is about bodies and, implicitly, also about the concreteness or physicality of bodies in particular.

A largely physical understanding of disability leads Davis simultaneously towards an unsatisfying parallel drawn between disability and neoliberal consumer choice rhetoric on one hand and a largely unmalleable understanding of disability identity on the other. He writes that "ultimately what I am arguing is that disability is an identity that is unlike all the others in that it resists change and cure" (2013: 14).[13] What is most interesting given the present effort, however, is that in raising the issue of the materiality of impairment in general as he does (2013: 7), Davis finds himself turning to Down syndrome as an example and writing: "It is patently not possible to be born a person with Down syndrome and become someone who does not have Down syndrome (though some cosmetic surgeries to normalize the faces of people with Down syndrome are available, and now drug therapies are being researched to improve cognitive skills) … Why is it that disability is often the identity that is left out – not choosable?" (2013: 11).[14] What I read in this statement is that Davis believes that the stubborn materiality of disability is best expressed, in fact, by IDD or cognitive disability. Is it a contradiction to think that disability best engages with materiality by moving towards issues of cognition? If so, I regard this contradiction as a fundamentally productive one.

It should be recognized that Mitchell and Snyder's *The Biopolitics of Disability* takes direct issue with Davis's purported premise, but also that the authors simultaneously reaffirm disability as "a nuanced experiential condition" (2015: 30). It is also reasonable to compare the recognition of materiality suggested in Davis's phrase "kicking the stone" with Mitchell and Snyder's recognition of impairment in their question, "If we are all effectively 'disabled,' then what is to mark disability as a nuanced experiential condition?" (2015: 30).[15] This represents, in my view, a practical turn towards the promise of "new materialist approaches" (2015: 7).[16] The scholars describe their work as part of a push that "dares to name diagnoses or conditions as something other than forms of medical false consciousness" and state quite boldly that "perhaps it is time to return to the scholarly suppressed topic of impairment" (2015: 160).[17] At its root, what both books reveal is a continuing preoccupation with fleshing out the role of materiality and biology in a field that has for so long focused on barrier removal at the expense of impairment. In doing so, each text in its own way asks important questions about the deep schism that exists between medical and social models of disability. In this sense, the books by Mitchell/Snyder and Davis share a common goal – they both want to assess what the social model has left out as a result of its focus on barrier removal and strong constructivism.

There has to be room in disability studies – despite its trenchant critiques of simplistic inclusionism and neoliberal forms of diversity that are held to be suspect because they reify normative power structures[18] – for recognizing the materiality of impairment without assuming the inherently able-bodied bias pointing to rehabilitation as a sufficient or even appropriate response.[19] A pertinent question is posed by the afterword in Mitchell with Snyder: "What, ask politicized disabled people, bodily capabilities does one need in order to actively participate in social democracies?" (2015: 210). Here I read the same slippage identified by Stuart Murray in his book *Representing Autism: Culture, Narrative, Fascination* (2008), a slippage whereby the general term "disability" is frequently used to mean "physical disability," specifically.[20] If disability studies is to consider more deliberately how cognition impacts active participation in society, the issue of impairment must be addressed more thoroughly than it has been until now. If we want to go beyond mere inclusionism to address pernicious and pervasive structural and ideological forms of ableism – as *The Biopolitics of Disability* encourages us to do – the field would be helped by turning to those issues of cognition, impairment, and medication that are currently located largely at the margins of humanities work if not ignored altogether. Directing our attention to severe cognitive disabilities in particular can help us think through the current limitations of disability studies approaches that frame the health sciences and the social sciences/humanities as mutually exclusive.

The Varieties of Humanities Scholarship

Readers should understand that my work throughout this book – and in the applied chapters centred on visual cultural products from Spain in particular – reflects the engagement of a particular kind of humanist. The fact that interest in visual representations of cognitive disability – as opposed to disability representations in prose literature – has been relatively slow to emerge can be attributed in part, in my estimation, to matters of discipline. That is, study of traditional print literature has continued to dominate Departments of English and Departments of Languages and Literatures in the United States – and is still dominant in American programs of graduate study. Notably, this has been the case even well into a twenty-first century characterized by the effects of the disciplinary shifts brought about by cultural studies methods. In my home discipline of Hispanic studies (Spanish Language and Literature), for example, recent publications on the subject of literary canon have made clear just how persistent the traditional definition of culture in terms of prose literature really is (see Brown 2010; cf. Fraser, Larson, Compitello 2014).[21] (And while study of film by language and literature scholars may still be proportionally rare, the study of comics/graphic novels is even more rare.) It is clear, however, that the upsurge in cultural representations of cognitive disability – not only in prose literature but also in cinema and even the comic/graphic novel – increasingly requires humanistic interpretation. There is a risk to such work in that readers interested in the broad theme of disability are not always interested in the formal or artistic dimensions of specific expressions of visual culture, nor are they fully aware of how the nuances of artistic genre impact the disability representations discussed.

In addition, readers from Anglophone fields often have diverse and conflicting expectations regarding work covering other global areas. I have found, for example, that scholars of Hispanic studies who engage in disability research seeking a broader interdisciplinary audience are often asked to recapitulate the insights of a specific Anglophone corpus of disability work. They may also be expected to outline formulations of disability studies from other global traditions that may be underdeveloped, and/or that effectively tropicalize cultural difference of a given location in a form easily digested by non-specialists. Such non-specialists frequently are, after all, eager to read encyclopedic introductions to an exceptional foreign land rather than jump into the analysis of specific humanities texts in a non-Anglophone cultural context.[22]

It is necessary to underscore that even in Anglophone contexts the number of humanities studies seeking to correct for the relative invisibility of cognitive disabilities in theoretical, historical, and/or representational fields is small. I wrote my previous book *Disability Studies and Spanish Culture: Films, Novels, the Comic, and the Public Exhibition* (2013a) precisely to address the need for further studies of cognitive disabilities. There I focused on Down syndrome, autism, and agnosia/alexia but also included discussion of other intellectual disabilities, cerebral paralysis, deafness, and more. Though I analysed prose literature as well as cinema and the graphic novel in that publication, in every case I used a cultural studies method to give equal weight to both the artistic form of each product and the social context in which it was produced (see Williams 2007). As a way of continuing that move, here I turn also to issues of Alzheimer's dementia and schizophrenia, while maintaining an interest in Down syndrome and autism. Though the examples from cultural production that I explore later in this book may come from Hispanic studies – the field in which I have been working for more than a decade – I am more interested in the general principle of visibility they illustrate rather than in making the claim that disability representations are uniquely framed by contested constructs of nationhood or by inadequate models that homogenize experiences of language or culture.

Given the surging interest in the "global turn" in disability studies (see Mitchell and Snyder 2010; Murray and Barker 2010; Fraser 2013a,

2016a), my hope is that the structure of this book will bring Anglophone readers exposure to the Spanish context, and that it will similarly push readers from Hispanic literary and cultural studies to find a balance between issues of embodiment and issues of cognition as they continue to explore disability studies as a specialized discipline on its own terms. The interest in disability evidenced by scholars situated within the disciplinary moorings of Iberian and Latin American literature and culture has been relatively slow to develop when compared with Anglophone work on disability. For scholars in Anglophone fields, it may even be difficult to understand that book-length texts specifically and directly engaging the topic of disability (and not just embodiment) in Hispanic studies only first appeared in 2009. Recent editions by Hispanic studies scholars have attempted to broaden the global scope of Anglophone study of disability: Susan Antebi's *Carnal Inscriptions: Spanish American Narratives of Corporeal Difference and Disability* (2009), Matthew Marr's *The Politics of Age and Disability in Contemporary Spanish Film* (2013), Encarnación Juárez-Almendros's special section of the *Arizona Journal of Hispanic Cultural Studies* titled "Disability Studies in the Hispanic World: Proposals and Methodologies" (2013), Julie Avril Minich's *Accessible Citizenships: Disability, Nation, and the Cultural Politics of Greater Mexico* (2014), and Susan Antebi and Beth Jörgensen's *Libre Acceso: Latin American Literature and Film through Disability Studies* (2016), for example. Such editions have of course built on a range of pioneering essay-length contributions in Hispanic studies (e.g., Conway 2000, 2001; Gámez Fuentes 2005; Juárez Almendros 2010; Marr 2009; Minich 2010; Prout 2008; Rivera-Cordero 2009, 2013a, 2013b) – a tradition I hope will receive greater attention within disability studies proper.

The tensions explored in this introduction are complicated issues to be sure, but it seems that now is the time for a book that returns to impairment precisely as a way of taking another look at cognition. At the risk of repetition, I affirm once again that this does not need to mean that we shift away from a social model to a medical model of disability, but it may mean that some articulation between these polarized approaches can be beneficial. I hope to speak from my disciplinary positioning to an issue around which studies of disability – taken in the broadest sense – might take steps to reorganize. I want to broaden the academic understanding of cognitive disability to include intellectual disabilities, developmental disabilities, and psychiatric disabilities. At the same time, I hope to reduce the theoretical and cultural distance between cognitive disability and physical disability. The fulcrum for closing this gap is the concept of the visible world. Exploring the intersection of visual culture, signification, cognition, representational practices, material experiences of impairment, and social constructions of disability can bring more attention to how attention to severe cognitive difference can potentially inform a more capacious disability studies.

Book Structure and Chapter Summaries

Cognitive Disability Aesthetics has two parts. Part 1 consists of historical and theoretical chapters, written for a wide Anglophone readership interested in cognitive disability no matter their global area of expertise. Part 2 consists of applied chapters focusing on individual expressions of recent cultural production in Spain, with translations to accommodate all readers of English. In this book I prioritize issues of cognition as a way of outlining what a more inclusive disability studies might be like. I admit that in recent years, the largely physical orientation of the academic field has been changing to include cognitive disabilities – as documented more thoroughly in chapter 1 – but I stress that this move has only just begun. That is, key foundational texts of disability studies have responded specifically to the social circumstances regarding physical disabilities and have not been historically focused on the specific social dimensions of constructions of cognitive disability. As explored in chapters 2 and 3, we need to reflect on how this bias may have shaped approaches to disability representations in traditionally literary fields, and how giving more attention to visual disability representations can simultaneously benefit exploration of the material experiences of cognitive disability. Thus the first half of this book serves as a call to think through the friction that exists between a long tradition of work on physical disability and more recent advances in the field that focus on cognitive disability. To analyse and understand visual disability representations, I argue, the field will need to create different conceptual tools. In the same way, if disability studies is to approach cognitive disability representations on their own terms, it may even need to reconsider the long-held assumptions that were forged in traditions of academic work focusing primarily on physical disabilities. Readers should note that while I refer on occasion to Spanish-language examples in the body text or accompanying notes, in the chapters making up Part 1 of the book I am more interested in exploring the theoretical and methodological ground that can be applied more broadly to visual disability representations in a range of international contexts.

"On the (In)Visibility of Cognitive Disability" – the first chapter of the book – explores the largely physical orientation of disability studies from historical, theoretical, and cultural perspectives. I explain why readers in the field tend to encounter deafness, blindness, and exceptional bodies much more frequently than persons who embody cognitive exceptionality, how this may be changing, and what humanities scholarship can contribute to the increased visibility of cognitive disabilities within the interdisciplinary field of disability studies. This chapter also serves to ground more general readers in previous disability studies work, mentioning canonical books from the close of the twentieth century (Davis 1995, [1997]2013; Wendell 1996; Garland-Thomson 1996, 1997; Mitchell and Snyder 1997, 2000; Brueggemann 1999), as well as earlier work (Fiedler 1978; Bogdan 1988; Stiker [1982]1997), more recent theoretical texts (Murray 2008; McDonagh 2008; Siebers 2008, 2010) and a continuing tradition of scholarship on photography and film (Norden 1994; Enns and Smit 2001a; Chivers 2011; Chivers and Markotić 2010; Mogk 2013).

Chapter 2, "Signification and Staring: Icon, Index, and Symbol in Visual Media," shines a theoretical light directly on the links between the social and cultural/artistic representations of disability. While much has been written on the social representation of disability (e.g. Siebers 2008, 2010; Davis 1995; 2013), and while much has been written on the cinematic representation of disability (e.g. Chivers 2011; Chivers and Markotić 2010; Enns and Smit 2001a; Fraser 2013a, 2016a; Marr 2013; Mogk 2013; Norden 1994; Riley 2005; Smith 2011; Wijdicks 2015), there have been very few attempts to bridge discussions of both representational processes explicitly. I contend, however, that what is common to both is the visual bias that underlies our thinking and our construction of socially negotiated representations of disability. To make this argument I draw inspiration from a specific line of cinema criticism throughout the twentieth century – expressed concisely in the work of film theorist Peter Wollen (1972) – that prioritizes the interrelation of indexical, iconic, and symbolic forms of representation. Filmmaker and theorist Pier Paolo Pasolini (1988), who was himself a part of this undervalued yet continuing critical tradition, once wrote that the cinema expressed the "cognitive code of reality." This semiotic premise borrowed from the discourse of art is of significant interest to disability studies scholars precisely because it reveals the way in which our social constructions of normalcy are mediated by images, by a presence in the visual field, even in non-artistic contexts. Moreover, the emphasis Rosemarie Garland-Thomson (2009) places on the "visual work" of staring (2009) and the identification of the "new disability documentary cinema" by Snyder and Mitchell (2010) suggest that the iconic/indexical forms of signification that predominate in visual media have great potential to impact social relationships through the connections they provide with material experiences of cognitive disability off-screen, and by extension when considering the graphic novel, off-page.

Chapter 3, "Disability Scholarship at the Seam: The Materiality of Visual Narrative," adapts Mark Jeffreys's use of the phrase "the seam where body joins culture" (2002: 33) to describe the methodological premise of a disability studies scholarship focused on visual culture. Jeffreys points to the limitations of social constructivism in disability studies and asserts the importance of attending to matters of biology and impairment. While I believe that a certain amount of social constructivism was necessary in order for first-wave disability studies scholarship to advance some strong claims to autonomy for disabled populations, the consequence has been a focus on bodies at the expense of minds. Therefore, in Jeffreys's claim I find reason to tread carefully: "Outright hostility to biology and to the natural history of our flesh," he warns, "all too easily plays into mind-body, theory-matter dualism and may turn out to be just another effort at the erasure of the body by culture" (2002: 33). As this quotation itself suggests, Jeffreys's insight is just as applicable to the needs of those disabled by a cognitively abled society. This chapter explores in depth the distinction between how prose literary representations and visual representations of disability operate with reference to Mitchell and Snyder's *Narrative Prosthesis* (2000) and Ato Quayson's *Aesthetic Nervousness* (2007). It also builds on the iconic/indexical basis of film and comics art to suggest that visual narrative expresses a material connection with extra-artistic matters of biology and impairment and renders cognitive difference visible through the ontological assertion of iconic redundancy (Groensteen 2007; Postema 2013). It thus advocates for a strain of disability studies in the humanities that operates "at the seam" where biology and culture are joined. By conceiving of visual representations as a bridge to the material disability experiences of real people, criticism can complement the metaphorical/metacognitive concerns articulated by literary scholarship (Bérubé 2005) and a mode of critique developed for physical disability studies (Garland-Thomson 2005) with an exploration of the role of cognition in a second-wave disability studies.

Part 2 of this book applies insights from earlier chapters to the visibility of cognitive disability representations in three areas of cultural production in Spain: visual art in urban space, graphic novels, and documentary cinema. The representation of severe cognitive disability figures prominently here. One of the things that comes from acknowledging the material reality of severe cognitive impairment is the need to consistently recognize the potential of collaboration. From this recognition there may come, possibly, a stronger commitment to fostering collaborative critique of cognitive ableism. I am particularly interested in collaboration that involves the spheres of art and culture, but heeding the call of cultural studies method this interest extends beyond the border of the text to approach the way in which culture intersects with social formations and institutions. This is to embrace a focus on representation that involves both artistic and social modes and that admits the necessarily collective nature of all representation.

Chapter 4, "Visualizing Down Syndrome and Autism: The *Trazos Singulares* (Singular Strokes; 2011) Exhibition and *María cumple 20 años* (María Turns Twenty; 2015)," looks at a public event and at a graphic novel as collaborative representations of developmental disability. The exhibition was held in Madrid during May 2011 at a metro station in the north-central area of the city and comprised some sixty works by artists with developmental disabilities. Significantly, the work of artistic production was itself performed on site between 5 and 8 April of that year. Thus, although the issues of art, advocacy, and embodiment expressed in this exhibit are far from simple and receive their own consideration, ultimately I argue that the novel character of this exhibition demonstrates a somewhat more sophisticated understanding of the historical legacy of the paradoxical visibility/invisibility of cognitive disability than would be reflected in the decision to showcase the artistic products alone. Disability philosopher Licia Carlson compellingly writes in her work *The Faces of Intellectual Disability* of the way in which "intellectual disability … has been made both socially visible and invisible" (2010: 46). Historically speaking, then, the institutionalized classification/codification of people with intellectual disabilities made them highly visible from a clinical (and social) standpoint just as their incarceration in "institutions far from public view" was intended to render them seemingly invisible to the public at large (Carlson 2010: 46; see also Davis 1995: 73, 94–5, 173; Siebers 2008: 99–109). Trazos Singulares thus arguably succeeds in that it renders the contributing artists as socially visible (momentarily – a fact not without its own problems), in the process drawing attention to the embodied nature of all artistic production. The second half of this chapter looks at the representation of autism in *María cumple 20 años* (2015), itself a follow-up to the earlier graphic novel *María y yo* (2007). Graphic artist Miguel Gallardo here collaborates with his daughter María Gallardo to create a shared autobiographical portrait that builds on the representational strategies of the pair's earlier comic, pushing readers beyond neurotypical understandings of cognition. In particular, this sequel incorporates María's own artistic work to create a fusion of voices and focuses more on issues related to the autonomy and support she might enjoy as an adult. The end result is an artistic work that implicitly recognizes the materiality of cognitive impairment, celebrates neurodiversity, and presents a collaborative model for approaching autism representations.

Chapter 5, "Sequencing Alzheimer's Dementia: Paco Roca's Graphic Novel *Arrugas* (Wrinkles; 2008)," explores an acclaimed graphic novel that was later turned into a film directed by Ignacio Ferreras. First published by the French publishing house Guy Delcourt as *Rides*, *Arrugas* was subsequently edited by Astiberri Ediciones in Bilbao, País Vasco, to critical acclaim. Its debut in France had earned it recognition as one of the top twenty of the year, and in Spain it subsequently received two awards in the prestigious Salón del Cómic de Barcelona: the prize for Best Script and the prize for the Best Work by a Spanish Author. Significantly, it has since been translated into Japanese, Dutch, Finnish, and Italian, winning awards also for Best Album at Expo Cómic, Madrid, the Premio Nacional de Cómic 2008, the award for Best Album in the festivals of Lucca and Rome, and the prize of the Ministry of Culture in Japan. *Arrugas* is not only an award-winning graphic novel, however; it is also a moving portrait of aging and of the effects of Alzheimer's-related dementia. The graphic novel emphasizes the everyday lives and frustrations of residents in a transitional care facility through its central protagonist – the recent arrival Emilio. *Arrugas* describes not only his blossoming friendships and newfound hardships, but also a range of characters and everyday situations. Building on recent scholarship on senescence and intellectual disability in Spanish film, cultural studies of Alzheimer's dementia, and work on interdependency within disability studies approaches more broadly, this chapter explores key formal aspects of the graphic novel's iconic representation.

Chapter 6, "Screening Schizophrenia: Documentary Cinema, Cognitive Disability, and Abel García Roure's *Una cierta verdad* (A Certain Truth; 2008)," chronicles the distance between conceptions of psychiatric disabilities as theorized by two distinct groups: health care providers and patients. The work of Michel Foucault is mobilized to connect explicitly with the contemporary disability studies frameworks that his work in many ways inspired. In particular, this chapter interrogates the way his works *The Birth of the Clinic* (1994) and *History of Madness* (2006) both focus on the visibility of infirmity and the role of vision in the contemporary clinical gaze. The case of the informational documentary *1% esquizofrenia* (1% Schizophrenia; 2006) here illustrates how cultural representations of schizophrenia are likely to be portrayed as spectacular. By contrast, the second half of the chapter explores the representation of schizophrenia that obtains in *Una cierta verdad* (A Certain Truth; 2008), directed by Abel García Roure. García Roure studied filmmaking with noted cineaste Joaquim Jordà at the Universitat Pompeu Fabra de Barcelona, and his film is at once a compelling portrayal of the everyday individual experience of schizophrenia, a denunciation of the brutality that systematically accompanies its medical treatment, and perhaps something of an apology for our collective failure to bridge the distance between the cognitively abled and those living with this illness. The battle of voices we watch unfold on-screen, then, is not constituted by the medicalized self-talk of the person with schizophrenia, but is instead a social dialogue between two polarized groups of actors: providers and patients. Ultimately, the film suggests that it is the clinical paradigm's low tolerance for nuance and lack of precise tools that in fact perpetuates this ongoing battle of voices.

PART ONE
Theorizing Visual Disability Representations

1 On the (In)Visibility of Cognitive Disability

"Are we justified, however, in historically separating rehabilitation from the treatment of madness? … and separating the physically disabled from the mentally deficient? Today, when the same legislation affects them all together, when institutions are so similar to one another, when the boundaries are often indistinct, how are we to speak of this century that is about to close, which from a divorce made a union?"

– Henri-Jacques Stiker ([1982]1997: 139)

This book is motivated by a simple premise: cognitive disabilities, when juxtaposed with the increased theoretical, social, and cultural visibility of physical disabilities, have tended to remain disproportionately unseen. That is, those disabilities that might be classified as intellectual disabilities, developmental disabilities, and psychiatric disabilities have not enjoyed as much critical attention by humanities scholars. They have not been as visible in society, historically speaking, or as frequently represented in cultural and artistic products, as have those disabilities judged to be physical in nature. In theoretical monographs, in the wider social environment, and in all manner of artistic texts it has historically been the case that one encounters deafness, blindness, and exceptional bodies much more frequently than one does persons who embody cognitive exceptionality. This chapter explains why this has been so, how this may be changing, and what humanities scholarship can contribute to the increased visibility of cognitive disabilities within the interdisciplinary field of disability studies.

The fact that cognitive disabilities today enjoy less theoretical, social, and cultural attention than do physical disabilities is a barrier to disability studies, understood "as both an academic discipline and as an area of political struggle" (Davis [1997]2013: 1). My starting point is to affirm that, to date, much attention has been placed on the need to correct a normative and able-bodied social gaze, and not enough attention has been given to its complementarily normative and "cognitively abled" gaze (a term employed by Carlson 2001, 2010; see also Kafer 2013: 16). Following from this assertion, this chapter explores the relationship between visibility and cognitive disability at three levels: the theoretical or discursive, the historical or social, and the representational or cultural. It is important to note that each of these levels is also a window into the others. For example, how disability is theorized – what we write about it, what categories or divisions we employ, whether we distinguish between physical disabilities and cognitive disabilities in a given context – all of this informs how disabilities are seen in society, literally and figuratively speaking. At the same time, the images of disability that appear in art, culture, and various media routinely consumed can also have a significant impact on spectators. These representations – which are never neutral – render disabilities in visible form. Throughout this work I am particularly concerned with those disabilities that tend to be invisible in society just as I am also concerned primarily with their visible representation in cultural production.

Readers will note that the titles of both this book and this chapter highlight the terms "cognitive disability/cognitive difference." By using this umbrella term, I hope to capture a range of experiences that might alternatively be labelled as intellectual disabilities, developmental disabilities, and psychiatric disabilities. Because these groupings share the simultaneously social and aesthetic condition of relative invisibility on which I focus throughout this volume, there are some more nuanced discussions implicit in the use of this umbrella term to which I have intentionally avoided contributing. Chief among them is the philosophical question of how, if at all, we are justified in separating the mind from the body. This separation points to a limiting and dualistic classification with much deeper roots in the history of Western thought and philosophy than can be explored here.[1] It may seem that the attempt to isolate cognitive disabilities on their own terms in this book elides the more complicated relationship between the body and the mind, one that, I would say, is certainly recognized by disability studies scholarship. I emphasize, too, that this work is a corrective; treating cognitive disabilities alone, as I do here, is a necessary step if we are to foreground cognitive disabilities in the humanities. These discussions will necessarily complicate the existing political and academic work on disability, which emphasizes the physical. Although this chapter concisely describes the persisting effects of this differential mind–body classification, which can be observed generally as a residue in modern theory, society, and culture, it is more interested in matters of representation than in questions of ontology. After the work of this chapter is completed, rather than explain the philosophical or historical motivations for the persistent theoretical, social, and cultural marginalization of cognitive difference, I argue that a focus on visuality changes the tools we use to explore cognitive disability representations in the humanities.

Another important discussion implicit in my use of the umbrella term "cognitive disability" involves what are nonetheless important distinctions and possibly nuanced overlaps between intellectual disabilities, developmental disabilities, and psychiatric disabilities. Of course, readers should be aware that these terms clearly reflect a wide range of cognitive experiences and that these experiences themselves are not always without a physical component or coexisting disabilities that are seen as physical. Of the three categories of cognitive disabilities that are the focus of this book, the inclusion of psychiatric disabilities here may perhaps seem the most out of place to some readers. But attending to this group – precisely *because* it may seem out of place – is perhaps the most essential component of this project, for it speaks to the way in which disabilities related to cognition are more likely to be seen through a medical rather than a social lens.

Historically, the distinctions between what are today termed intellectual disabilities, developmental disabilities, and psychiatric disabilities were neither clearly observed nor recorded as such – as is suggested in Patrick McDonagh's wonderful book *Idiocy: A Cultural History* (2008). Mark Rapley's *The Social Construction of Intellectual Disability* (2004) also signals the way in which the boundaries established between each of these categories may be negotiated differently in certain contexts. Here it is of interest that even today use of the term "psychiatric disability" is extremely rare in disability scholarship in the humanities. In Hispanic studies, for example, I consider Candace Skibba's use of the term in her book chapter "The Other Body: Psychiatric Disability and Pedro Almodóvar (1988–2011)" (2016) to be highly significant. Following her lead, I employ this term here as an attempt to stake claim to humanities study of the representation of psychiatric disabilities among disability studies scholars; schizophrenia is the psychiatric disability that perhaps most frequently captures the public imagination and is discussed in chapter 6. While disability studies theorists, with much success, have worked to wrest discursive control of those disabilities taken to be physical – such as blindness, deafness, and missing limbs – from the clinical gaze, medicalized discourse has continued to be a predominant theoretical voice speaking on issues related to Down syndrome, autism, Alzheimer's disease, and schizophrenia, for example. It is currently the case that intellectual disabilities, developmental disabilities, and what goes by the name of madness or mental disorder continue to be disproportionately explained by health field practitioners and not by humanists, even given the rise of humanities interest in the subfield of Mad Studies.[2]

A time of opportunity has arrived. The same humanistic inquiry that has invigorated the study of physical disabilities through the lens of a social model can now similarly reclaim cognitive disabilities from the medicalizing gaze. What makes this a time of great opportunity is the increased attention given to cognitive disabilities in cultural production. In the last decade, intellectual, developmental, and psychiatric disabilities have enjoyed a relatively high level of cultural representation that humanities scholars are in a unique position to explore. I mention a range of examples from the Spanish context in chapters 4, 5 and 6, but this trend can arguably be observed also in Anglophone contexts – consider the spectacular representation of Down syndrome in A&E's reality show *Born This Way* (2015–16, currently in its second season), Alzheimer's in the Hollywood film *Still Alice* (2014), starring Julianne Moore, and possibly schizophrenia in *Shutter Island* (2010), with the protagonist role played by Leonard DiCaprio. Scholarship in the humanities can comment on the way disability representations operate in artistic texts and simultaneously on their greater resonance within social discourse. Here I apply the somewhat broad notion of cultural production as an approach to discussing how cognitive disability is represented in artistic products such as the comic/graphic novel and the feature-length documentary film, as well as in the staged and embodied production of paintings by cognitively disabled artists in the urban environment itself. As will be revealed in this book's exploration of these and other examples, I am particularly interested in visual representations of cognitive disability. Apart from some considerations addressed in chapter 3 – which are necessary as a contrast to foreground the characteristic aspects of visual representations – here I do not engage prose literature at length. Instead I seek to blend a humanities approach to visual culture with disability studies method, in every case prioritizing the need to attend to those artistic properties particular to the form of cultural production under study. In addition, I want to push disability studies scholars to embrace a dual emphasis on embodiment and cognition. Although it is beyond the scope of this book to explore the insights towards which this dual emphasis might lead, acknowledging the commonalities and distinctions between physical and cognitive disability representations will be an important step in strengthening academic and political discourse related to disability.

Before moving forward, I draw the reader's attention to the question that serves as the epigraph for this chapter. In his foundational *A History of Disability* ([1982]1997, translated from the French by William Sayers), Henri-Jacques Stiker asked whether we are justified in "separating the physically disabled from the mentally deficient" ([1982]1997: 139). Although his remark may have been intended as a comment on particular historical circumstances, which I explore briefly below, readers may sense correctly that it has an even greater resonance. Stiker's question works on all three of the levels with which the present book dialogues (the theoretical, the social, and the cultural). It is clear to me – as I believe it was to Stiker – that these two populations have been separated in historical reality – that is, that the modern histories of the physically disabled and the cognitively disabled are not the same. Of the fact that this uneven history has resulted in an uneven contemporary moment there can be no doubt. Echoing Stiker, the next three sections of this chapter briefly illustrate how the "physically disabled" and the "mentally deficient" have been approached theoretically, socially, and culturally through very different and very uneven levels of attention.

The Theoretical or Discursive Field

In their book *Narrative Prosthesis* – a text that since its publication in 2000 has become a touchstone for the field of disability studies – David T. Mitchell and Sharon L. Snyder (2000: 39) wrote of the need for work on cognitive disabilities. It is helpful here to briefly contextualize Mitchell and Snyder's remark for contemporary readers. When we look at some of the canonical texts in the humanities that launched disability studies scholarship in its contemporary form, we find that mention of cognitive disabilities is extremely rare. Out of the twenty-seven chapters in the first edition of the *Disability Studies Reader* (1997, edited by

Lennard J. Davis) and the twenty-six numbered chapters in *Freakery: Cultural Spectacles of the Extraordinary Body* (1996, edited by Rosemarie Garland-Thomson), for example, cognitive disability is not central to a single one. The *Disability Studies Reader*'s first edition mentioned audism (1997: 286), but not autism; dwarfism (1997: 336), but not Down syndrome; stigma as cognitive processing (1997: 221–3), but not schizophrenia. Garland-Thomson's volume, focused as it is on spectacles made of the exceptional body, pushed no further into cognitive terrain, although it is valuable on its own terms. Simply put, cognitive disability did not appear in these foundational scholarly approaches to disability.

Lingering, for a moment, on Davis's brief introduction to that first edition of the *Disability Studies Reader*, readers will note that the text consistently emphasizes the body at the expense of cognition. Drawing attention to ableist misperceptions, it risks reducing disability to an identifiable physical trait: "a missing limb, blindness, deafness. What could be simpler to understand?" (1997: 2). Davis there critiques writing that "tended to be written so that 'normal' people might know what it is like to be blind, crippled, deaf, *and so on*" (1997: 4, emphasis added). In the passage that leads up to mention of the passing of the ADA (Americans with Disabilities Act) in 1990, the text reads: "there have been people with disabilities throughout history, but it has only been in the last twenty years that one-armed people, quadriplegics, the blind, people with chronic diseases, *and so on*, have seen themselves as a single, allied, united physical minority" (1997: 3, emphasis added). Culminating on the last page of the introduction, references to "received truths of culture and the body," "able-bodied writing," and a "grand unified theory of the body" transparently reflect the physical emphasis of the chapters to follow (1997: 5). His final sentence in that first edition points towards a future when "the marginalized being *in the wheelchair or using sign language*, the person with disabilities will become the ultimate example, the universal image, the modality through whose knowing the postmodern subject can theorize and act" (1997: 5, emphasis added). Nowhere in this account is any intellectual, developmental, or psychiatric disability mentioned, except perhaps as an implicit echo in the "and so on" that repeats in the material quoted above. Rather than being seen as a failing of that individual publication, the lack of interest in cognitive disability on display in the first edition of Davis's nonetheless valuable edited volume should be taken as an expression of the kind of disability studies scholarship that humanists were engaged in at the time. If that edition of the *Disability Studies*

Reader was indeed the culmination of a decades-long first wave of humanities interest in disability studies, as I take it to be, its approach spoke specifically – and, as the present view would have it, in a somewhat limited fashion – to the high degree of visibility of physical disabilities in areas as divergent as the Disability Rights Movement, government legislation such as the ADA, popular culture and media representations, and the wider social realm itself.[3]

Another revealing case in point concerns the publication of book-length monographs focusing on disability and emphasizing the physical over the cognitive. Those titles appearing on a short list of what were arguably the most important humanities books in the interdisciplinary field of disability studies prior to the year 2000 would reveal how widespread was this emphasis on the physical. The predominance of physical disability can be gleaned merely from glancing at these titles, which should surely figure near the top, if not *at* the top, of any such list: Lennard J. Davis's *Enforcing Normalcy: Disability, Deafness, and the Body* (1995), Susan Wendell's *The Rejected Body: Feminist Philosophical Reflections on Disability* (1996), Rosemarie Garland-Thomson's *Extraordinary Bodies: Figuring Physical Disability in American Culture and Literature* (1997), David T. Mitchell and Sharon L. Snyder's *The Body and Physical Difference: Discourses of Disability* (1997), and Brenda Jo Brueggemann's *Lend Me Your Ear: Rhetorical Constructions of Deafness* (1999). Unfortunately, despite its undeniable value, the volume *Disability Studies: Enabling the Humanities* (2002), published by the Modern Language Association and edited by Sharon Snyder, Brenda Jo Brueggemann, and Rosemarie Garland-Thomson, included no sustained conversations regarding cognitive disabilities.

It would be unfair, however, to say that the field has not opened up quite a bit since the year 2000. Developments in intersectionality and queer studies have led disability studies scholars to reinvest in the relationships among physical, psychological, social, and political forces in the process of negotiating subjectivity as constructed within normative power structures. These developments have been particularly significant over the past decade. In addition to Robert McRuer's already classic *Crip Theory: Cultural Signs of Queerness and Disability* (2006), more recent books like Julie Avril Minich's *Accessible Citizenships: Disability, Nation and the Cultural Politics of Greater Mexico* (2014) have addressed humanities texts through a synthesis of approaches (in Minich's text: prose literature, film, and theatre via LGBTQ studies, Chican@ Studies, and disability studies).[4] It is also promising that more and more studies on cognitive disability have been published in article form in the twenty-first century. One need only look at the essays published in two of the field's top-tier journals: *Disability Studies Quarterly* (DSQ) and *Journal of Literary and Cultural Disability Studies* (JLCDS). The special sections appearing therein – for example, on cognitive impairment, edited by Lucy Burke (JLCDS 2.1 [2008]); on emotion and disability, edited by Elizabeth Donaldson and Catherine Prendergast (JLCDS 5.2 [2011]]); on disability and madness, edited by Noam Ostrander and Bruce Henderson (DSQ 33.1 [2013]); on autism and neurodiversity, edited by Emily Thornton Savarese and Ralph James Savarese (DSQ 30.1 [2010]); and on learning disabilities, edited by David J. Connor and Beth A. Ferri (DSQ 30.2 [2010]) – are significant contributions that precede the present book in the attention they place on intellectual, developmental, and psychiatric disabilities.

Moreover, the differences between the first edition of *The Disability Studies Reader* published in 1997 and its fourth edition published in 2013 are significant. The fourth edition expanded its contents from twenty-seven to forty-two contributions and included a number of new selections perhaps solicited precisely to push beyond a purely physical understanding of disability. Five of the newly included chapters are particularly poignant additions in this sense: Bradley Lewis's "A Mad Fight: Psychiatry and Disability Activism" (ch. 9), Liat Ben-Moshe's "'The Institution Yet to Come': Analyzing Incarceration through a Disability Lens" (ch. 10), Catherine Prendergast's "The Unexceptional Schizophrenic: A Post-Postmodern Introduction" (ch. 18), Margaret Price's "Defining Mental Disability" (ch. 22), and Joseph N. Straus's "Autism as Culture" (ch. 34).

Yet even with these productive and inclusive shifts, in the main cognitive disability remains a secondary interest in contrast to the much more widely appreciated intersection between physical disability and – as Davis put it in the first edition – "the differences implied in gender, nationality, ethnicity, race and sexual preferences" (1997: 5). It is still the case, for example, that many of the outstanding disability studies monographs published since 2000 have continued the primacy of the visual (i.e., physical disability) in disability studies work. Garland-Thomson's *Staring: How We Look* (2009), while a wonderful and powerful "anatomy of staring" (2009: 9), tends to emphasize corporeal over cognitive exceptionality.[5] Tobin Siebers's masterful *Disability Aesthetics* (2010) is also a path-breaking humanities analysis of the body in visual art, but is no less physical in orientation.

Stuart Murray's *Representing Autism: Culture, Narrative, Fascination* (2008), however, is an important exception and as such is essential reading for a second wave of disability studies research focused on cognitive difference. Although it focuses on autism specifically, the book's introduction speaks broadly to the invisibility of cognitive difference within disability theory. It is easy to agree with his characterizations there: that Snyder and Mitchell's *Cultural Locations of Disability* (2006), for example, "has little to say about cognitive exceptionality generally," that the "centrality that the *body* occupies in contemporary disability studies that focus on narrative is nearly ubiquitous," and that otherwise impressive contributions to the field by significant scholars "often make the linguistic slip whereby 'disability' in their writing comes to mean physical impairment" (Murray 2008: 8, original emphasis).[6] Murray suggests that the notion of visibility may figure into the tendency by disability scholars to avoid autism in particular (2008: 8-9), and one might extend this point more generally to explain avoidance of the topic of cognitive disabilities. Simply put, disability studies theory avoids exploring those disabilities that are less visible in society. The problem with this evasion is, as Murray explains, that "of course, seen in these terms the brain is as physical if not as markedly visible, as part of the body as a limb" (2008: 8). Those with cognitive disabilities are less visible in theoretical inquiries, and those same inquiries tend to theorize the social marginalization of people with physical disabilities as representative of people with all manner of disabilities. As Murray points out (with his reference to the autistic body in particular, of course), the bodies of those with cognitive disabilities are also subjected to physical control by social, political, and cultural forces. This cannot and should not be disputed. In this sense, theory and academic discourse hide nuances related to cognitive disabilities from theoretical consideration and thereby obscure the ideologies that are particular to the cognitively abled gaze. It is possible, then, that disability scholarship has – inadvertently, perhaps – aided in constructing a homogenized view of disabled populations by prioritizing the exceptional physical body.

The question that disability studies scholars should be asking is whether cognitive disabilities merit their own attention, and if so, how this attention impacts the wider field. This question is decidedly not meant to take authors of previous works in disability studies to task; rather, it points to a way of accounting for difference in what would otherwise be imagined as an undifferentiated physically disabled population. Elevating cognitive disability to the same level of theoretical interest as that enjoyed by physical disabilities is a crucial step towards recognizing that the social environment is disabling in both a physical and a cognitive sense. Focusing sufficient critical attention on the mind, and not merely on the body, will surely strengthen disability studies critique. This is, of course, a field that due to its historical links with programs in gender and sexuality studies has long underscored the significant relationships between sociopolitical formations and subjectivity. How is it that a field so aware of the physical, social, and psychological dimensions of identity has neglected, almost wholesale, those populations experiencing cognitive disability? As indicated by the title of this chapter – "On the (In)Visibility of Cognitive Disability" – this neglect makes sense only if we are willing to recognize the visual moorings of the able-bodied gaze to which the vast majority of disability studies scholars speak. This gaze is a social and political power that has harnessed the visible world towards its own ends. Scholars working in disability studies have done well in combatting this visual mechanism of subjugation, discrimination, and marginalization on its own terms – on its home terrain of the visible world. (This way of combatting power is not unique to disability studies.) To the able-bodied colonization of the visual field, disability studies opposes the cult of the visual; yet in privileging the notion that social power is anchored purely in the visual, much of the theoretical work on disability has limited the field's scope to what is visible in the simplest sense.

The above is intended as a concise snapshot of the history of physical bias in disability theory. I do not want to question the value of work in disability studies either pre-2000 or post-2000, but merely to call attention to what is being left out. Once this bias is acknowledged it cannot come as a surprise that the medical and health fields continue to dominate discussions of cognitive disabilities. Yet if we are to understand those disabling power structures that are less visible in society, another complementary approach is needed. This approach will need to be more inclusive of the cultural locations of cognitive disabilities, specifically. It will have to grapple more thoroughly not merely with the lack of demonstrated interest in developmental, intellectual, and psychiatric disabilities among humanities theorists but also with the blurry and insufficiently recorded history of how those with cognitive disabilities have been marginalized within cognitively abled societies. The concise account I provide as introductory context in the next section should in no way be seen as a substitute for carrying out more thorough historical work on cognitive disabilities from a disability studies perspective.

The Historical or Social Field

If disability studies has for decades been about confronting and investigating the disabling conditions experienced by "exceptional bodies," we must understand that this emphasis recapitulates the prehistory of a majority able-bodied society's understanding of disability. Previous disability studies research reveals that this prehistory was driven by visual forms, chief among them the photograph and the freak show. (I save discussion of the cinema for the next section focusing on cultural or artistic representation, though I admit it is not possible to fully separate the historical or social from the cultural or artistic realms or even to clearly define these.) Although both of these forms necessarily draw upon what Elizabeth Stephens has called "the culture of public spectacles emergent during the mid-eighteenth century," which was itself related to "the rise of modern medicine over the same period" (2011: 5), the photograph and the freak show are relatively distinct visual forms of cultural representation that reached their apogee during the nineteenth century.[7] As such they unfolded in a historical context in which able-bodied encounters with physical disability and cognitive disability were defined by the trope of (in)visibility in specific ways. Through the social power invested in institutions and the proper conduct continually reproduced through adherence to everyday able-bodied norms, disabled populations were frequently kept from the view of the able-bodied majority; and through the alienated forms of visible spectacle made possible by photography and the freak show, disability was exposed for visual consumption by able-bodied publics. As scholars have noted, the visible representation of disability functioned as a distillation of "otherness" intended to reaffirm the produced notion of normalcy for able-bodied audiences.

With research drawing on thousands of photographs, Robert Bogdan's *Picturing Disability: Beggar, Freak, Citizen, and Other Photographic Rhetoric* (2012, with Martin Elks and James A. Knoll) provides a comprehensive look into how the photograph represented disability for public visual consumption in various forms (e.g., sideshow souvenirs, begging cards, poster children, advertisements, art photography, personal keepsakes, and more). The chapter in that volume authored solely by Martin Elks, "Clinical Photographs" (ch. 6), looks specifically at the way "feeble-mindedness" was represented through photography in order to validate the agendas of late-nineteenth- and early-twentieth-century eugenicists in the United States, but it is fair to say that overall the book's contents emphasize physical disability. This book, along with David Hevey's foundational text *The Creatures Time Forgot: Photography and Disability Imagery* (1992), helps readers understand a principle inherent in the social practice underlying disability photography. Contextualizing photographic representation within an ableist society reveals how visual consumption of disability is always tied to the extra-artistic oppression of disabled people (Hevey 1997: 345).[8] It is clear from these and other studies that photography of disability in both its clinical and commercial forms since the nineteenth century has been exploitative, and furthermore, the visual form of exploitation in question has largely centred on the representation of physical disability.

Inspired by the pioneering work of Leslie Fiedler (*Freaks: Myths and Images of the Secret Self*, 1978) and Robert Bogdan (*Freak Show: Presenting Human Oddities for Amusement and Profit*, 1988) – and tying in to earlier work on stigma by Erving Goffman (1963) and more recent theorizations of performativity by Judith Butler (1993) – Garland-Thomson's edited volume *Freakery* (1996) invigorated academic interest in investigating the cultural resonance of freak shows. These shows, which reached their peak between 1840 and 1940 (Garland-Thomson 1996: 23), found widespread resonance through the efforts of P.T. Barnum. Photographs could be viewed privately by individuals or smaller groups; the freak show entailed a much more public performance of normalcy. Through such performance, staged and spectacular encounters with visible disabilities – most frequently those of a physical nature – worked to produce what Garland-Thomson calls the "common" and "indistinguishable" bodies of able-bodied observers:

> The exaggerated, sensationalized discourse that is the freak show's essence ranged over the seemingly singular bodies that we would now call either "physically disabled" or "exotic ethnics," framing them and heightening their differences from viewers, who were rendered comfortably common and safely standard by the exchange … A freak show's cultural work is to make the physical particularity of the freak into a hypervisible text against which the viewer's indistinguishable body fades into a seemingly neutral, tractable, and invulnerable instrument of the autonomous will, suitable to the uniform abstract citizenry democracy institutes. (Garland-Thomson 1996: 5, 10)

The nineteenth-century popularization of both photography and freak shows, however, was largely directed towards sensationalizing the exceptional body, not the exceptional mind. These display practices reaffirmed the power of the able-bodied gaze, while the cognitively abled gaze was relegated to a secondary role. These earlier visual practices were engaged in the act of producing a persisting rift between physically disabled and able-bodied people, actively heightening public interest in physical disability as spectacle while, simultaneously, cognitive disability remained hidden from view.

It is important to note that even while the photograph and the freak show were being harnessed to reaffirm able-bodied normalcy through the vehicle of the exceptional body, populations with physical and cognitive disabilities were isolated from each other. Henri-Jacques Stiker suggests a historical explanation for the distance between the relative social visibility of physical disabilities and the relative social invisibility of cognitive disabilities that is worthy of our consideration.[9] The physically disabled and the mentally ill – as the text's author puts it – were historically subjected to social power in two distinct ways. As a result, these populations were confined in two distinct social environments: the asylum for those with mental disorders, and the rehabilitation centre for those with bodily impairments:

> Before the war of 1914–18, and this will confirm the rupture as our reference point, there existed only the psychiatric institutions on one side and some establishments for those with sensory impairment on the other. The latter were not connected with the asylum. They sprang up beside it, even in opposition to it. For someone aware of the history of the treatment of insanity, this is not surprising at first glance: the "mad" were isolated, both on the level of the knowledge that was available (or that was projected) of mental disorder and on the level of institutions. By the end of the nineteenth century the Asylum was firmly in place. Alienation was the ruling concept: medicalization would be added to this moral and social action; internment is henceforth the preferred and single form of intervention; the expert psychiatrist, absolute master of the rationalized space of the asylum where all madness ends up, the benevolent leader of the phalanxes of citizens without rights, is one of the quintessentially important personages of society. The physically disabled are not in the asylum and the sequestration of the mentally ill puts an end to the mixture of the two categories. Establishments for the bodily deficient will not be born of the asylum system. ([1982]1997: 138–9)

Stiker prefers to use the term *sequestration* rather than write of social invisibility explicitly, but it is clear that internment in the asylum removed the mentally ill from the cognitively abled gaze more completely than the physically disabled were sequestered from the able-bodied gaze (see also Carlson 2010).

The result of this historical shift was a split between two different ways of seeing: each gaze – the cognitively abled and the able-bodied – rationalized and justified itself by defining and arguably producing a distinct population in its own image. Inside the asylum, the underpinnings of a psychiatric specialization were introduced, complete with a corresponding spatial environment. The clinical gaze exercised its dominion in the sheltered and relatively autonomous institution, where both its activity and the objects of its attention remained largely unseen by the wider society. By contrast, people with physical disabilities, who in this account remained outside of the asylum, were progressively distinguished as a social group in and of themselves.[10] Subsequently, as Stiker's text captures, the physically disabled gradually emerged from the ranks of the poor and began to be seen by the public eye as a distinct population (Stiker [1982]1997: 139). It is to this historical circumstance that the word "handicap" refers, as physically disabled populations were habitually associated with beggars by the able-bodied gaze.[11] In a double-move, then, those who were seen as physically disabled were left out of the total institution of the asylum and progressively distinguished from the poor and thus became historically and socially visible in a way that those with cognitive disabilities did not. This is not to downplay the new oppressions faced by the physically disabled due to their social visibility, nor is it to suggest that the institution/asylum was a place of refuge from ableism for those with cognitive disabilities. Instead, it is important to understand that rehearsing this history can help readers glimpse a historical precedent for the differential treatment of two groupings of persons disabled, arguably, by a single ableist power structure.[12]

Much as with the point elucidated by Stiker's work on the nineteenth and early twentieth centuries, part of the reason for the sustained predominance of attention given to physical disabilities over cognitive disabilities in contemporary critical theory, quite plausibly, lies in historical circumstances that predate the nineteenth century. Margaret A. Winzer's contribution to the first edition of the *Disability Studies Reader* – a chapter titled "Disability and Society before the Eighteenth Century: Dread and Despair" (1997) – prompts readers to trace this generalized differentiation even further into the past. She points out that "until the close of the eighteenth century those who fell under the broad, elastic categories labelled as insane or blind or deaf and dumb commanded most notice. Madness particularly attracted attention, although 'idiocy' (mental retardation) as a discrete and separate condition was rarely mentioned" (1997: 80).[13] As Patrick McDonagh concurs in the introduction to *Idiocy: A Cultural History* (2008), historically speaking, generalizations have abounded "that muddied the idea of idiocy – and for that matter, continue to muddy the contemporary concepts of intellectual disability, or mental retardation, or cognitive impairment, or developmental delay, or learning disability" (2008: 5; see also discussion over 5–6). This insight is supported by Winzer's account, in which she notes that historically there was no "consistent, sound means of discriminating between those who had physical disabilities (i.e. were crippled, dwarfed, epileptic, or deaf) and those who were intellectually impaired or mentally ill. All were considered to form one, all-encompassing category" (1997: 80).[14]

Physical disabilities in particular have progressively become more socially visible to an able-bodied majority population, which makes it possible to trace their historical documentation even as shifts in the sociological imagination, patterns of knowledge. and political power have changed how they are viewed by an able-bodied majority. This can be seen quite clearly, for example, in the case of deaf populations throughout history – it is possible to trace a recorded history of the deaf through time and place even though understandings of deafness have changed significantly.[15] What should be clear from even this cursory and comparative exploration of the social and historical visibility of physical and cognitive disabilities is that from the nineteenth through the twenty-first centuries, an able-bodied majority has consistently found reason to distinguish physical or sensory disabilities from cognitive disabilities that would have been classified as madness or mental disorder in a general sense. Moreover, as the next section explores in broad strokes, the investigation of both physical and cognitive disabilities in cultural or artistic representations has demonstrated similarly unequal levels of attention.

The Representational or Cultural Field

As Tobin Siebers convincingly explores in *Disability Aesthetics* (2010), visual art has long portrayed and even depended on disabilities even while rendering them invisible. He writes that disability has been present even if "rarely recognized as such" throughout the history of modern art; the presence of disability – of "strangeness" and the "convulsive," of "misshapen and twisted bodies" – has allowed "the beauty of an artwork to endure over time" (2010: 4–5; see also Siebers 1998, 2000, 2008, 2013). Of course, Siebers focused in his 2010 text mostly on sculpture and painting, not on cinema. Nevertheless, Martin F. Norden's earlier book *Cinema of Isolation: A History of Physical Disabilities in the Movies* (1994) should be seen not only as anticipating Siebers's book but also as a precursor that traces a comparable thesis through a popular art form.[16]

As the subtitle of his book indicates, Norden – like Siebers after him – had no intention to address cognitive disabilities. He writes that "as powerful cultural tools, the movies have played a major role in perpetuating mainstream society's regard for people with disabilities, and more often than not the images borne in those movies have differed sharply from the realities of the physically disabled experience" (1994: 1). Norden's is a valuable study in its own right and deserves no criticism other than to suggest that his focus on physical disability is – as with Siebers's own much more recent book – consistent with the high levels of interest regarding the exceptional body that predominate in what I am calling first-wave disability studies work. What is interesting in relation to the present study is not merely the way in which Norden captures cinematic representation's recapitulation of the presence and presumed enduring artistic value of physical disability previously rendered visible in sculpture and painting. Readers of his text will note that cinema spectatorship also reinvigorates the performance of able-bodied normalcy through visual consumption found in social practices involving nineteenth-century cultural forms such as the photograph and the freak show.

Norden's thesis, expressed concisely in his main title *Cinema of Isolation*, is that "most movies have tended to isolate disabled characters from their able-bodied peers as well as from each other" (1994: 1). He traces this thesis over approximately one hundred years of US cinema, from silent film to talkies, through the postwar era and into the late 1980s. His conclusion, titled "Reel Life after the Americans with Disabilities Act," takes on even early-1990s American films and continues to critique "Hollywood's deep equivocation on physical disability concerns" (1994: 311). This critique – which in my view is appropriate and accurate – is consistent throughout the book.[17] Readers may find that Norden is ultimately ambivalent about the value of these images. This ambivalence is evident in his suggestion that one can talk about some degree of "progress" in cinematic representation of disability. He even remains hopeful about the future of cinema:

> Progress has been particularly evident in independently produced and often modestly budgeted works ... In addition, more positive depictions have surfaced in other mainstream media, particularly television commercials and print advertising. As people with disabilities continue to make gains in our society (gains that a majority of U.S. citizens will learn of through mainstream news media, of course), their movie images will presumably begin to reflect the lives of people with physical disabilities with a greater degree of accuracy and sensitivity. (1994: 314)

Given the likelihood of intense debate surrounding what constitute "positive depictions" of disability, I suspect that not all readers from disability studies will see this hope as realistic. Nevertheless, it is important to understand that Norden's ambivalence regarding both the distortion and the potential of cinematic representations – an ambivalence that echoes sentiments expressed in an earlier 1985 essay by Paul K. Longmore[18] – is also evident in an increasing number of publications by disability scholars.[19]

Screening Disability (2001a), edited by Anthony Enns and Christopher R. Smit, published seven years after Norden's monograph, is an important further step forward in recognizing the importance of cinematic representations of disability. The book follows up on an event in March 1999, "when scholars in both Film Studies and Disability Studies gathered at the University of Iowa for the first conference on cinema and disability" (Enns and Smit 2001b: xi). Its collected essays deal largely with physical disability at the expense of cognitive disability;[20] however, the chapter titled "The Fusion of Film Studies and Disability Studies" by Thomas B. Hoeksema and Christopher R. Smit marks what I consider to be a significant and still underappreciated advance in theorizing disability on-screen. Hoeksema and Smit write that

> cinematic depictions of people who live with disability have been enormously diverse. Sometimes they contain negative and erroneous images; at other times their portrayals of disability are accurate and positive. Sometimes they respond to or reflect societal attitudes and beliefs; at other times they influence society's perceptions. We believe that it is inaccurate and insufficient to characterize cinematic depictions of disability as primarily negative and stereotypic. (2001: 35)

The claim that follows this statement is the one I regard as significant and underappreciated: "We also think that taking an activist, advocacy perspective when critiquing disability cinema risks missing insights that may be obtained by reviewing films using additional tools from the field of Film Studies" (2001: 35). One must understand this statement in the context of the entirety of the authors' chapter, which pushes disability studies scholars to grapple with the unique artistic and formal properties of film. Well into the twenty-first century, the complaint made by Hoeksema and Smit remains a familiar one to film studies scholars working in traditionally literary departments, even where disability is not considered. I note a general tendency for humanities scholars not specifically trained in cinema to reduce films to their arranged content – events, dialogue, plot, for example. This practice thus strips cultural products of their artistic specificity and meaning and reduces them to narrative documents in a simple sense. The authors call for disability studies scholars to go further and pay close attention to the formal attributes of a unique artistic medium – such elements of cinematic form as shots, angles, sound, the mobile frame, and the conventions of cinematic genre – when making sense of portrayals of disability on-screen (2001: 35, 39). I read their warning not as confirmation that activism, advocacy, and "political agency" (2001: 41) are incompatible with cinematic criticism, but rather as pointing to their frustration with how disability studies perspectives at the time tended to produce "bland and one-dimensional" interpretations (2001: 35) instead of attending to and exploring in depth the formal properties of specific visual art forms.[21]

Almost a decade after *Screening Disability* (2001a), *The Problem Body* (2010), edited by Sally Chivers and Nicole Markotić, was published. The book implicitly privileges the cinema's place in a social history of the visual exhibition of exceptional bodies, as when the editors note that "before the screen lies a place where many people can take an extended look at the disabled body and live comfortably or even uncomfortably with their reactions, be they to shudder, to desire, to identify, to pity, to turn away" (2010: 4). A valuable contribution, the book nonetheless focuses overwhelmingly on the representation of physical disability.[22] Similarly, in *Different Bodies* (2013), published three years later and edited by Marja Evelyn Mogk, only two out of nineteen essays centre on cognitive disability: "Seeing the Apricot: A Disability Perspective on Alzheimer's in Lee Chang-dong's *Poetry*" by Sally Chivers, and "*Chocolate*'s Ass-Kicking Autistic Savant: Disability, Globalization, and the Action Cinema" by Russell Meeuf. As Mogk's introduction makes clear, books such as these are carrying out important work, especially so when disability on-screen is not "seen" as such (2013: 2) and when curricula "continue to address disability predominantly or exclusively in applied fields as a category of medicine, rehabilitation services, or educational specialization" (2013: 3). Nevertheless, more work is needed if we are to foreground cognitive disabilities along with physical disabilities in a critique carried out in the humanities.[23]

In conclusion, by tracing how cognitive disabilities have historically been invisible in the theoretical, social, and cultural realms, this chapter has paved the way for those that follow. Subsequent chapters continue to dialogue with the themes established from the introduction up until now. These themes include not only the invisibility of cognitive disability but also the need to consider issues of impairment when addressing cognition and the need to pay attention to the specific formal and artistic aspects of a given medium of visual representation. The wider argument to which chapters 2 and 3 contribute involves the notion that visual representations require a different approach than has been marshalled in disability studies up until now. Chapter 2 underscores the unique properties of visual media, emphasizing the need to attend to the primary functions of iconic and indexical signification. These aspects of visual media, in particular, have tended to be underappreciated, ignored altogether, or overshadowed by the routine transposition to film of a literary model of disability research relying on metaphor, symbol, plot device, and disability as the foil for an ableist norm. This approach can continue to shed light on how disability representations work in mainstream film, but it often misses the opportunity to value the ontological assertion of visual media regarding cognitive disability – an assertion that can be particularly important in culture at the margins of mainstream discourse such as independent film and comics. What Rosemarie Garland-Thomson (2009) writes about the "generative potential" of staring reinforces the value of these representations. Chapter 3 builds on the importance of attending to iconic and indexical signification in visual media as a material connection between artistic representations and social representations of disability. It explores carefully the ways in which disability representations operate in prose literature, explicitly distinguishing the function of visual disability representations in film and comics from this prose narrative model. I use film theory and, briefly, comics theory to establish this distinction between prose and visual representations in order to prepare the ground for analyses of painting and the graphic novel in chapter 4, the graphic novel in chapter 5, and documentary film in chapter 6. In each case I attend to the potential value of cultural representations that make cognitive disability visible; I also assert the materiality of disability experience as made up of both biology/impairment on one hand and aesthetics/culture on the other.

2 Signification and Staring: Icon, Index, and Symbol in Visual Media

"Thus it should be observed that the object which becomes a film image is characterized by a degree of unity and determinism. And it is natural that it be so, because the lin-sign used by the writer has already been refined by an entire grammatical, popular, and cultural history, while the im-sign employed by the filmmaker ideally has been extracted – by the filmmaker himself, and no one else – from the insensitive chaos of objects in a process analogous to the borrowing of images from a dictionary intended for a community able to communicate only through images ... [The filmmaker] chooses a series of objects, or things, or landscapes, or persons as syntagmas (signs of a symbolic language) which *while they have a grammatical history invented in that moment* – as in a sort of happening dominated by montage – *do, however, have an already lengthy and intense pregrammatical history* ... This is probably the principal difference between literary and cinematographic works (if such a comparison matters). The linguistic or grammatical world of the filmmaker is composed of images, and [filmic] images are always concrete, never abstract."

– Pier Paolo Pasolini (1988: 171, original emphasis)

Film theorist and noted director Pier Paolo Pasolini wrote an intriguing essay titled "The 'Cinema of Poetry,'" reprinted in the anthology *Heretical Empiricism* (1988, trans. Ben Lawton and Louise K. Barnett). In it, he compares literary and filmic forms of representation through a basic semiotic vocabulary inspired by the work of Charles Sanders Peirce and reflected in the above epigraph's use of lin-signs (or linguistic signs) and im-signs (or image signs). After discussing the key elements of this basic lin-sign and im-sign terminology, this chapter calls for greater awareness regarding the unique properties of visual media and their potential for disability studies. It also sets up chapter 3's continued exploration of distinctions between literary and visual (filmic/comics) representation. To understand how the im-sign functions, scholars must balance what Pasolini calls the grammatical and pre-grammatical aspects of filmic signification. Grammatical aspects are the structural and compositional decisions conveyed in art linearly, whether in prose narrative or film; pre-grammatical aspects are the existential or perhaps even ontological properties of signs, which are rendered concrete in the visual forms of signification commonly encountered in films and graphic novels.[1] As developed by film theorist Peter Wollen, the notions of icon, index, and symbol are fundamental to understanding the weight of the im-sign's concreteness when compared with the more abstract signification that characterizes the lin-sign. Visual disability representations derive both their risk and their reward from the concreteness and materiality that iconic and indexical forms of signification provide.

Disability approaches have tended to undervalue the concreteness of the visual image. The indexical (in film) and the iconic (in both film and graphic novels) are forms of signification that have great power to connect with material experiences of disability. It should be recognized that, just as with literary narratives of disability, visual media representations can either essentialize normative disability constructions or disrupt entrenched perspectives on disability. As happens with all cultural products – novels, memoirs, theatrical productions, popular music, and so on – films and graphic novels are frequently the bearers of contradictory meanings that stem from the holistic assessment of factors related to artistic construction and composition, authorial intention, and audience reception. Nevertheless, visual representations of disability are intimately connected with embodied experience in ways that prose literary art forms are not due to a reliance on these iconic and sometimes indexical forms of signification. This chapter affirms the unique nature of these visual representations using a basic semiotic vocabulary and explores the ways in which viewers interact with these disability images. It also links these discussions to the potential value of what scholars have identified as a "new disability documentary cinema" (Snyder and Mitchell 2010: 193).

The first step carried out below is to explore the notions of im-sign and lin-sign addressed by Pasolini, and the iconic and indexical aspects of filmic signification theorized by Wollen, to assert "The Concreteness of the Filmic Image." While mainstream representations of experiences of disability have arguably been widely and historically normative and thus negative, there are reasons to look more carefully at screen images of disability in the twenty-first century. In particular, Sharon Snyder and David Mitchell's notion of a "new disability documentary cinema" supports the potentially transgressive properties of visual disability representations. This approach can underscore how symbolic approaches build on the fundamentally iconic/indexical links between textual (or aesthetic/cultural) representation and extra-textual (or more properly social) representation of material experiences of disability.

In order to theorize how the study of cognitive disability in film might begin to move forward on its own terms, the second section of this chapter, "Pre-Grammatical and Grammatical Disability Representations," begins with a discussion of director Jaco van Dormael's short film *The Kiss* (1995). Framing the aesthetic realm of cinema as one in which the "cognitive code of reality" identified by Pasolini continues to operate, this section illustrates how filmic disability representations rely on iconic/indexical signification to constitute an ontological assertion that need not conflict with the strong social model of disability. Also integrated are the productive aspects of staring as identified by Garland-Thomson in her book *Staring: How We Look* (2009), aspects that are relevant to how the meaning of visual media hinges on material links between artistic and social representation. While visual media have the potential to bring greater social visibility to cognitive disabilities, their messages risk being conditioned by normative codes of ableism. Acknowledging this nuanced tension between the potentially disruptive and normative poles of visual representation, using the cinema as a primary example, is necessary if we are to move beyond the somewhat reductive approach that has seen visual disability representations as largely negative. Overall, this account allows for a twenty-first-century disability cinema to actually induce new forms of thinking in viewers, thinking that is in principle transferrable to other visual art forms and social situations outside of the work of art. In this paradigm the issue of cognition is thus doubly important. Cognitive disabilities are increasingly rendered visible on-screen, thus potentially correcting for a legacy of historical invisibility in the social realm; in addition, cognition is implicated in the way film viewers convert what Garland-Thomson calls the "visual work" of staring into new knowledge about the social origin of disability and its non-spectacular, material experience in everyday life.

The Concreteness of the Filmic Image

As asserted in this chapter's epigraph, the im-signs encountered in film "are always concrete and never abstract." Due to their concreteness, filmic images possess and necessarily communicate immediately *"an already lengthy and intense pregrammatical history"* – that is, a history that exists prior to, and thus predates, their incorporation into the grammatical and thus linear "language" of cinema. By contrast, the verbal and necessarily abstract lin-signs used in prose narrative are conditioned more by their immersion in grammatical webs of meaning or in the organizational structures of novelistic form. To illustrate Pasolini's point about the cinema, let us use a purposely simple and concrete example. Consider the possibility that in a given prose narrative written in English, readers encounter the lin-sign "tree." There is no question that – in the context of literary representation – this "tree" exists. Readers will likely immediately picture this "tree" visually, or said another way, they will give form to this tree "in their mind's eye." But consider for a moment that there is not, in fact, any such material object outside of the text that corresponds to this "tree" – for "tree" is a verbal moniker that refers to a general conceptual category of objects, and not to a specific object. Note that this lin-sign, the word "tree," is culturally and socially defined. Its imagined existence is highly dependent on readers' experiences. The visualization of this lin-sign by readers in the context of an imagined scene prompted by the text is not likely to be completely abstract – it is necessary to point out that some readers may supply layers of definition and concreteness to their imagined referent. That is, some may visualize a "pine tree," others a "pecan tree," others still perhaps even a "quince tree." Thus, as this example shows, much if not almost all of the concreteness that arises with such a visualization is lacking in the literary text itself and is necessarily produced through the reader's encounter with it. This itself is evidence of the abstraction characteristic of what Pasolini calls the lin-sign, and of what are the primarily arbitrary and symbolic dimensions of signification as encountered in prose narrative.

Let us substitute "quince tree" for "tree." Here we will note that not much has changed regarding the abstractness of the literary sign. The lin-sign "quince tree" is still an arbitrary sign whose full attributes readers are called upon to supply in their mind's eye. The size and shape of the tree, its height, its branches, its attributes in general, are not completely and thoroughly specified in literary signification. Even in the most exacting description of a referent by a literary text there are, unavoidably and necessarily, gaps of a certain nature. Neither do we see, concretely, what surrounds the "quince tree" in the collectively imagined space of prose narrative. We do not see the sun's rays cast against it producing a shadow; nor do we see it moving with the breeze. The pre-grammatical history of this lin-sign is thus limited and conditioned – but also made possible, it is important to point out – by the reader's experience or lack of experience with the presumed referent. By its very nature, any such lin-sign in prose narrative is from this perspective an incomplete or half-drawn signifier.

Furthermore, there are wider cultural forces at play that must be addressed. Does the "quince tree" function as a symbol conditioned by social convention? Does it evoke a certain socially determined mood? Is it received differently across global readerships or in specific cultural contexts? Does it remind contemporary readers in Madrid, for example, of the various quince tree images painted by Madrid-based artist Antonio López García or of images from filmmaker Víctor Érice's Madrid-based cinematic essay *El sol del membrillo* (The Quince-Tree Sun) (1992)?[2] In brief, whether the example is "tree," or "quince tree," or any other lin-sign whatsoever, the premise is the same. Readers of prose narrative are immersed in a realm of relatively abstract signification – all the more so when compared with the visual signification of the cinema. Adopting the perspective of a reader of literary narrative entails being thrust into a signifying arena where meaning is primarily and heavily impacted by social convention and everyday experience.

All of this background is necessary to make a simple point: in visual representations one will never encounter an im-sign possessing the sheer weight of abstractness evidenced by the lin-sign "tree." A filmic image, for instance, is always concrete and never abstract, as Pasolini asserts. That is, a "tree" in film is always necessarily and unavoidably a "pine tree" or a "pecan tree" or a "quince tree." More than that, since film is both a spatial and a temporal medium, we will see the object's contour, shape, outline, texture, and so on clearly and concretely represented on the screen. This is true whether the object is cropped extremely close or shot at a distance, whether is it captured in a long take or barely visible on account of a quick edit. The object in film necessarily always appears in a spatial context (fictional or not) that is explicit or implicit – admitting, that is, the continual existence of off-screen space as a necessary, unavoidable, and pervasive element of the cinema. Taking into account the temporality of cinema, we may in all likelihood see the sun's rays cast a shadow upon the im-sign "tree"; we may see its leaves and branches move with the breeze. On film, as viewers we will bear witness to the spatial and temporal existence of the tree. This general premise is one that can be described here in terms of the ontological quality of photography or in terms of cinema's commitment to material or physical reality.[3]

As an entire counter-tradition of film theory has worked to establish throughout the twentieth century and into the twenty-first, it is possible to separate out three different aspects of filmic signification that directly inform our discussion of filmic disability representations and that are of relevance, too, in discussions of the visual representations found in comics/graphic novels. (1) The indexical aspect of the im-sign derives from the fact that, in celluloid film, the impression of light upon sensitive material directly supplies the image that viewers of cinema perceive. (2) The iconic aspect of this im-sign is defined as the similitude between the form, outline, shape, or contour of the concrete image and the form, outline, shape, or contour of its material referent. (3) The symbolic aspect of this im-sign would be layered onto this iconic aspect and also heavily conditioned by social convention. The example of the "quince tree" given above broached the topic of artistic convention – as evinced by the potential links to the work of painter Antonio López García or director Víctor Érice. Links with a more historically rooted and conventionalized cultural symbolism are also operative, however – for example, the fact that the "quince tree" might evoke love, fertility, and even health when viewed in Japanese contexts.[4]

Film theorist Peter Wollen's main thesis, in the underappreciated but nonetheless classic work *Signs and Meaning in the Cinema* (1972), is that meaning in the cinema is constructed simultaneously through these three modes of signification: icon, index, and symbol. It is important to note that this general thesis has been continued by a somewhat marginal line of theorizations that continue into the twenty-first century, even as it has also been widely ignored by more mainstream traditions of film theory (as Stephen Prince [1999] details). Wollen elaborates on the coexistence of these aspects of filmic signification thus: "The cinema contains all three modes of the sign: indexical, iconic and symbolic. What has always happened is that theorists of the cinema have seized on one or more of these dimensions and used it as the ground for an aesthetic firman" (1972: 125).[5] His insight has been a touchstone for arguments sustained since the late 1960s and 1970s that the iconic and indexical aspects of cinema need to be reasserted in film theory as complements to the arbitrary and symbolic aspects of film "language."[6] This move to restore iconicity and indexicality to film theory, to which Wollen contributes, is one that can be productive for disability studies, and for studies of cognitive disability in particular, as this chapter explores. Complicating this move, however, are the current contradictions inherent in existing studies of filmic disability representations. Current approaches to the filmic representation of disability largely take the material experience of disability to be self-evident while at the same time leaving the iconic and indexical aspects of that disability representation undertheorized.

With this context in mind, we can transition towards two central points. The first of these is that the medium-specific aspects of filmic signification outlined briefly above have not been sufficiently articulated with disability studies scholarship. Broadly speaking, the humanities have emphasized literary disability representations at the expense of filmic disability representations, and prose narrative over visual narrative. This is because the MLA disciplines have been somewhat slow to break with their own (i.e., literary) traditions. Rapidly evolving and high-profile methodological innovations are gaining ground in the field, and newer generations of researchers are pursuing other forms of cultural production such as film, graphic novels, popular music, and video games; yet English departments and top-tier journals continue to prize traditional studies of print literature – disproportionately so. In a high number of MLA departments, including but not limited to those in my own field of Hispanic studies, faculty researching cultural products beyond prose literature frequently opt to present their work in non-MLA-field conferences and to publish it in journal venues grounded outside of or at the margins of MLA fields.[7] It is also significant that existing interest in the humanities in the topic of disability on film has often entailed merely transposing a literary model onto the realm of cinema, without a full appreciation of the nuances of visual signification.

The impact of this traditionalism has been that, on the whole, disability representations in film have been seen as operating in the same way as disability representations in literature. By this I mean that analyses have most frequently paid attention to notions of artistic structure, literary device, plot, metaphor, and symbolism in terms relevant to prose literature, but have not specifically addressed those elements of film that distinguish the cinema from literature. In studies of disability representations, this literary emphasis is, of course, testament to the enduring value of the way that Mitchell and Snyder explored disability narrative in their foundational book *Narrative Prosthesis* (2000). The approach outlined in that foundational text is generally applicable to sociocultural representations in the broadest sense, including those appearing in film contexts, and it continues to have an effect on the field's current directions. In the introduction to their edited volume *The Problem Body: Projecting Disability on Film* (2010), in fact, Sally Chivers and Nicole Markotić directly establish a link with Snyder and Mitchell's concept:

> As David Mitchell and Sharon Snyder point out in *Narrative Prosthesis*, disability in narrative is both excessively visible and conversely invisible (15). Rather than absent, as other stigmatized social identities can be (for example, films can entirely avoid lead female or racialized roles), disability is highly and continuously present on-screen. However, it is not always agential. Often disabled bodies appear in order to shore up a sense of normalcy and strength in a presumed-to-be able-bodied audience. In this book we follow this argument into narrative film, noting the contradiction between how many characters in films display disabilities and how seldom reviewers and audiences "notice" disability as a feature within the film.

The editors' intention to focus on "filmic narrative" (Chivers and Markotić 2010: 1) is productive from a disability studies perspective, as is their focus on how viewers "project" disability in their interaction with the screen. But it is important to point out that this twin focus does not in any sense exhaust analysis of the nuances specific to filmic disability representation.[8] Emphasizing what happens in the film's action – with the question of who says what to whom, for example, often figuring prominently in such accounts – can be a meaningful way of dialoguing with able-bodied viewers' attitudes and reactions. Critiquing disability films from a perspective grounded in literary conventions can certainly help expose the normative social codes and the metanarratives embedded in visual storytelling; nonetheless, visual storytelling by its very nature overflows these explanations in its reliance on iconic and indexical signification and the concrete character of its visual representations.

The second point is that the physical orientation of disability studies has largely been continued in the study of filmic disability and that more work on cinematic representations of cognitive disability is sorely needed. I adopt a dual perspective on cognition that emphasizes its crucial role both in the lives represented on-screen in disability cinema and in the imaginative thought processes by which viewers connect with disability representations. Snyder and Mitchell in their own co-authored contribution to *The Problem Body* make some intriguing and relevant points in the section titled "New Disability Documentary Cinema" (2010: 193–201) on which this chapter seeks to build. This term underscores the gradual emergence of films that push back against the ableist tropes of disability commonly found in big-budget cinema. These films are generally screened and circulated outside of established and ableist (inter)national circuits, and it might be fair to say that they achieve their greatest recognition at "in(ter)depedent" disability film festivals (see Mitchell and Snyder 2015, 2016).

> One could argue that the primary convention of the new documentary genre is the effort to turn disability into a chorus of perspectives that deepen and multiply narrow cultural labels that often imprison disabled people within taxonomic medical categories … While disability documentary films *do not seek* to repress, suppress, or erase the fact of differing biological capacities and appearances (as is sometimes charged in critiques of disability studies), they *do* seek to refute pathological classifications that prove too narrow and limiting to encompass an entire human life *lived*. (Snyder and Mitchell 2010: 198; original emphasis)

I agree with Snyder and Mitchell that too little attention has been paid to the potentially positive contributions of new disability documentary cinema. There are ontological and critical aspects to the point that Snyder and Mitchell are making here: this new documentary cinema testifies to the existence of a life and asserts this life lived against the limitations of medical paradigms. Importantly, they leave room in their assessment for "differing biological capacities and appearances." Their phrase "a chorus of perspectives" is equally significant, in that it resonates with their insistence on "the portrayal of disability *ensembles*" (2010: 198, original emphasis). Using these phrases, Mitchell and Snyder implicitly recuperate Norden's critique, in *Cinema of Isolation* (1994), of the "lone figure" disability representation – a "staple and contrivance of popular genre filmmaking" (2010: 198).

Part of the potential power of this reconfigured disability cinema comes from how film can present the biological or material experience of disability through iconic/indexical signification while embedding that experience in a specifically social context. This category of new disability documentary cinema certainly should not include all documentaries or fiction films containing disability representations or emphasizing the theme of disability. A great number of films depicting disability undoubtedly continue to do so from a normative perspective, expressing a harmful reliance on the personal tragedy model, the figure of the supercrip, or other ableist attitudes and stereotypes. Yet as Snyder and Mitchell seem to indicate, new disability documentary cinema may prove to be significant because of the potential balance such films establish between biological or experiential impairment and social context. As they assert, "the point of the new disability documentary cinema is not to refuse impairment (as many contend even in disability studies)" (2010: 199).[9] What is significant is not merely that impairment is not refused in such new disability documentary films, but that it is presented more directly via the concreteness of iconic and indexical signification. This does not mean there are no metaphorical, symbolic, or socially/culturally constructed aspects of disability representation in documentary cinema, but it does mean – contrary to what happens in the arbitrary, metaphorical, symbolic, and highly socially conditioned signification that pervades literary narrative (see chapter 3) – that disability on film is not *solely* a discursive construction. This does not mean that we mistake cinema for reality and essentialize disability, locating it in bodies. It does mean that disability studies has more reason to pay attention to the way in which icon, index, and symbolic modes of signification all interact to produce complex cinematic texts. The return to biology and impairment can thus reinvigorate the study of visual art in general and documentary cinema in particular. A focus on cognition in film can help expand on the physical orientation of much work in disability studies and bring visibility to socially and historically invisible populations.

Pre-Grammatical and Grammatical Aspects of Disability Representations

It is important to understand what occurs when viewers interact with visual disability representations. There is a great difference between those representations that may be normative or ableist in construction and the more progressive depiction that Snyder and Mitchell allow for in their discussion of the new disability documentary cinema. For the moment, however, it is necessary to attend to the mechanism of viewership itself, and to continue to do so within a comparative approach outlined by Pasolini, one that juxtaposes the lin-sign and the im-sign. The concept of "the gaze" has been a central component of a whole tradition of critical film theory – expressed perhaps most famously in Laura Mulvey's essay "Visual Pleasure and Narrative Cinema" (1975). Nevertheless, though this tradition is still very much applicable to the study of disability representations, I believe that Garland-Thomson's notion of "staring," which she explicitly contrasts with "the gaze," better elucidates the potentially transformative aspects of new disability documentary cinema. I underscore here Garland-Thomson's assertion that visual work is cognitive work (Garland-Thomson 2009: ch. 5), but I am also interested in how cognition applies to represented material as well as what makes the act of representation possible or knowable. I believe that what she calls "staring's generative potential" in the social realm can be adapted also to the artistic realm – to filmic disability representations directly and to other visual disability representations (e.g., those in comics/graphic novels) as well.

This section is grounded in a simple but underappreciated idea: at the level of signification in literature (Pasolini's "lin-sign"), it is possible to suggest constellations of disability that are not concrete or specific – imprecise hints of bodily exceptionality/cognitive capacity, tropes of presence and lack, and a disembodied, discursive resonance with disability carried out via an author's style. Such representations do not have to reflect the specificities of biology or impairment or the material experience of disability. Even when we are discussing realism in literary production – whether understood as trope, stylistic mode, or movement – at the level of signification, literary disability representations are not required to be, for lack of a better term, realistic. Michael Bérubé's book *The Secret Life of Stories: From Don Quixote to Harry Potter: How Understanding Intellectual Disability Transforms the Way We Read* (2016) engages this aspect of literary disability representations from a nuanced critical perspective that allows for both ableist and disruptive, non-normative literary treatments of disability. He even notes the possibility that readers may "find in fictional modes of intellectual disability a way of imagining other ways of being human that expose and transcend the limitations of our own space and time" (2016: 116).[10] Bérubé's argument, however, remains relatively contained within prose literature and is not easily extended to the analysis of visual forms of representation. This is because in visual media, and especially so in the concreteness of the filmic image, disability representations are unlikely to be diffuse. This is all due to the iconic and indexical aspects of film.

In filmic representations, the material experience of disability has the potential not simply to *mean* – a process of primarily symbolic signification structurally informed by the normate – but also to merely *be*.

Belgian filmmaker Jaco van Dormael's intriguing short film *The Kiss* (1995) can shed light on how the iconic/indexical aspects of filmic signification unavoidably exploit the ontological qualities of photography that are reorganized in the cinema. Made to commemorate the hundredth anniversary of the first Lumière screening, *The Kiss* was included in the collection *Lumière et compagnie* (*Lumière and Company*, 1995), a project in which forty directors from around the world were asked to shoot a short film using a model of the original cinematograph machine employed by the Lumière brothers a century earlier. Van Dormael's fifty-two-second black-and-white film opens with actors Pascal Duquenne and Michele Maes in an outdoor environment and looking directly at the camera in a mid-close-up.[11] Although not much of the background can be seen, the presence of a building and the movement of passers-by clearly demonstrate the publicness of the space in which they are captured. From a perspective that acknowledges the relevance of the same cognitive code of reality to both film and life, it is significant that viewers will note that both actors have the physical (biological/material) traits associated with Down syndrome. After eight seconds, they turn toward each other, smile, and kiss. Their kissing becomes more passionate and, between caresses, they once again smile and look at the camera.

There are many ways to view this short film, and two may jump immediately to mind. Viewers may see it, for example, as part of a tradition of "objectifying ethnography."[12] Alternatively, it may be a subversion of the way disabled bodies more routinely serve as a "vehicle of sensation" related to trauma and threats to able-bodiedness (Snyder and Mitchell 2006: 163). We should not overlook the way that disability has been harnessed for exploitation by narratives – literary, filmic, or otherwise – that reaffirm the denigrating discourse of disability as lack from the perspective of a medical model or as a product of an ableist imaginary. Nor should we ignore that disability has been systematically differentiated from a socially and politically constructed able-bodied or neurotypical norm. It may be relevant to keep in mind, too, that narratives of disability – filmed or otherwise – rarely incorporate sexuality, preferring a sanitized image of platonic or amorous love instead.[13] Neither should we forget, more generally, the problematic on-screen portrayal of disability by able-bodied actors, a topic that has rightly received much attention in disability studies scholarship, as well as a continuing historical tendency that is seemingly counteracted here. Nor still, however, should we ignore the risks of categorizing van Dormael's production as a "disability film," given advances in intersectionality theory that warn of the dangers of adhering too closely to identity politics, narrowly defined (see Siebers 2008: 27–30).

Cinematic representation is not just about the indexical or iconic meaning of images, of course; these meanings themselves provide the basis for viewer engagement with cinema's metaphorical and symbolic value. Thus another perspective on this particular film might tie *The Kiss* to cinema's oft-cited ability to turn images into metaphors. This is cinema as a form of thinking, and specifically as a form of thinking through, via, by way of, representations. From this perspective, cinema serves as a visual form that stages for us the way we think through, via, by way of, concepts. Pasolini's notion of cinema as the "cognitive code of reality" (1988: 250) is relevant here. Informed by this perspective, cinema becomes a reflective mirror, a productive expression or a theoretical ground for the integration of perception and concepts that informs our socially negotiated understanding of disability. Due to the way indexical, iconic, and symbolic/arbitrary signification are layered over one another in the cinematic sign, film becomes, like reality, a cognitive code that requires active questioning and complex understanding. This might of course be said of all art, or of all artistic representation and engaged spectatorship. To deal with film's symbolic signification is always to deal with social convention/social history on one hand, and individual consciousness/individual interpretation on the other. Viewers are perhaps encouraged to assess where van Dormael's film – considered as represented thought, images as socially mediated concepts – coincides with their own thinking.

For some viewers, the significance of *The Kiss* may seem to come from the way it reconciles two times as well as the perceived distance between the "real" and the "reel." Restaging the material conditions (equipment), limitations, and stylistic conventions of 1895 for contemporary audiences, the short film boasts an organic simplicity – a black-and-white image, length of approximately one minute, static camera, no apparent editing or postproduction, unity of time and place, everyday topic, situated in public space, natural lighting, no sound. With the knowledge of when *The Kiss* was filmed assured, however, the images it captures speak to a more contemporary moment. Van Dormael's film seems to take on greater meaning in light of the growing awareness of disability in Europe towards the end of the twentieth century. Given the metaphorical value of cinema stemming from the symbolic signification of the filmic image, one might see the film as a vehicle for abstraction. From the stark reality of the couple's filmed moment, viewers can easily move towards consideration of the abstract and embattled concepts through which they make sense of this image: Publicness? Emotions? Relationships? Love? Nationhood? Progress? Rights? Humanity? But such abstraction is always held in tension with the concrete (i.e., the indexical and iconic) aspects of film, which assure that such a moment is not abstract but embodied. From this perspective, one might suggest that the question posed by Van Dormael's film is precisely how far the socially mediated concept of disability – perceived through the ontological assertion of material bodies represented through the iconic and indexical aspects of cinema – intertwines with other concepts such as community, nation, and human-ness.

To ask this question is to explicitly consider the imbrication of indexical, iconic, and symbolic modes of signification in the filmic image. Even in the more casual practice of spectatorship, however, viewers necessarily draw upon their own experiences with the "cognitive code of reality" to fuse together notions of existence and interpretation, biological or material experience and social and cultural representation – notions that, of course, can never fully be pulled apart. The application of Pasolini's "cognitive code of reality" to disability film should not be seen in limited terms as an essentialization of disability, but rather as a call to recognize that viewers call upon the same socially mediated concepts, categories, and representations in analysing van Dormael's screen images as they do in making sense of extra-filmic perceptions. It is to recognize that, whether in the realm of art or in social life, thought influences perception and vision affects knowledge. Through film, viewers may confront their own socially mediated perceptions of disability in other cultures, and they may potentially form knowledge of how concepts of disability are embedded in social environments. The vehicle for this engagement with disability on film is the notion of representations as a presence. The individual and social forces that construct and shape the presence of disability on film draw their power – whether seen as pernicious, progressive, neutral, or some combination thereof – from those forces that construct and shape the presence of disability in an extra-filmic, embodied everyday life. In dismissing the power of this on-screen presence – however problematic it may be – we risk dismissing the presence of disability in arguably less artistic, but similarly sociopolitical, contexts off-screen.

When audiences view filmic disability representations, such as those found in *The Kiss*, there are arguably two distinct analytical levels of the viewing experience that can be parsed out, levels that Pasolini identifies as the pre-grammatical and the grammatical. The one I would say is more immediate in film, and the one that interests us in this section, involves the ontological or existential experience of disability outside of film. This is the level Pasolini terms the pre-grammatical (1988: 171). This level is heavily conditioned by the material connections between art and social life that iconic and indexical aspects of film sustain. As a result, the visual act of staring is key for an engagement with the pre-grammatical in film. Though staring at *filmic* images may be somewhat different from other forms of staring that do not involve artistic production, attending to the insights explored by Rosemarie Garland-Thomson in her book *Staring: How We Look* (2009) can nevertheless be productive here as well. Staring, she suggests is intimately tied to knowledge, and "staring that leads to knowing thus requires the arduous visual work of reconciling the curious with the common" (2009: 49). It is extremely important to understand how Garland-Thomson distinguishes the act of staring from the gaze:

> The stare is distinct from the gaze, which has been extensively defined as an oppressive act of disciplinary looking that subordinates its victim ... Starers engage in several variations of intense looking: among them are the blank stare, the baroque stare, the separated stare, the engaged stare, the stimulus-driven stare, the goal-driven stare and the dominating stare. At the heart of this anatomy is the matter of appearance, of the ways we see each other and the ways we are seen. It unsettles common understandings that staring is rudeness, voyeurism, or surveillance or that starers are perpetrators and starees victims. Instead, this vivisection lays bare staring's generative potential. (Garland-Thomson 2009: 9–10)

With regard to the way in which cognitive disabilities have been historically invisible in society (see chapter 1), film constitutes an opportunity to visually engage material experiences of disability that do not figure routinely in the everyday lives of many able-bodied and cognitively abled people. Thus when certain conditions are favourable in the realm of the cinema, staring can be an opportunity to disrupt habits or at the very least, potentially and not necessarily, to revisit assumptions and misunderstandings surrounding cognitive difference. In disability film the notion of the stare is thus complementary to the gaze – taken together, they help us adopt a productively ambivalent perspective on the value of twenty-first-century filmic representations of disability.

In Garland-Thomson's words, "because we come to expect one another to have certain kinds of bodies and behaviors, stares flare up when we glimpse people who look or act in ways that contradict our expectations. Seeing startlingly stare-able people challenges our assumptions by interrupting complacent visual business-as-usual. Staring offers an occasion to rethink the status quo" (2009: 6). Thus, while staring may have a "generative potential" in visual social arenas or in visual media, its disruptive effects may not transfer to literary disability representations. The visual world, with its immediacy, is quite distinct from the discursive world encountered in prose precisely, as Pasolini writes, "because the lin-sign used by the writer has already been refined by an entire grammatical, popular, and cultural history" (1988: 171). The im-sign, on the other hand, enjoys a "lengthy and intense pre-grammatical history" (1988: 171). To put this another way, the pre-grammatical (iconic and indexical) aspects of visual disability representation in documentary contexts – those aspects that testify to a "human life *lived*" (Snyder and Mitchell 2010: 198, original emphasis) – are crucial to the generative potential of visual images.

It must be acknowledged that in the cinema, just as in social environments more broadly, "starees, of course, are sometimes reluctant participants in their starers' visual search for something new" and "have their own lives to live" (Garland-Thomson 2009: 7). Filmic representations complicate the social consequences of staring through the displacement and hidden machinations of the production process, but also mitigate some of these consequences by introducing a certain kind of representational distance between starer and staree that only aesthetic representations can offer. Certainly the potential for genuine spatio-temporal audience interaction with the filmic image, in a way that would be possible in a social encounter at least, is sacrificed. It cannot be ignored that Garland-Thomson's book consistently emphasizes the active role of starees, who are "subjects not objects" (2009: 11; see also 33). Yet the inclusion and analysis of still images, photographs, and paintings as well as individual films in her book indicates that even where interaction is not possible in real time in a given social context, the act of staring at static representations still potentially "makes meaning" (2009: 9). Contributing to the book's more extensive exploration of curiosity, Garland-Thomson suggests that the perceived "strangeness" (2009: 82) of visual disability representations in the context of familiar artistic genres can be productive and meaningful.

It is worth asking whether film – in the same way as the portraits by Doug Auld and Chris Rush discussed in *Staring*'s chapter 7 (Garland-Thomson 2009: 80–3) – holds the potential to give us what the critic calls "permission to stare," potentially "gratifying our 'deep curiosity' while at the same time inviting 'empathy' and 'sensitivity'" (2009: 81). Regarding the represented woman with Down syndrome in Chris Rush's portrait titled "Swim II," Garland-Thomson describes the subject's stately features in the context of the "familiar commemorative portraits of the Italian Renaissance" (2009: 82). She affirms that "the portrait invites us to stare, engrossed perhaps less with the 'strangeness' of this woman's disability and more with the strangeness of witnessing such dignity in a face that marks a life we have learned to imagine as unliveable and unworthy, as the kind of person we routinely detect in advance through medical technology and eliminate from our human community" (2009: 83). The specific biological/material traits of Down syndrome figure prominently in her discussion of the iconic aspects of Rush's painting, just as they do in the cinematic example from *The Kiss* explored above.[14] Due to the visual nature of the disability representation, it is not the prosthetic function of disability in the artistic representation that is primary. Instead, the biological links of Down syndrome with the material and social experience of a specific disability provide the basis for Garland-Thomson's discussion of the piece's symbolic meaning.[15]

It is underappreciated that literary representations do not, in fact, render (cognitive) disabilities visible. Whereas in long-form cinema in particular, the generative potential of staring – evident, too, in still images – can become even more productive. To put the matter somewhat more crudely, what Garland-Thomson calls the "generative potential" of staring is made possible by the mere fact that visual art renders disability visible. It is relevant that Pasolini writes the following of the pre-grammatical dimension of film:

> And so it will be immediately necessary to make a parenthetical observation: while the instrumental communication which lies at the basis of poetic or philosophical communication is already extremely elaborate – it is, in other words, a real, historically complex and mature system – the visual communication which is the basis of film language is, on the contrary,

> extremely crude, almost animal-like. As with gestures and brute reality, so dreams and the processes of our memory are almost prehuman events, or on the border of what is human. In any case, they are pregrammatical and even premorphological (dreams take place on the level of the unconscious, as do the mnemonic processes; gestures are an indication of an extremely elementary stage of civilization, etc.). *The linguistic instrument on which film is predicated is, therefore, of an irrational type:* and this explains the deeply oneiric quality of the cinema, and also its concreteness as, let us say, object, which is both absolute and impossible to overlook. (1988: 169).

The material experience of disability displayed in film has the potential to correct the pervasive and historical effects of the normative stigmatization of cognitive disabilities in particular. In her book, Garland-Thomson writes that "avowing disability as tragic or shameful, we have hidden away disabled people in asylums, segregated schools, hospitals, and nursing homes ... This hiding of disability has made it seem unusual or foreign rather than fundamental to our human embodiedness ... When we do see the usually concealed sight of disability writ boldly on others, we stare in fascinated disbelief and uneasy identification" (2009: 19–20; see also Stiker [1982]1997). It is thus the pre-grammatical dimension of film – whether this is understood as the ontological, existential, properties of photographic representation in general or in terms of the iconic and indexical aspects of cinematic signification (especially in the new disability documentary cinema) that testify to a material experience, a social relationship as actually *lived* – that is primarily responsible for making possible cinema's generative potential. This pre-grammatical dimension, of course, must be analysed subsequently in relation to the grammatical dimension of disability representation. If the pre-grammatical dimension of film engages the director's selection of images, prioritizing the medium's iconic and indexical relationships, then the grammatical dimension of film builds on these relationships through the medium's temporal and symbolic properties.

As Snyder and Mitchell have written, "the analysis of film images of disability provides an opportune location of critical intervention – a form of discursive rehab upon the site of our deepest psychic structures mediating our reception of human differences" (2010: 182). If film analysis of disability is to become a critical intervention, however, it must blend the cinema's pre-grammatical dimension with its grammatical dimension. Disability studies scholars approaching film have not always paid close attention to the grammatical, formal, structural, stylistic, and artistic dimensions of film that unfold over time – that is, those aspects of film that make it a unique artistic discourse (see Enns and Smit 2001b). If the pre-grammatical dimension of film emphasizes the link between representation and referent, the grammatical dimension of film tends to reflect the construction of film narrative in temporal terms.

Garland-Thomson is similarly attentive to temporality. She suggests that if the productive aspects of staring are allowed to unfold over time, potentially "converting the impulse to stare into attention" (2009: 22), viewers can be prompted to think much more deeply about disability as a social relation. This does not merely mean that analysis must pay attention to the action of narration – what happens, who says what to whom, and so on. Perhaps more importantly, disability scholars approaching cinema need also to pay more attention to artistic form as it is produced over the length of the film product. While film form has not been entirely absent from previous disability studies approaches, scholars have been more likely to privilege insights that draw implicitly from semiotic theories centred on actors emplotted in a narrative. Such "actantial" theories (Vladimir Propp 1968, A.J. Greimas) were made fashionable in traditional literary analysis over the course of the twentieth century and were arguably derived from if not also supported by studies of the role of narrative in epic traditions, as evidenced in the anthropological approach to symbol and ritual. When the role or the function of disability is privileged in a certain artistic emplotment (be it in literature or film) – the notion of disability as a plot device would be a rough equivalent (Mitchell and Snyder 2000) – the story of a disability narrative is isolated from its formal presentation. There is nothing inherently wrong with analysing how disability figures into narrative at the level of story; indeed, such work has yielded valuable insights into the pervasive nature of ableist paradigms of disability. That said, the limitation of actantial theories of filmic disability representation, or theories that centre on the role or function of disability relative to the actions of other actors in the story, is that they necessarily prioritize the symbolic or grammatical value of disability within an art form whose most immediate and powerful dimension is pre-grammatical. This model separates iconicity and indexicality from symbolism in the cinema. That scholars have tended to use this model when studying disability representations in film is not surprising, given the way in which semiotic theories of film throughout the twentieth century themselves prioritized the arbitrary nature of the filmic sign over its iconic and indexical qualities.[16] The contradiction within this approach has been that such scholarship in practice actually assumes the disabled character as im-sign without putting that im-sign into a relationship with an extra-filmic referent through awareness of the iconic and indexical dimensions of filmic signification. It is perhaps most important to ask whether this model for studying disability representations is adequate for independent, small-budget films that might belong to the category of a new disability documentary cinema.

Viewers of film must understand that the meaning of cinematic representation comes from the way in which it folds iconic/indexical signification into symbolic signification. If cinema is a language, it is one in which the pre-grammatical im-sign of disability, referring to an extra-filmic referent, is rendered grammatical through the formal decisions embedded in the film as an artistic product.[17] There is nothing about the artistic genre of film itself that would ever ensure a positive or negative representation of disability; even so, cinema arguably allows disability representations to serve a non-normative purpose in a way that prose literature and even static images cannot because of the way in which disabled characters are seen to move on-screen. Here I am referencing the way that disabled characters act and/or are situated in relation to their environment and the way they interact and communicate – whether verbally, non-verbally or both – with others in their environment over time. This perspective emphasizes the power of presence, the potential for action to convey thought and for movement to render cognition visible. Consider that the cinema actually shows thought through visible actions, and cognition through visible movements and not merely through spoken language.

An example can prove helpful here. Take the case of American fibre artist Judith Scott (1943–2005), who appears on film as the protagonist of an intriguing documentary from Spain titled *¿Qué tienes debajo del sombrero?* (What's Under Your Hat?) (2006).[18] Profoundly deaf, with Down syndrome, and having dealt with a long history of undiagnosed impairment and institutional isolation, Scott became recognized around the world for her enigmatic mixed-media sculptures, which she created at the Center for Creative Growth in Oakland, California. As Lola Barrera and Iñaki Peñafiel – the directors of *¿Qué tienes …?* – certainly seem to understand, it is not easy to explain either Scott's artistic creativity or the significance and meaning of her artistic production without first understanding her connections with others. These involved the opportunities forged through her relationship with her sister Joyce and the supportive connections she enjoyed with staff and other artists at Creative Growth. Due to severe impairments, Scott could not communicate her needs to others verbally, nor could she reflect on her position within the world of art. She could not critique society's disabling conditions in the same way as cognitively abled populations. The visibility she brought to experiences of cognitive disability through her fibre art cannot be discussed without mention of her collaborations: with her sibling, with an organization, with art scholars and others, and even with documentary directors from Spain. Viewers of *¿Qué tienes ...?* will not hear Scott communicate in verbal language; but they will nevertheless see her communicate through her actions, her bodily movements, and ultimately also her visual art as showcased on-screen. This example illustrates the opportunities that visual media provide for viewers to widen their understanding of what cognition actually looks like in the social (and artistic) relationships of non-verbal people with severe cognitive disabilities.

There is no inherent reason why film would be immune from the pervasive ableism evidenced in historical practices of disability photography and the freak show. Disability representations in the cinema can be just as ableist and spectacular as disability representations in prose literature, and the number of valuable analyses that look at disability and film in this way is growing.[19] Yet I contend that in cinema's representation of time, in the work of committed directors and actors, and perhaps most frequently in non-mainstream circuits of cultural production, it is possible also to represent disability as something other than a spectacle or an exception. The transgressive potential of film comes from the fact that it can represent the material experience of disability in terms that are quite ordinary and decidedly unspectacular. In the right circumstances, viewers can spend time with these represented experiences of disability, dwelling with characters, doing the visual work of engaging with their material experience through the act of staring, and thus potentially also confronting their own internalization of ableist norms and expectations. If staring has a generative potential in social life as Garland-Thomson suggests, then staring in the cinema may be equally productive when disability is contextualized within everyday social relationships unfolding over time. If we allow for art/aesthetics in general to draw from and influence/reinforce our collective thought and social practice, we must also allow for the potential value of staring in film.

This potential arises from cinema's relationship with the everyday. Even outside the context of disability studies, everydayness has been a potentially transformative aspect of different world cinemas at particular moments – the French new wave, Italian neorealism, and the New Latin American Cinema, for example. Regarding the latter, Susan Antebi and Beth Jörgensen's edited volume *Libre Acceso* (2016) contains a number of film analyses that reveal the potential of filmic im-signs to reorient consciousness through disability representation, emphasizing everyday activities through the temporal aspect of cinema. For example, Ryan Prout's chapter titled "*Otras competencias*: Ethnobotany, the *Badianus codex*, and Metaphors of Mexican Memory Loss and Disability in *Las buenas hierbas* (2010)" illustrates how the cinematic representation of Alzheimer's disease can be approached simultaneously at the concrete level of iconic/indexical signification and the abstract level of symbolic signification, preserving a notion of disability "in its own right" (2016: 92) and avoiding the use of "Alzheimer's as a metaphorical vehicle" (2016: 93). Susan Antebi's chapter in that same volume, "Cripping the Camera: Disability and the Filmic Interval in Carlos Reygadas's *Japón*," argues that the 2002 film "disrupts the viewer's expectations … by splintering the visual continuity it at first appears to offer, and hence releasing bodies into unpredicted patterns of affective continuity and symbolic circulation" (2016: 105). As these and other essays seem to suggest,[20] the power of the everyday in cinema, the filmic image's potential for disruption, comes from the cinema's reliance on icon and index. Film's power comes from its unique mixture of the ontological and existential qualities of photography and how these qualities intertwine with the symbolic meaning woven into the cinema's artistic form.

Filmic disability representations have evolved in certain respects during the twenty-first century that are worth recognizing. It is intriguing that it has become somewhat more common to represent disabled characters as embedded in social contexts and not as isolated outsiders (compare Norden 1994 and Snyder and Mitchell 2010). For all their potential faults, there are a number of contemporary global films that explore disabled characters in the everyday contexts of familial relationships, working relationships, and sexual relationships – a significant change from the characteristic isolation that Norden investigated in American Hollywood cinema. In the Spanish context, for example, the film *Yo, también* (Me Too) (Pastor and Naharro, 2009) featured not only a protagonist with Down syndrome but also a number of secondary characters with intellectual disability.[21] I do not intend this as an apology either for the current spate of ableist screen images of disability or for the paucity of disabled directors and actors one can still find in mainstream film cultures. Instead, I believe that the continued rise of disability film festivals (see Mitchell and Snyder 2015, 2016) as well as the still infrequent but nonetheless visible presence of disabled character protagonists and disabled directors in selected mainstream and independent films are important shifts that will require a more nuanced form of disability film criticism.[22] Garland-Thomson notes that "the modern world, in our particular era, is ocularcentric; it depends on sight as the primary sensory conduit to the world" (2009: 25). In seeing disabled characters embedded in social relationships on-screen, film viewers can be prompted to do some visual work and, potentially, reach a new understanding about the social nature of disability. Such representations potentially go beyond the way in which "*disabled bodies have been constructed cinematically and socially to function as delivery vehicles in the transfer of extreme sensation to audiences*" (Snyder and Mitchell 2010: 186, original emphasis). Such films, if viewed by spectators who are open to what Garland-Thomson calls the "generative potential" of staring and who are willing to engage in visual work, may actually work to counteract the sensationalism habitually attached to filmic disability representations.

Though it may not have been intended in this way, Garland-Thomson's comment that "the extraordinary excites but alarms us; the ordinary assures but bores us" (2009: 19) can be tied to the power of cinematic representations of the everyday. Such representations can be seen as a reaction to the history of disability as narrative prosthesis in ableist cinema. Prosthetic disability narrative in the cinema has undoubtedly served a function similar to that of prosthetic disability narrative in literature. In both cases, it has been relatively common to tell stories in which "persons with disabilities somehow manage to overcome their difficulties and live a happy life within the realm of art" (Quayson 2007: 25). Such a representation "serves a pragmatic/cathartic function for the audience and the reader" (Quayson 2007: 25). It is precisely the lack of such catharsis in cinema privileging the everyday material experience of disability, however, that makes new approaches to representing disability in cinema potentially transgressive. Non-prosthetic, everyday disability narrative in film tends to focus on unresolved, everyday, and even adverse consequences of the normate, on the experience of disability within a normative, able-bodied, cognitively abled culture.

Film's temporal flow and its representation of the everyday allow viewers to see not merely a physical dimension but more importantly a cognitive dimension to disability representation. It is important to understand that both the pre-grammatical and grammatical levels of filmic disability representations are deeply intertwined with cognition.[23] Films that represent intellectual disabilities, developmental disabilities, and psychiatric disabilities render cognition visible. This may be a simple point, but it is one to which disability studies should pay careful attention in the twenty-first century. In the next chapter, I build on this simple premise by continuing to explore the opportunities presented by visual media representations in direct contrast to literary representations. Visual media provide a particularly appropriate arena in which disability scholarship can work to connect issues of biology/impairment with matters of aesthetics/culture. Borrowing a term from Mark Jeffreys (2002: 33), I refer to this scholarly activity as embracing a methodological premise to work "at the seam where body joins culture."

3 Disability Scholarship at the Seam: The Materiality of Visual Narrative

"At the seam where body joins culture every construction of the body begins and ends. On the efforts of cultures to hide that seam, every oppression ends."
– Mark Jeffreys (2002: 33)

The investigation of cognitive disability in the realm of aesthetics requires a completely new approach, different from the one that has been already articulated in pioneering work on first-wave studies of physical disability representations. Questions of materiality and biology are at the core of one of the contradictions in humanities scholarship on disability – a contradiction that remains unresolved. In asserting a strong social model for disability, scholars have pushed material and biological matters to the side. Somewhat paradoxically, this has been the case even despite the field's persistent focus on physical bodies. Here I make the case – one that may itself seem paradoxical – that in foregrounding issues of biology and impairment in disability studies, we also foreground issues of consciousness; that in returning to materiality, we actually move beyond the field's physical focus to embrace cognition. This does not require that we release the strong social model of disability, merely that we broaden it to include cognition more intentionally.

The notion of visual culture allows for stronger connections between the cognitive and the physical. The previous chapter used a basic semiotic vocabulary to assert iconicity and indexicality as the defining properties of visual signification through Pier Paolo Pasolini's discussion of the "im-sign"; this chapter builds on that discussion to explore in greater depth the distance between prose disability representations and visual disability representations. Drawing from that discussion of the unique aspects of signification in visual representations, here I focus on the opportunity offered by the material aspects of narrative in visual media. I argue that visual narrative offers disability studies in the humanities the chance to investigate the seam between the material and immaterial forces that impact disability representations. Disability scholarship operating at the seam between biology and culture can reaffirm disability as a material experience at the same time that it recognizes the way in which this materiality is impacted by discursive constructions and symbolic meanings organized by an ableist society. This endeavour is particularly important if disability studies is to tackle the topic of severe cognitive disability.

The present discussion of biology, impairment, and culture is inspired directly by Mark Jeffreys's chapter titled "The Visible Cripple" included in the landmark volume *Disability Studies: Enabling the Humanities* (2002, edited by Brueggemann, Garland-Thomson, and Snyder). As I usually do when reading disability studies scholarship, I was thinking of my brother in-law when I read Jeffreys's essay.[1] In it he uses the phrase "the seam where body joins culture" to point out the limitations of social constructivism in disability studies. "At the seam where body joins culture," he writes, "every construction of the body begins and ends. On the efforts of cultures to hide that seam, every oppression ends" (2002: 33).

> Now however, the constructivist epistemology that has powered disability studies thus far needs to be more critically examined. Outright hostility to biology and to the natural history of our flesh all too easily plays into mind–body, theory–matter dualism and may turn out to be just another effort at the erasure of the body by culture. Just as society needs to learn how to accommodate rather than stigmatize those of us with unusual and extraordinary bodies, so too humanist cultural theory needs to learn how to accommodate rather than demonize the study of the biological aspects of our bodies. (2002: 39)

As should be clear given this book's focus, I see Jeffreys's point from a perspective that acknowledges the links between cognitive disability and biology/materiality. In my reading, he concisely expresses the need for disability studies in the humanities to pay attention to both body and mind. For this reason, when I read the phrase "the biological aspects of our bodies" in his essay, I take the word "biological" as incorporating both physical and cognitive disability. I understand his insistence on joining biology and culture more intentionally as a call to think of materiality in terms of culture, and to think of culture in terms of materiality. Just as culture has the ability to erase the body – as Jeffreys suggests above – it similarly has the ability to erase the mind. Still, it also has the power to bring connections between body and mind into sharp focus. My understanding of culture acknowledges the connections between material cultural production and immaterial cultural codes, as well as the dialectical relationship between these two. Culture is productive in this sense: it can induce alienation or assert ontological primacy, cleave body from mind or reflect the complicated imbrication of cognition and the physical body. Taken in the artistic sense, culture can both reflect and impact social practice, either enforcing normalcy and the status quo (acting as a conditioning or norming force), or prompting hesitation, sustained reflection, and criticism and ultimately even disrupting normative practice (thus acting as a re-norming or counter-norming force). Visual culture also has the potential to draw attention to the materiality of cognitive disability experiences in unique ways, as explored in this chapter.

It is significant that Jeffreys challenges the traditionally accepted constructivist approach of disability studies research in the humanities by asserting the materiality of disability. His is one of a handful of clear and significant attempts to warn against the pitfalls of a position that uncritically accepts an un-nuanced perspective on the social constructedness of disability. The full recognition of the reality of biological or material impairment as a part of disability experience is key to his essay, just as I believe it is key to any approach that acknowledges the reality of severe cognitive disability. Whether they are looking at physical or cognitive disabilities, disability studies scholars might follow Jeffreys's lead in seeking to bridge the hallmark social critique of a strong constructivist position with the reality that addressing biology and impairment can extend that social critique further into health sciences territory.[2]

In borrowing Jeffreys's term to signal the potential of carrying out disability studies scholarship positioned "at the seam" of biology and culture, I address two concerns. This notion of the seam is both a tool for disability studies and a tool for humanities method. In disability studies, this term calls on us to reconsider the significance of attending to notions of impairment. I believe this can be done in a way that does not sacrifice the gains made by the historical focus (in both the academic field and the political realm) on barrier removal, a focus that emphasizes disability as a product of the ableist social environment. Regarding humanities method, this notion of the seam also suggests to me, perhaps indirectly, a methodology for linking aesthetics/cultural production and the material experience of disability.

The first section of this chapter, "On the Surface: Literary Disability Representations," assesses the primacy established in prose narrative between literary conveyances of form, shape, and appearance on one hand, and symbolic, socially grounded meaning on the other. Insights from Mitchell and Snyder's *Narrative Prosthesis: Disability and the Dependencies of Discourse* (2000) and Ato Quayson's *Aesthetic Nervousness: Disability and the Crisis of Representation* (2007) reveal how an able-bodied society frames the disabled body as a question whose ontological proof seemingly resides in the contour that society itself has outlined by distinguishing able-bodied constructions from disabled bodily constructions. In the process of the social construction of disability, this contour, this outline, this shape, this form – this physical, material, and visible reality – is imbued with a signifying power that points elsewhere, towards a social or cultural meaning over which the body and mind so delineated itself has no control. It is in this sense that the literary disability representation is a signifying surface – just as the social construction of disability is also itself a signifying surface. I assert that the trope of the surface has been mobilized in practice in the humanities by way of reinforcing the perceived distance between the physical and the cognitive. What is needed instead is an approach to disability representation situated at the seam of biology/impairment and aesthetics/culture that condenses the physical and the cognitive from the outset as part of a material experience of disability. If we content ourselves with the study of literary disability representations as a surface, instead of combining this direction with newer work on disability representations carried out at the seam, in the context of visual media studies, then disability studies in the humanities will miss out on a great deal.

In the second section, "Materiality, Visual Narrative, and Cognition," I assert that visual disability representations insistently and simultaneously render cognitive disability visible in both the aesthetic and social worlds. Here I emphasize the materiality of iconic and indexical forms of signification as visible links with extra-artistic experiences of disability, and investigate how visual narrative allows the force of these visible links to accumulate. The concept of "iconic redundancy" – borrowed from comics theory and applied here both to graphic novels and to film

– is crucial to this effort. Visual narratives present an opportunity to recognize being over meaning, an opportunity that is crucial for representing populations with severe cognitive disabilities, as explored through the examples of María in chapter 4, Emilio in chapter 5, and Javier and Rosario in chapter 6. Relying on iconic/indexical signification, visual narratives acknowledge the existence of cognitive impairments without strongly correlating that existence with webs of social signification. As such, representations of cognitive disability experiences in visual narratives can sidestep the persistent problems of self-representation in community and mindedness in narration as described by Joseph N. Straus (2013) and Michael Bérubé (2005, 2016). The value of visual representations of cognitive disabilities, in particular, is that they can express the cognition of disabled characters through movement and action, rather than literary discourse, thus avoiding the polarized extremes whereby cognitive difference is either rendered as a stigmatized spectacle or avoided entirely. The brief conclusion of this chapter outlines in broad terms how these insights inform the analyses of visual cultural production in part 2 of the book.

On the Surface: Literary Disability Representations

In *Narrative Prosthesis*, Mitchell and Snyder ask a series of compelling questions: "Why does the 'visual' spectacle of so many disabilities become a predominating trope in the nonvisual textual mediums of literary narratives? … What is the significance of disability as a pervasive category of narrative interest? Why do convolutions, distortions, and ruptures that mark the disabled body's surface prove seductive to literary representation?" (2000: 53, 57). It is easy and of course valuable to see this questioning as part of the authors' larger move to denounce the ideology of ableism, to expose the foundational role it plays in the structuring of prose disability representations. There is also, however, another sense in which these questions can be taken, and that is as a provocation to investigate more thoroughly the semiotics of disability representation in the aesthetic realm. Mitchell and Snyder investigate the way entrenched social constructions of disability impact literary narrative, but they do not explore in great depth the functioning of the literary construction of disability itself, that is, the semiotic and imaginative process by which authors and readers themselves participate in visualizing literary disability representations. Their perspective is best positioned to account for ideology's role in the production of literary narrative (the act of creation or composition), but they do not necessarily explain how literary narrative operates (how readers actively participate in it, how it is received). This process is important to investigate for two reasons: first, as a way of marking the distinction between how literary and visual narratives function, and second, as a way of asserting the materiality of disability experiences, and also the materiality of visual narrative, as a corrective to historical patterns of the social (in) visibility of cognitive difference.

It can be productive to contrast literary with visual disability representations. Doing so can help us understand further the potential of visual media to represent cognitive difference while sidestepping the pitfalls of how these representations have been mobilized in prose. Those pitfalls have been somewhat extensively documented by disability scholarship, with the focus usually on physical disabilities. Thus, for example, the disabled body of *Richard III* in Shakespeare's play is mobilized symbolically as "a social burden; metaphysical sign of divine disfavor; evidence of the machinations of a divine plan in history, that a disabled child is retribution for parental weakness; that a disabled child follows a deterministic trajectory in life," and so on (Mitchell and Snyder 1997: 14; see also Williams 2009).[3] In this way, countless disabled characters in prose have long functioned as charged symbols whose presence does not point outside the text towards the material experiences of disability in society but is instead designed to reaffirm normative social constructions of ability, capacity, and health. This has also been the case with literary characters whose appearance in narrative spectacularizes the experience of cognitive difference, as Alice Hall suggests in *Literature and Disability* (2016). In "Cognitive Difference and Narrative," for example, chapter 7 of Hall's extensive scholarly overview, she writes of William Faulkner's "struggle to represent cognitive difference" (2016: 105) in his novel *The Sound and the Fury*.[4] It is particularly interesting that Hall's discussion of the representation of cognitive difference in literature broaches the topic of diagnosis (2016: 109–10).[5] That is, while the topic of diagnosis can unnecessarily introduce the dehumanization that accompanies a medical paradigm when discussing the physical disability experiences that have been obsessively represented in ableist society and aesthetics, in the case of cognitive difference the lack of a diagnosis can actually obfuscate the materiality of a disability representation.

Prose narrative may allude to cognitive capacity or ability without having to illustrate clear dimensions of the material experience of cognitive difference. It may seem counter-intuitive, but in the context of written literature, the fact that matters of cognition are not named, defined, or medicalized may indicate that authors are dealing with cognitive disability merely as a literary spectacle and ableist symbol. Because it need not clearly illustrate its referent, literary representation of cognitive disability can more easily turn on normative and harmful misunderstandings of material experiences, and it can do so in a way that misrepresents the textures of these experiences, exploiting them for an ableist audience. By contrast – and especially so given the concreteness of the filmic image as discussed in chapter 2 – visual disability representations are unlikely to be as diffuse as they are allowed to be in literary texts. Such diffuse visual images of disability would only be possible in cinema under certain unlikely conditions – for example, if a film were of an experimental genre, if disabled characters were to appear very sporadically, in undeveloped form, at the margins of the filmic narrative, at a distance in the frame, solely in the film's audio or otherwise formally obscured or minimized. In documentary films centring on disabled characters played by disabled actors, for example, disability representations are going to trend towards a more specific range of material experiences of disability. This will be true unless the disability representation is faulty, questionable, overly creative, or, in other words, not "realistic."[6] This is all due to the iconic and indexical aspects of film, which can represent the material experience of disability without relying predominantly on the forms signification that are prioritized in written language and that I consider with a degree of scepticism below.

Visual depictions of disability in cinema or comics may tend towards the iconic and indexical poles of representation, whereas prose literature effects a curious distancing that must be accounted for in theories of disability representation. This is because it relies on the written word and thus on a preponderance of arbitrary signification directed by social convention. The distancing of prose literature's characteristically arbitrary signification is effected by a foundational reliance on the symbolic, by a privileging of symbol/metaphor over icon and index. As a whole corpus of linguistic study has indicated, iconicity is present even in spoken language (whether written or oral).[7] It remains, however, that arbitrary signification predominates in the spoken or written word, and it follows that in an ableist society this social convention is going to tend to be dominated by normative understandings. Compared explicitly with visual texts, the meaning of literary prose is highly conditioned by a hermeneutic excess shaped by collectively negotiated understandings and enforced (and/or contested) social and cultural norms. Individual readers necessarily bring their own experience to bear on the malleable grouping of collective understandings with which an author and a prose narrative play, just as they bring their own experience to bear on visual disability representations. Still, there is an immediacy and a concreteness to the iconic and indexical properties of visual media whose contrast with the signifying processes characterizing prose literature can prove meaningful.[8]

This does not mean that literary prose representation lacks a visual component. As readers visualize the disabled characters appearing in prose literature in their mind's eye, this more or less diffuse visual image is necessarily linked with a more or less diffuse constellation of avatars of the normate that permeate able-bodied culture. This image is not a purely visual one, by which I mean it is not physical in the simple sense. That is, it is not an iconic representation of a material body as would occur in comics or in visual media generally, nor is it a reference or an index to a material body outside of the text, as would occur in filmic signification specifically. Instead, this prose literary representation presumes a higher degree of mediation through arbitrary signification than would images of disability rendered in visual media. As literary representations are not concrete but rather fragmented or half-drawn – they are neither iconic nor indexical in the way that images from visual media are – readers must necessarily supply their own information to complete the basic outlines of literary representations of disability. In the process, they draw extensively on their own experience or lack of experience with disability, on their own visual memories or lack of visual memories. From a visual perspective, the result of this necessary interaction with the prose literary text depends on a number of factors that lack a clear hermeneutic hierarchy. As a result, the impact of literary disability representations varies considerably from reader to reader; semiotically speaking, readers lack a material basis for connecting disability representations in prose with disability experiences outside of the literary text.

Two important issues are addressed both by Mitchell and Snyder in *Narrative Prosthesis* (2000) and by Quayson in *Aesthetic Nervousness* (2007) whose exploration can shed light on the contrast between disability representations as they appear in prose and as they appear in visual media. The first involves a critique of the way in which prose disability representations function within the literary text. In both cases, critique attends to the practical benefits these representations seem to offer authors – either the false promise or illusion of materiality (Mitchell and Snyder) or a complex and nuanced connection to ethical content (Quayson). The second issue raised by these books involves the connection of literary disability representations with disability representations in the social sphere. Because they necessarily draw from extra-literary social constructions of disability, literary authors unavoidably reflect the normative presumptions of those constructions. Exploring these arguments makes clear that literary disability representations are distanced from material experiences of disability precisely *because* they are discursive products. As such, their meaning is more subject to the hermeneutic variability of reader engagements with arbitrary, metaphorical, and symbolic language than would occur in visual media.[9]

Narrative Prosthesis emphasizes how literary disability representations offer literary authors the illusion of materiality. Mitchell and Snyder assert the constructed nature of both the literary representation of disability and the social representation of disability from which it draws. Thus they are able to develop the compelling metaphor of the notion of surface as a way of denoting what might be described as the relative autonomy, the malleability, and even the normative co-optation of disability representations. They write that "the narration of the disabled body allows a textual body to *mean* through its long-standing historical representation as an overdetermined symbolic surface" (2000: 64). Put another way, the process governing the literary representation of disability can be taken as an echo of the process governing the discursive construction of disability outside the literary text in our wider social world.[10] The notion of the surface mobilized here conveys a certain inadequacy of literary representation to represent material experiences of disability unfolding in society. It connotes a superficiality or lack of depth, and it seems to denounce an ableist contentment with the depthless appropriation of symbol for another purpose. In even simpler terms, Mitchell and Snyder are suggesting that disability operates as a symbol in literary narrative because it is already a symbol outside of literary narrative. It is a surface within literature because it is a surface outside of literature in the wider social world. And in this sense, literary disability representation it is not, strictly speaking, a metaphor or symbol but more of an aesthetic re-rendering of pre-existing metaphorical, symbolic, conventional social practice. To return to Mitchell and Snyder, "textual bodies" *mean* because extra-textual bodies themselves also *mean*.[11]

In asserting the disabled body in prose literature as a construction whose signifying practice ties it to social signifying practices outside of the text, Mitchell and Snyder also call attention to the ways in which authors exploit the presumed materiality of disability representation. They suggest that authors are tempted by the thought that disability might bring concreteness to literary metaphor: "the corporeal metaphor offers narrative the one thing it cannot possess – an anchor in materiality" (2000: 63). (As we will see below, Quayson advances a related but somewhat more nuanced argument, suggesting that the disability representation offers prose authors not materiality but instead an ethical content added to literary narrative). The implication is that the representation of disability in literature involves the textual act of cloaking a material body in symbolic trappings: "the extreme examples of those with physical disabilities and deformities invited the armchair psychology of the literary practitioner to participate in the symbolic manipulation of bodily exteriors"; "the disabled body also offers narrative the illusion of grounding abstract knowledge within a bodily materiality" (Mitchell and Snyder 2000: 59, 64). Their point is that prose literature frequently and even obsessively mobilizes the disabled body as a symbol of materiality in order to reaffirm the constructed norm of ableism: "the materiality of metaphor via disabled bodies gives all bodies a tangible essence in that the 'healthy' corporeal surface fails to achieve its symbolic effect without its disabled counterpart" (2000: 64). Their text makes clear that the materiality of disability exercises a basic function in the ableist literary text, in that it can serve as one of many literary strategies to imbue the literary world with an immediacy and a corporeality that it lacks due to its semiotic and compositional reliance on the forms of arbitrary signification predominant in the written word.[12] This perspective pinpoints prose literature's anxiety regarding the material world; it also allows literary narrative to turn to disability for at least one specific reason that would not apply to visual texts, whose reliance on iconic/indexical signification preserves materiality and immediacy to a degree impossible in prose.

Ato Quayson's *Aesthetic Nervousness* (2007) advances a focus on the ethical that allows the critic to discern the imbrication of social views and aesthetic structures without presupposing the existence of a material or "stable disability 'reality' that lies out there" (2007: 19). Regarding this issue of concreteness or materiality, there is a key distinction to be made with *Narrative Prosthesis*: instead of focusing on physical bodies as a way of critiquing the appearance of disability in literary narrative,

Quayson emphasizes social views. This in itself illustrates how, in connecting textual representations with extra-textual representations, room can be made for cognition. This approach prioritizes the social realm as an arena of contesting interpretations in which the notion of disability is itself constructed and negotiated, and for that reason, as an arena in which the division between the physical and the cognitive, the form and the content, the surface and the meaning, the text and the world, is not as clear as it might otherwise seem:

> Disability returns the aesthetic domain to an active ethical core that serves to disrupt the surface of representation. Read from a perspective of disability studies, this active ethical core becomes manifest because the disability representation is seen as having a direct effect on social views of people with disability in a way that representations of other literary details, tropes and motifs do not offer. In other words, the representation of disability has an efficaciousness that ultimately transcends the literary domain and refuses to be assimilated to it. This does not mean that disability in literature can be read solely via an instrumentalist dimension of interpretation; any intervention that might be adduced for it is not inserted into an inert and stable disability "reality" that lies out there. For, as we have noted, disability in the real world already incites interpretations in and of itself. Nevertheless, an instrumentalist dimension cannot easily be suspended either. To put the matter somewhat formulaically: the representation of disability oscillates uneasily between the aesthetic and the ethical domains, in such a way as to force a reading of the aesthetic fields in which the disabled are represented as always having an ethical dimension that cannot be easily subsumed under the aesthetic structure. Ultimately, aesthetic nervousness has to be seen as coextensive with the nervousness regarding the disabled in the real world. The embarrassment, fear and confusion that attend the disabled in their everyday reality is translated in literature and the aesthetic field into a series of structural devices that betray themselves when the disability representation is seen predominantly from the perspective of the disabled rather than from the normative position of the nondisabled. (2007: 19)

The notion of aesthetic nervousness in the literary realm is one, as noted in the above quotation, with a direct complement in the "real world." In Quayson's account, disability thus appears in literary narrative not as a referent but from the very beginning as a symbol whose meaning interacts with conceptions of the normate (Garland-Thomson 1997).

The indexical or referential link between text and world is here not focused on the materiality of the body but rather on an embodied and, most importantly, mental experience of the construction of disability in able-bodied society. In short, this is a cognitive reference. Here the symbolic, the arbitrary, and the metaphorical – and not the iconic and/or indexical – unite the appearance and construction of disability in both text and world. The use of the words "perspective" and "position" in the extended quotation above is of great significance. Quayson is emphasizing the inherent malleability or variation of disability representations ("when the disability representation is seen predominantly from the perspective of the disabled rather than from the normative position of the nondisabled"). The matter of perspective is crucial when not merely the meaning but also the nature of a disability representation is so highly dependent on the experiences of individual readers.

Instead of emphasizing the materiality of disability in a simple sense, Quayson's framing makes more room for the cohabitation of the cognitive and material realms. While Mitchell and Snyder frame materiality as an illusion mobilized by authors in literary narrative, here the notion of aesthetic nervousness accounts more capaciously for the materiality of disability outside of the text. Quayson writes of disability's "oscillation between a pure abstraction and a set of material circumstances and conditions" (2007: 23), explaining that generally speaking, "disability oscillates between a pure process of abstraction (via a series of discursive framings, metaphysical transpositions, and socially constituted modalities of [non]response, and so forth) and a set of material conditions (such as impairment, accessibility and mobility difficulties, and economic considerations)" (2007: 24). Instead of suggesting a purely arbitrary signifying chain where the literary disability representation "points to" or references disability representations in the real world, he emphasizes that "disability serves then to close the gap between representation and ethics, making visible the aesthetic field's relationship to the social situation of persons with disability in the real world" (2007: 24).[13]

One can make the argument, based on Quayson's text and on the nature of the signifying processes that undergird the literary text (identified above), that the presence of disability in literary representations has the effect of a suture: it ties the text world to the extra-textual world. *Aesthetic Nervousness* captures that there is a reciprocal energy surrounding the functioning of disability. Disability is a symbol in the literary domain that, though a symbol, resists signification through its ethical qualities, which call readers back to the materiality of the extra-textual world. This is why he writes that it "transcends the literary domain and refuses to be assimilated to it" (2007: 19).[14] Here it is ethics – a realm infused with cognition and not with the materiality suggested by the body in Mitchell and Snyder's analysis – that returns us to an extra-textual world where disability is itself awash in symbolic and signifying meanings, meanings built up over time and subject to able-bodied constructions and ableist discourse but potentially subject also to crip/queer challenges to ableism and the normate. In brief, Quayson's work allows us to be more intentional about how we imagine cognition to condition the surface appearance of disability in both literary and non-literary contexts.

The two books discussed here differ greatly in their perspectives on materiality. Quayson's account emphasizes, much more so than Mitchell and Snyder's, the nuanced way in which literary prose representations reference or interact with material practices. I want to make clear that materiality is a concept that is relevant to both areas of aesthetic production – both visual and prose media. That said, my concern is with the way in which materiality operates at the semiotic level of artistic production and the way it is prioritized in a certain way in visual media. Specifically, the material correspondence suggested between the body as literary representation and the body as material, social reality deserves closer consideration. One can say that in prose the connection, the index, the reference, the relation, comes after the symbolic and the metaphorical, and not before it; and that the literary reference to bodies in the external world is predicated and made possible by the primary productive and representational activity of literary symbol and metaphor. It is not that literary representation references an extra-textual body; instead, it is that the bodily literary representation is from the outset a symbol or metaphor, already mediated and constructed by extra-textual social forces. It is because the body in literary representation functions as a symbol that it may be then, in a second pass, linked with bodily representations and material practices outside of the text. While in literature the arbitrary/symbolic serves as the basis for the referential/indexical, in visual media the referential (iconic/indexical) serves as the material basis for the arbitrary or symbolic. This may seem like a minor distinction to some, but it is crucial, for it opens up visual media as a way of representing cognitive disability without explicit (or total) conditioning by discursive bias and normative social convention. It also underscores the potentially transformative path by which disability studies in the humanities can feel comfortable about carrying out analyses of cultural products (visual texts, but not literary texts *per se*) that, as in the new disability documentary cinema, may indeed be seen to deal with "real people" (Bérubé 2005: 570). The next section continues to emphasize the material connections with disability experiences offered by visual media while addressing the value of seeing visual texts as representations of human lives lived off-screen or off-page.

Materiality, Visual Narrative, and Cognition

Visual representations of disability require a more distinct theoretical apparatus than has been developed up until now. They necessitate that we shed many of the methodological priorities that have been built up in the development of a predominantly literary engagement of disability studies in the humanities. The previous section explored what it means for disability in literature to be considered a signifying surface, focusing on how this surface operates to connect literary texts and extra-literary worlds, and noting the limitations of asserting such material correspondences. Embedded in this exploration, however – and particularly in the transition from Mitchell and Snyder's to Quayson's work effected above – is the important question of how we understand materiality and culture in relation to disability representations. If the literary disability representation may be a dubious "anchor in materiality" (Mitchell and Snyder 2000: 63) and promise the "illusion" of materiality (2000: 64), disability representations in films and graphic novels offer a way of connecting aesthetics with social representations through a more immediate and perhaps less consistently dubious form of materiality. The iconic/indexical basis of visual media constitutes its signifying ground, but it is the way in which this iconic/indexical basis acquires accumulative force through narrative that is most important. The deceptively simple principle referred to as iconic redundancy is a way of highlighting the generative potential and accumulative ontological force of visual narrative with respect to cognitive disabilities.

The notion of iconic redundancy has been introduced and explored as a hallmark element of comics theory (and is relevant also to the cinematic image). In his influential work *The System of Comics* (1999, translated into English in 2007), Thierry Groensteen distinguishes between the way characters are referenced, in the semiotic sense of the term, in prose literature and visual media: "the insistent character of the protagonist finds itself in all narrative forms, comprised in the novel where it is a proper noun, or the pronoun that takes its place, and which is tirelessly repeated ('I,' 'he,' or 'she,' depending on whether the narration is effectuated in the first or third person). It is only conspicuous when it is a matter of a story *in images*" (Groensteen 2007: 115).[15] As he remarks, it is significant that what we call character "description" in prose literature is generally introduced infrequently, and perhaps it is not an overstatement to say only once – when the character in question is initially introduced to readers, for example.[16] In comics, however, and in visual narrative more broadly (so as to include cinema), this basic form of character description is a narrative process "infinitely restarted" (2007: 124) with each visual appearance of the character.[17] The insistent character of this visual representation amounts to a strong ontological assertion. In the case of characters with cognitive disability, this assertion repeatedly renders the existence of cognitive difference visible, an act that can be particularly powerful given the historical invisibility of corresponding populations with cognitive disabilities.

Iconic redundancy is important in visual media not just because of the way it foregrounds the visibility of characters through strong ontological assertion but also because of the role this assertion takes on in a narrative in which iconic and indexical forms of signification predominate. As Barbara Postema explains in her monograph *Narrative Structure in Comics: Making Sense of Fragments*, where she compares comics to other (prose literary) narrative forms, "somewhat less common in comics are symbolic representations, where an image represents or stands for something else based on arbitrary or conventional signification" (2013: xvi). Given the predominance of icon and index in visual narrative, and the concomitant relegation of symbol and metaphor to a secondary (though not insignificant) position in semiotic processes of meaning-making, the ontological assertion of character arguably assumes a greater portion of the narrative impact. That is, in practice, visual narrative actually relies heavily on the repetition of visual information to advance itself. "Though panels create narrative, they need a point of reference to create the cohesion between the separate images," writes Postema (2013: 57). Description, in this sense, becomes in visual media a generative mechanism for plot advancement. Its intimate involvement with iconic/indexical signification ensures the continual reactivation of material connections with those same cognitive codes that structure our experience of social embodiment. By contrast, in prose literature description is routine, easily forgotten, necessarily incomplete, and more susceptible to the normative social convention that pervades the arbitrary character of linguistic signification and literary discourse.

On the basis of these relatively simple observations regarding iconic redundancy and its role in visual narrative we can articulate the value of attending to visual disability representations in disability studies in the humanities. Specifically, the nature of these visual representations suggests a new perspective on two long-standing problems that disproportionately affect populations with severe cognitive disabilities. In the introduction to this book I cited Joseph N. Straus's essay "Autism as Culture," in which he outlined two ways in which cognitive difference can constitute a barrier to constructing a political identity (2013: 462). The "problem of narration" highlights how neoliberal capitalism requires those engaging in rights-based discourse to speak for themselves and narrate their own experiences. The "problem of community" highlights the expectation that social groups frame themselves as minoritized identities through self-aware communication and self-organization. If we acknowledge that material experiences of disability involve not just social constructions but also biological factors and issues of impairment – if we acknowledge the materiality of cognitive impairment along with socially constructed barriers to full participation in neoliberal society – we must understand that populations with severe cognitive disabilities face material barriers to resolving these matters of narration and community.

In order to consider material barriers to narration and community while acknowledging biological factors and cognitive impairment, disability studies scholars need to reassess the way in which the notion of the disabling social environment responds to the questions raised by cognitive difference. Rosemarie Garland-Thomson expresses this notion, which has proved powerful for populations with physical disabilities, quite well in her essay "Disability and Representation":

> Disability studies points out that ability and disability are not so much a matter of the capacities and limitations of bodies but more about what we expect from a body at a particular moment and place. Stairs disable people who need to use wheelchairs to get around, but ramps let them go places freely. Reading the print in a phone book or deciphering the patterns on a computer screen is an ability that our moment demands. So if our minds can't make sense of the pattern or our eyes can't register the print, we become disabled. In other words, we are expected to look, act, and move in

> certain ways so we'll fit into the built and attitudinal environment. If we don't, we become disabled. (2005: 524)

The question is whether the needs of populations with severe cognitive disabilities can be fully addressed by a model that was conceived to address "what we expect from a body at a particular moment and place." This argument denouncing a disabling social environment is in effect a situational or task-based one that, while valuable, assumes a certain degree of able-mindedness. Is it sufficient to address the situational needs of populations with severe cognitive disabilities? Or is a more collaborative model needed?

For populations that cannot represent themselves or that cannot organize themselves as a political identity under the individualistic paradigm of neoliberal and representational democracy, visual narratives potentially offer a collaborative model for addressing the need for societal changes in response to the material experience of cognitive difference. I do not claim that visual culture is a panacea. There is nothing inherent in visual media that ensures transgressive or counter-normative representations of disability. Nevertheless, I believe that more can be done to understand what visual media do in fact make possible. In the chapters comprising part 2 of this book, I implicitly revisit what has been a traditional point of contention in disability studies work in the humanities – namely, the question of whether representations of cognitive disability by cognitively abled producers are by this very fact of their creation flawed, colonizing, and therefore easily dismissed.[18] There are those scholars, for example, who would suggest that "any narrative involving a character who cannot narrate themselves is somehow exploitative" (commented upon in Bérubé 2005: 572; see also Hall 2016: 107). In "Disability and Narrative," Michael Bérubé does not include himself in that group of scholars, but neither does he address the unique properties of non-literary representations of cognitive disabilities. Discussion there focuses on the textual representation of cognitive disability as a device,[19] and in that essay Bérubé simultaneously uses cognition as a way for criticism to return its focus to the representational strategies of literary narrative in general. He is ultimately concerned with the intersection of literary narrative and cognitive disability, and he affirms that characters in literary texts should not be "read simply as representations of real people" (2005: 570) – a call to which he returns in *The Secret Life of Stories* (2016: 29).[20] Yet if disability studies wants to move away from metaphorical use of disability, we might also pursue further how to complement the work on disability as metaphor in scholarly criticism with work that does indeed address the needs of real people. I ultimately see this as a complementary move, in the context of visual media, to the method advocated by Bérubé, in the context of literature – a move he describes as finding "a way to talk about function without repudiating the key insight into the social character of disability … The point is not to try to pretend that all disabilities are purely a matter of social stigma; the point, rather, is to insist that 'function' can never be a meaningful measure of human worth" (2016: 57).

Given the historical invisibility of cognitive disability representations, I wonder if it might actually be beneficial to reinvest in the material connections between artistic representations of cognition and the existence of cognitively disabled populations outside of the artistic text. Visual media in particular offer disability scholars in the humanities a way of balancing both sides of this connection without feeling they have to sacrifice nuances related to questions of aesthetics. Put most simply, if populations with severe cognitive disability cannot self-narrate the subject position required by representational democracies and neoliberal capitalism in prose literature, then perhaps it is time for scholars in the humanities to turn more towards visual aesthetic forms, which arguably offer greater potential for collaborative forms of representation. Visual portrayals of cognitive disability – particularly so in the case of what Snyder and Mitchell call the new disability documentary cinema, and also in the biographical strain of comics art that lends priority to non-spectacular everyday experiences – offer the opportunity to recuperate the value of reading screen and page images of disability as representations of real people. Importantly, Bérubé's own words contain the seed for conceiving of disability studies as a collaborative project, even though this point may be clothed in the language of literary analysis:

> In one world, cognitive disability remains irreducibly alien, and self-representation depends on one's capacity to distinguish oneself from those incapable of self-representation; in another world, cognitive disability is part of a larger narrative that includes an indeterminable number of characters, only some of whom have the capacity to narrate but all of whom shed light on the mechanics of narrative and narration. (2005: 576)

What the critic refers to as "another world" might as well be taken as the world that awaits humanists in what I take to be the richly collaborative potential of visual media analysis.

In the next three chapters I explore the collaborative potential of cognitive disability aesthetics and in one case the limitations of that collaboration. Perhaps by necessity, these chapters analyse cultural production at the margins of ableist society. It should not be surprising that with few exceptions, cognitive difference remains a topic that mainstream visual media either ignores entirely or else presents through a normative lens. Currently it may be that it is only at the margins of (inter)national circuits of cultural production that material experiences of cognitive disability are explored in art with a greater degree of social critique. Even these endeavours are not wholly unproblematic, of course. For instance, as evident in chapter 4's exploration of an art installation produced by artists with intellectual disabilities at the Nuevos Ministerios Metro Station organized by the Metro de Madrid company, the (in)visibility of cognitive difference in society is still subject to the desires of powerful corporations. Nonetheless, the reality is that populations with severe cognitive disabilities necessarily rely on forms of social collaboration to assert themselves as a community if not a minoritized group, and for that reason, scholarship in the humanities should pay close attention to the way in which art is mobilized as a vehicle for inclusion. As the second half of chapter 4 explores, the complicated issue of collaboration for populations with severe cognitive disability can also be analysed on a more intimate scale. There I consider the case of *María cumple 20 años*, a graphic novel composed by a noted artist with the collaboration of his daughter, who has autism, as another pathway to rendering cognitive difference visible. In both cases it is important to note that each of these discussions of cultural production involves the existence of real people with cognitive disability, instead of focusing on cognitive difference as a metaphor, symbol, or vehicle for constructed normalcy.

The ontological assertion conveyed in comics form through iconic redundancy is implicitly a part of chapter 5's exploration of another graphic novel, *Arrugas*, which focuses on the experience of Alzheimer's-related dementia. Here I adopt the perspective that the artist's fictionalized representation of his visits with specific residents living in a skilled-care facility should be seen through the lens of collaborative narration. Since I intend to recognize the reality of severe impairment, I do not shy away from portraying Alzheimer's as cognitive decline. Some readers will surely find this objectionable.[21] I think, however, that the graphic novel, and also my analysis of it, acknowledges cognitive impairment as a material experience of Alzheimer's-related dementia.

This does not mean that Alzheimer's disease is not overmedicalized in ableist society, only that it is also important to attend to the material experience of Alzheimer's. An additional aspect of the comic worth highlighting is that it embraces the ensemble thinking that Snyder and Mitchell attribute to the new disability documentary cinema (2010: 198), in that it presents multiple characters with cognitive disability. In prioritizing the textures of everyday experience, in focusing on the relational aspects of its characters' lives, and in the end also by not avoiding the topic of diagnosis, it resists the spectacularization of cognitive difference that so often obtains in mass-marketed cultural products.

The ontological assertion of iconic redundancy is also a significant factor in the filmic representations of schizophrenia analysed in chapter 6. The documentary *Una cierta verdad* by Abel García Roure also employs ensemble thinking, rendering visible for audiences the experiences of multiple persons living with schizophrenia. It explicitly foregrounds the question of a patient's right to live autonomously from the violence of the medical paradigm's imprecise doses of medication and forced hospitalizations while grappling with the material reality of severe impairment in some cases and with a more pervasive lack of community support for cognitive disabilities. Through iconic and indexical signification, the film allows the voices and the actions of its characters to communicate on their own terms to a degree impossible in prose narrative. In this case it is the sophistication of the film's aesthetic engagement with its topic that sets it apart from other, more instrumentalist and informational documentary projects. I read the earlier film *1% esquizifrenia*, which takes its title from the percentage of the population identified as living with this form of psychiatric disability, as a counter-example in precisely this sense.

Whether the chapters that follow explore representations of Down syndrome, autism, Alzheimer's disease, or schizophrenia, in every case they recognize the seam between culture/aesthetics and biology/impairment. They address and problematize this seam, refusing to reduce cognitive disability representation to a symbol, metaphor or discursive formation in the simple sense, and focusing on the opportunities offered by visual media. These are chapters about representation that purposely adopt a naive view on the connection between representation and referent – this is a way of recognizing that art loses none of its aesthetic complexity when it addresses the experiences of "real people." We need to recognize that this is possible in visual media to a degree that it may not be in literary narrative and also that this is important for populations with cognitive disabilities in a way it may not be for populations with physical disabilities. In the end, disability scholarship in the humanities carried out "at the seam where body joins culture" (Jeffreys 2002: 33) fully assumes neither the constructivist argument that disability is solely a social relationship nor the essentializing premise that disability is located purely in the individual body or the individual mind. Instead it inhabits that persistently uncomfortable middle ground where cognition and embodiment, material experience and normative social convention, intertwine.

PART TWO
Cognition, Collaboration, Community

4 Visualizing Down Syndrome and Autism: The *Trazos Singulares* (Singular Strokes) (2011) Exhibition and *María cumple 20 años* (Maria Turns Twenty) (2015)

"Inclusion and equity are mighty tasks that require artful social imagination and the commitment of material resources."

– Leslie Roman (2009a: 61)

"The dynamics of disability compel us to recognize that there will always be among us people who cannot represent themselves and must be represented."

– Michael Bérubé (2005: 572)

This is the first of three chapters in part 2 of *Cognitive Disability Aesthetics* that analyse specific examples of representations of cognitive disabilities in contemporary Spanish culture. The twin purpose of these explorations is to correct for the invisibility of cognitive difference in society and in scholarship and to acknowledge the value of attending to the notion of impairment when approaching cognitive disabilities in particular. Both of the examples discussed in this chapter explore the social (in)visibility of cognitive disability and situate the question of impairment in a decidedly collaborative context. I am interested here in the way that the artistic production of disability representations can reinforce collaborations between those who experience cognitive disability in an ableist society and those who do not. A focus on collaboration affirms that all in human societies are interdependent (Kittay, Jennings, and Wasunna 2005; Carlson 2010) and that all artistic production, reception, and connection is a necessarily social activity. Discussions of the value of collaboration are particularly significant when those collaborations involve populations with severe cognitive impairments, for the disability experiences of these populations tend to be among the least visible. This is true whether we think of visibility in terms relevant to historical documentation, social supports, cultural representations, or all three at once.

Arguing for inclusion and equity in the field of cognitive disability aesthetics does not mean affirming the theories of dependency that align ableism with the individualistic myth of contemporary capitalism. The individual artist is never a monad, but is instead always part of a larger social web of artistic traditions, motivations, supports, and opportunities. Moreover, to expect that those experiencing severe cognitive disabilities have the social power to communicate their needs or to critique society's disabling conditions individually or as a group – without the assistance of others – may be another form of affirming individualism and the myth of independence, both of which are, in truth, forms of ableism.[1] What this means for disability studies in the humanities is that we must more thoroughly investigate the pathways and limitations of collaborative modes of critique.

In this chapter I look at two ways in which collaborative modes of cultural production can help render cognitive disabilities visible. The first centres on an attempt to use the discourse of art to lend greater visibility to developmental disabilities in the urban space of Madrid. This is a large-scale endeavour that exposes the limitations, but also the potential, of organizational (and, perhaps more controversially, even corporate) outreach. The Trazos Singulares exhibit involved the participation of a large number of artists with developmental disabilities, who created art at a metro station in Madrid during 2011. Sponsored by the Metro de Madrid company, the art focused on images of transportation. Symbolically, it posed basic questions about the visibility of developmental disabilities such as Down syndrome and autism in society, about access and mobility, and about the contested value of art both in and beyond corporate projects.[2] These are not simple questions. Consideration of the issues involved in this exhibition reveals the ableist dimensions of a necessarily shared collective imaginary that permits visibility of cognitive difference in public spaces only in an uneven and inconsistent fashion. I hope that readers do not dismiss the exhibition wholesale or, on the other hand, tout it unequivocally as a success. Instead, I see Trazos Singulares as an imaginative prompt to help us all think through what more might be done at the urban scale to return "the right to the city" to populations with cognitive disabilities in theory and in practice: through imagination, access, community supports, and the potentially radical power of artistic discourse.[3]

The second collaborative mode of artistic production unfolds at the much more intimate scale of the family. The graphic novel *María cumple 20 años* (2015) – a sequel to the earlier graphic novel *María y yo* (2007) – brings a father and daughter together in the collaborative representation of a shared everyday life foregrounding the social experience of autism.[4] Here, just as in that previous work, María and Miguel Gallardo deliver an autobiographical comic centring on their shared experience of María's autism. This work continues several strategies used in *María y yo* – such as two-tone print, innovative panel transitions, and intriguing whole-page layouts – and returns to core themes of travel, behaviours, the everyday value of pictograms, social marginalization, and the strength of relationships with friends and family. To the degree that the work invests in the iconic signification particular to the visual form of the graphic novel, its depictions of María and its other characters connect with matters addressed in chapters 2 and 3 of this book. Here a preponderance of iconically motivated representations connect readers with specific human beings outside of the artistic text and testify to real experiences of cognitive disability. The original comics text from 2007 was in spirit already a collaborative venture, as signalled there in the byline that provided the names of its co-creators: "María Gallardo y Miguel Gallardo." In the sequel *María cumple 20 años* this tradition of co-authorship is continued, but also evident is the significant decision to include images drawn by María herself. In particular, the comic highlights the shared activity of drawing as a form of human connection and as a social *and* artistic collaboration. Through the practice of drawing, an inclusive community is formed at the scale of the family; that community is subsequently sustained and expanded – through publication – at the level of the graphic novel's readerly reception.

A close examination of these two divergent contexts – a collaborative public exhibition and a collaborative graphic novel – can help us think through the nature and potential of cognitive disability representations. An understanding of cognitive difference that attends to the question of impairment requires us to think differently about the fundamental interdependence of all who live in human societies. Whatever limitations readers may attribute to them, both the exhibition and the graphic novel discussed here have the potential, in the long term, to speak to issues of access, inclusion, and visibility for populations with cognitive disabilities. More than that, sustained scholarly exploration of these issues may help dismantle the pervasive ableism that thrives in the clear absence of such representations.

The Trazos Singulares Exhibition (2011)

During May 2011 (ending 15 May) an intriguing exhibition titled "Trazos Singulares [Singular Strokes]" was on display at Madrid's north-central metro station Nuevos Ministerios (New Ministries). The exhibition comprised some sixty works by thirty artists with developmental disabilities, and significantly, the work of artistic production was performed *in situ* between 5 and 8 April.[5] Very often, of course, the public appearance of the artistic work is separated in space and time from the moment of its production so that the artistic product takes on an existence separated from the producer. Those who appreciate art tend to become accustomed to this sort of disembodiment. Contemporary criticism thus tends to eschew the so-called biographical fallacy of interpretation whereby the meaning of a work of art is reduced to the life experience of its creator. Trazos Singulares, however, arguably not only recognizes the difficulty of separating artistic producer from artistic product but also underscores the artist's immersion in a decidedly social context. If we are to take to heart the somewhat predictably rhetorical spirit of the speech with which José Ignacio Echeverría inaugurated the exhibition at the Nuevos Ministerios station – "El arte no entiende diferencias ni conoce barreras sino que promueve *la integración* y la autonomía de las personas" (Art recognizes neither differences nor barriers. Instead, it promotes *the integration* and autonomy of people) ("Inauguración" 2011; my emphasis) – the artistic producers of the Trazos Singulares exhibition are not merely being integrated symbolically through the inclusion and integration of their artwork into the daily fabric of Madrid's transportation system. They are also being integrated physically, even if ephemerally.

While there clearly exists a certain kind of sporadic and somewhat showy form of outreach by companies using disabled populations for causes that have just as much to do with their own public relations plans as they do with the notion of "accommodating" such marginalized communities – one that certainly cannot abrogate the need for sustainable and lasting financial and institutional support from governments as well as the need to resituate the disabled/able-bodied dichotomy – there is something unconventional and intriguing about this particular event. Although it may admittedly be a far cry from sustainable and unconditional support for disabled populations, this small-scale decision to have the artists paint in the Madrid metro station nonetheless reflects a somewhat more sophisticated understanding of the historical legacy of the paradoxical visibility/invisibility of disability than would be reflected in the decision merely to showcase their works. Disability philosopher Licia Carlson compellingly writes in her work *The Faces of Intellectual Disability* of the way in which "intellectual disability … has been made both socially visible and invisible" (2010: 46). Historically speaking, the institutionalized classification/codification of people with intellectual disabilities made them highly visible from a clinical (and social) standpoint just as their incarceration in "institutions far from public view" was intended to render them seemingly invisible to the public at large (Carlson 2010: 46; see also Davis 1995: 73, 94–5, 173; Siebers 2008: 99–109). For all its potential limitations, then, Trazos Singulares does render the contributing artists as (momentarily) socially visible, in the process drawing attention to the embodied nature of *all* artistic production.

This section uses the social context of the exhibition and the subject matter of the artists' paintings as a way of asking more provocative questions about the "right to the city" (Lefebvre 1996) experienced by disabled populations in Madrid, specifically. The fact that the artistic products overwhelmingly represented themes of transportation and tended to depict scenes of various landmarks and public spaces in Madrid, including various specific buildings and metro stations, makes this an appropriate approach. Analysis draws equally from both disability studies scholars and Henri Lefebvre's urban theory while grounding the reader in the material conditions faced by disabled residents of Madrid. It highlights the insufficient public recognition of developmental disabilities in particular (as in the recent 2010 documentary *Capacitados*) as well as outreach efforts and televised spots supported by other agencies such as Down España, and even articles of the recent UN Convention on the Rights of Persons with Disabilities.

Generally speaking, disability studies has long signalled the importance of embodiment. To the extent that "the political unconscious upholds a delicious ideal of social perfection by insisting that any public body be flawless," this unconscious also "displaces manifestations of disability from collective consciousness … through concealment, cosmetic action, motivated forgetting, and rituals of sympathy and pity" (Siebers 2010: 62). Underscoring embodiment can serve to render these processes as visible if not also as susceptible to critique. Understanding that creative processes are necessarily embodied is particularly important when those producing bodies are marginalized through the normalizing discourse of "able-bodiedness" (see Carlson 2001, 2010). Tobin Siebers – who reminds us that "embodiment is, of course, central to the field of disability studies" (Siebers 2008: 23) – writes against the development of "a nonmaterialist aesthetics that devalues the role of the body and limits the definition of art" (Siebers 2010: 1), a critique we might extend also to the production of art and not merely to the "textual" result of creative process or to a detached hermeneutics seeking to explain artistic representation.[6] Thus bodies are important not merely because they are represented implicitly or explicitly through the discourse of art – a premise Siebers traces throughout his masterful work – they are also important because they actually *do* or *perform* the representing.

Dealing with the issue of embodiment from too general a perspective has its potential drawbacks. For example, scholars have pointed to the problems associated with viewing "disability culture" as more than merely an entry point into a syncretic and non-monolithic or non-homogeneous culture (see discussion in Johnston 2009: 155–6). It follows that if "disability cultures must be understood in the light of their artistic contributions" (Johnston 2009: 157),[7] and if the resulting understanding is to be productive, we must get specific. So in this section, I do not want to address generalities associated with the creative work of disabled populations. I refuse, for example, to engage debates surrounding whether disability affects the "ability to make art" in a positive or a negative way (commented on in Boeltzig et al. 2009: 753). Instead I seek to explore artistic production by a specific disabled (artistic) community (the artists with intellectual disabilities who produced the exhibit) in a given location (Madrid) at a given time (the spring of 2011). My implicit mobilization of the notion of embodiment suggests that we cannot avoid properly contextualizing the work of these artists socially, politically, or culturally. Furthermore, the necessarily urban context of the city of Madrid is important in terms of both form and content – both at the individual scale read through the represented content of the artistic products themselves and also at the broader social scale of artistic production.

Understanding the specific social and cultural context in which people with intellectual and developmental disabilities (IDD) live and work is an important first step in interpreting their artistic works. Zeroing in on the necessarily heterogeneous community of people with

Down syndrome living in Spain, we see that there have been strong advances in the form of public campaigns directed towards securing the rights of people with IDD as well as filmic representations of disability that challenge entrenched misunderstandings of IDD. Even so, many problems persist. The 2006 Convention on the Rights of People with Disabilities ("Convención" 2010) carefully articulated what remains to be done if populations with IDD are to live in society as equals with their cognitively abled counterparts. In fact, a series of televised spots broadcast on Spanish channels and reproduced on the Internet has drawn attention to specific articles of the convention through innovative dramatized clips as a way of challenging the public's misperceptions of IDD. These spots launch from specific articles of the UN Convention – such as Article 27, "Trabajo y empleo [Work and Employment]" (Campaña [1]), Article 19, "Derecho a vivir de forma independiente y a ser incluido en la comunidad [The Right to Live Independently and to Be Included in the Community]" (Campaña [2]), and Article 5, "Igualdad y no discriminación [Equality without Discrimination]" (Campaña [3]) – to dramatize how the rights of people with IDD might be better secured in Spanish society. These three spots feature a young woman with IDD whose employment shifts from temporary to permanent after her supervisor speaks to his boss on her behalf, a young man who moves out of his mother's house to live independently, and a bouncer who allows another young man with IDD to enter a club without being discriminated against.[8]

Such visual representations of IDD in televised spots are, of course, a welcome response to persisting inequalities suffered by and even within disabled populations. First, populations with IDD in Spain (and elsewhere) often face a form of social invisibility in that those disabilities that tend to be more publicly recognized tend to be more physical and less cognitive in nature. In her essay "Representing Disability in 90's Spain: The Case of ONCE," which takes on "the institution which has pioneered the integration of blind people in Spain," María José Gámez Fuentes informs the general reader of something that is well known among people in Spain – the fact that "the scope of the organization's activities has expanded in order to include groups dealing with other disabilities, such as hearing impairments or slight mental handicaps" (2005: 305). ONCE is undeniably the most widely recognized organization advocating for the rights of people with disability in Spain, and Gámez Fuentes makes sure to stress that, nevertheless, it "has been pivotal in the process of making a particular image of disabled people visible in the audience's mind since the beginning of its advertising campaigns in the eighties" (2005: 305). Traditionally and generally speaking (in Spain, just as elsewhere), "the media do not tend to offer unpleasant images of disability" but instead tend to show "people whose disabilities can be disguised or easily adapted to society. Therefore, audiences mainly encounter disabilities such as hearing, or visual impairments and wheelchair users" (Gámez Fuentes 2005: 306; cf. the video *Capacitados*[9]). Gámez Fuentes in fact takes many of Spain's disability organizations to task, contending that they base their discourse "on the idea that disability is the origin of the integration problem" (2005: 306). While I do not rush to apply this statement to other disability advocacy organizations too broadly – in particular, I think that major steps forward have been made since 2006, as shown by the Convention on the Rights of People with Disabilities and the work of DOWN ESPAÑA – it is nonetheless true that disabled Spaniards still face many obstacles to true social integration and that at the large scale, disability has not yet been sufficiently approached in Spain as an environmental/social (and not an individual) problem. A recent documentary produced by ONCE titled *Capacitados*, though a welcome invitation to the general Spanish public to view people with physical disabilities differently, confirms that intellectual disabilities in particular continue to be underrepresented, if not completely invisible, in mainstream discourses on disability in Spain. Nonetheless, it is reassuring that there are a growing number of academic studies on intellectual disability both within Spain and beyond. Research to gauge the quality of life and the satisfaction levels of people with intellectual disability living in Spain has only begun quite recently (Mirón Canelo et al. 2008), and, of course, people with disabilities continue to be disproportionately affected by unemployment both in and outside of Spain.[10]

I have addressed the issue of work for disabled populations more generally elsewhere.[11] Here I would like to focus on the realities of artistic production with an implicit nod also towards the possibility of careers/employment in the arts. As Heike Boeltzig and colleagues point out, "such careers are likely to be a viable and even desirable option for several reasons" – that is, the arts are a growing field that offers flexible employment options as well as arenas for self-expression/affirmation (2009: 753–4). The authors also emphasize the benefits of "art as a medium for communication and for sharing messages," art "as a coping mechanism," and art as "an escape from disability-related stigma" (Boeltzig et al. 2009: 758–9). While artistic production certainly offers benefits like these when viewed at the scale of the individual for both disabled and able-bodied/cognitively abled populations alike, there is undoubtedly a more profoundly discursive or social, even political value to be ascribed to the production and reception of artistic work by artists with cognitive disabilities specifically, given that heterogeneous population's relative social invisibility. Below, I use the Trazos Singulares exposition by Madrileño artists with IDD not only as a way of showing how important it is for artists with cognitive disabilities to "[find] opportunities to show their art" (Boeltzig et al. 2009: 765) but also as a way of looking at the question of integration from a perspective that is simultaneously artistic and urban, both social and political. I view this endeavour as a complement to existing work on the self-representation of people with disabilities rather than as a re-examination of that valuable critical tradition. David Hevey, for one, signals a core tenet of disability studies when he writes: "In the history of disability representation or 'arts and disability,' we find a history of representation that was not done by us but done to us"; and we must indeed take note of "the historical fact that disabled people have not had an input, let alone a controlling interest, in culture and representation done in our name" (Hevey 1993: 423).[12] Nevertheless, he also asks how we might "shift disability representation off from the body and into the interface between people with impairments and socially disabling conditions" (Hevey 1993: 426). While this comment is best understood as a call – so common and important for disability studies – to resituate the discourse of disability, to view disability not as a personal/individual trait but rather as a widely environmental and inherently social condition, I believe this move might also signal possible connections with other disciplines – here, with urban studies in particular. That is, understood in broad terms, the political fight (Davis 1997: 1) to socially and culturally include people with cognitive disabilities in today's urban environments presents commonalities with the more broadly defined urban struggles where urban dwellers must work to assure their voices are heard.

First among these is what urban theorist Henri Lefebvre has called "the right to the city" (Lefebvre 1996). I offer that this reconciliation of disability studies with urban studies in essence responds to what Kirsty Johnston has identified as "opportunities to engage with disability as an important identity rubric akin to race, class and gender" (Johnston 2009: 154). That is, while Lefebvrian thought has been applied to political (and cultural/artistic) struggles to reclaim city-space in the interests of specific formations of race, class, and gender, to my knowledge it has not yet been harnessed for disability studies critique. If it is valuable to critique "the notion that impaired bodies are disempowered by their own corporeality rather than by the conditions in which they find themselves" (Counsell and Stanley 2005: 91), then disability studies might seek out connections with other established traditions of social critique that speak to how the city is conceived and (re)produced, (re)imagined, and (re)shaped in certain interests. As an urban theory that from the outset admits the complex interaction between how space is "conceived, perceived and lived" (Lefebvre 1991a: 33) – that underscores the dialectical interaction between cultural and social imaginaries (mental space) on one hand and the materiality of urban built environments (physical space) on the other – Lefebvre's *oeuvre* provides a wonderful starting point for analysing the production of artistic works *in* urban space and *about* urban spaces by people with IDD in Madrid.

Urban studies may at first appear to be a discourse orthogonal to the contemporary debates at the heart of disability studies; even so, there is sufficient cause for us to understand some of the social/environmental problems faced by disabled populations living in cities also as urban problems. This is not at all to vitiate the insights offered by the wider field of disability studies, which have rightly focused on a number of problems that operate under a certain relative autonomy with regard to the urban problematic. For example, disability theorists in a variety of contexts have worked hard to unmask the ways in which the struggles disabled populations face on a daily basis are dependent on and reflective of harmful institutions and ideologies such as the medical model of disability (e.g., Brosco 2010; Lane 1993), the persistence of patriarchal and gender-biased discourses that have also historically marginalized women and LGBTQ populations (Butler 1993; Garland-Thomson 2002a; McRuer 2006; Mitchell and Snyder 2000), and the frequently flawed media presentation of people with disabilities (Enns and Smit 2001b; Riley 2005). Such relatively recent work has also argued strongly for the economic inclusion (Morris 2002), self-representation (Charlton 1998), and autonomy (Francis 2009) of disabled populations – in a word, for their rights (Carey 2009; Herr et al. 2003). Put plainly, disabled populations have a right to the city – that is, a right to the use of its specific sites just as to the material and social conditions governing its production and reproduction, both as a physical built environment and an imagined space – in the same way as do other urbanites.

The urban critique of Henri Lefebvre – though it was not conceived with disabled populations in mind – is compatible with disability studies on at least two levels. First, it is clear that the construction of cities has historically been carried out by way of the exclusion of such populations, in terms of both the planning and the execution of urban design. This fact can be partly explained by Lefebvre's understanding of the contemporary science of urban planning (in such works as *The Right to the City* and *The Urban Revolution*). For the urban theorist, modern urban design is a class project rooted in a (historically) bourgeois vision of the city not as a lived space but rather as a conceived space whose construction is heavily dictated by the interests of a small group of speculators and capitalists instead of being governed by a truly democratic process. An effect of the historical circumstances governing the rise of modern urban planning in the nineteenth century has been the creation of a (physical) built environment shaped by the interests of able-bodied people alone – a legacy that legislation such as the Americans with Disabilities Act of 1990 (to cite one example) has sought to correct. This fact, moreover, reflects the historical legacy of the exclusion of disabled populations from social dialogue as a whole – the lack of access to and control over space accompanies a lack of access to and control over social (and political) processes. The second way in which Lefebvre's work in urban geography is relevant to the struggles faced by disabled populations living in the city – generally speaking – is that he articulates a vision of space as social, as embodied, and as actually lived that is at odds with this disembodied and geometrical legacy of urban planning (see also Sennett 1992. We do not have to look too far to see how his work has been applied to more specific struggles of marginalized urban populations,[13] and we would be wise to see the relevance of his work to disability studies, even if this may not have been his original intent.

The central premise of Henri Lefebvre's approach to urban realities involves a notion of space that, though variegated and multidimensional, is nonetheless cohesive once seen through the lens of dialectical thinking.[14] In *The Production of Space* he writes of his intent to forge a "unitary theory of physical, mental and social space" (Lefebvre 1991a: 21), seeking to correct a static model of space as a physical built environment alone by recognizing how mental conceptions and social perceptions of space interact with urban environments over time. From this Lefebvrian perspective – one pursued by a number of other geographers who follow explicitly in the French theorist's footsteps (among them David Harvey and Edward Soja; see Harvey 1990; Soja 1989)

– space is a social process and not a mere static container for experience.[15] What this process model of space means is not necessarily that our contemporary cities are increasingly mobile places where the flow of modern urban life is accelerating (a thesis advanced in the early twentieth century by Georg Simmel 2000) – although that much is also true. Instead, the understanding of space as a process means that there is an evolving and dialectical relationship through which our mental conceptions of space and place are negotiated socially and then reflected in the static structures of the city, coming to reciprocally influence our understanding of the city and also our notions of ourselves and so on. Understanding space as a process – city-space as a process deeply entwined with social discourse – allows for a social critique. Furthermore, as Lefebvre highlights, this process has been, since its modern origins, inherently non-inclusive. City planning could easily be described also as ableist.

Throughout *The Right to the City*, Lefebvre privileges the nineteenth century as a key moment during which an understanding of the city as exchange-value trumped the use-value of the city (Lefebvre 1996: 167–8). The triumph of the notion of the city as exchange-value – which has persisted through the twentieth century and into the twenty-first – has thus led to a city produced in the interests and image of "capitalist spectators, builders and technicians" (Lefebvre 1996: 168). This process has traditionally failed to create an "urban reality for 'users'" (Lefebvre 1996: 168), with the result that those who inhabit the city are in effect alienated from input regarding the production of the very spaces in which they live. This is, for Lefebvre, further testament to the power of the various alienating forces of modernity that he describes from a multidimensional point of view. Alienation is for the French theorist simultaneously economic, social, political, ideological, and philosophical.[16] In the end, despite these pervasive modern forces of alienation, which affect all urban dwellers – both able-bodied and disabled – and despite the historical legacy of a planning culture that has concentrated control over the production of urban space in a few hands (Lefebvre 1996: 83–5; 2003), Lefebvre underscores that "the right to the city is like a cry and a demand" (Lefebvre 1996: 158). To realize a revitalized urban life we must recapture the city from the limitations of exchange value – that is, that cities are bought and sold, as are their images, and shaped purely in the interests of capital.

In "What *Kind* of Right Is the Right to the City," geographer Kafui A. Attoh writes that "the right to the city for Lefebvre thus signifies a great deal. It signifies the right to inhabit the city, the right to produce urban life on new terms (unfettered by the demands of exchange value), and the right of inhabitants to remain unalienated from urban life" (2011: 674). Nevertheless, as Attoh's essay also underscores throughout, the precise notion of what is meant by "rights" has varied considerably among geographers and even among Lefebvrian geographers. I view this not as a problem but as an opportunity to explore potential connections with disability studies. If, as Kirsten Simonsen argues, Lefebvre's pathblazing understanding of space as social and as lived might be applied fortuitously to feminist approaches grounded in notions of embodiment and performance (2005: 1), it might be equally important for disability scholars to do the same. Returning to Lefebvre's own *The Right to the City*, one of his many important remarks is the following one, which relates both to the topic at hand (disability art) and, more generally, to a set of needs that have not been addressed by modern urban planning and that thus constitute one of the key methods of disrupting the spatial logic of contemporary capitalist planning culture:

> The human being has the need to accumulate energies and to spend them, even waste them in play. He has a need to see, to hear, to touch and to taste and the need to gather these perceptions in a "world." To these anthropological needs which are socially elaborated (that is, sometimes separated, sometimes joined together, here compressed and there hypertrophied), can be added specific needs which are not satisfied by those commercial and cultural infrastructures which are somewhat parsimoniously taken into account by planners. This refers to the need for creative activity, for the *oeuvre* (not only of products and consumable material goods), of the need for information, symbolism, the imaginary and play. Through these specified needs lives and survives a fundamental desire of which play, sexuality, physical activities such as sport, creative activity, art and knowledge are particular expressions and *moments*. (Lefebvre 1996: 147, original emphasis)

"Creative activity, art and knowledge"; "symbolism, the imaginary and play"; for Lefebvre these are some of the privileged tools through which the city may be taken back by those who have been alienated from it. Lefebvre intends these measures as a disruptive response to the univocal logic and reductive notion of capitalist spatiality – such that festivals (*la fête*), protests or events that "take back the streets," and other, perhaps more playful expressions or reappropriations of city-space (for uses other than consumerism) come to symbolize if not actually enact (ephemerally) an oppositional, countercultural, and by nature necessarily inclusive understanding of the right to the city.

In this Lefebvrian context, I want to return to the 2011 Trazos Singulares art exhibition as a way of pointing to both its limitations and its potential. On one hand, the exhibit was in a sense limited by its connections with Metro de Madrid corporation, which perhaps sought self-aggrandizement through the use of disabled artists – a use that some may have seen through the objectionable lens of "charity" and that without a doubt was promotional. On the other hand, however, the event – through the symbolic weight of the nature of the art produced as well as the performance itself, which counteracted the perennial social invisibility of disabled populations in the city – points to the future possibility and potential of forging a more intimate relationship between people with cognitive disabilities and the city in which these populations live, work, and create. As the company sponsoring this exhibit was Metro de Madrid, it is not surprising that many (but not all) of the images feature trains, depictions (including signage) of specific metro stations (e.g., Nuevos Ministerios, Delicias, Chamberi, Miguel de Vergara), or even street-level metro entrances (e.g. Plaza de España, Banco de España, Callao, Cartagena), focusing also on elements of the built environment such as staircases, escalators, elevators, doors, turnstiles, and ticket machines. On one level, the prevalence of such images points somewhat directly to the extent to which the social meaning of the exhibition has been structured from the outset and later limited by the involvement of Metro de Madrid. From this point of view, the artworks function merely as illustrations of the image that Metro would like Madrid's citizens to have of their corporation. This perspective emphasizes the exhibit as a collection of (embodied) representations of perceived values such as creativity, inclusivity, accessibility, and – going back to the words from the speech cited earlier ("Inauguración" 2011) – the lack of barriers and (specifically) the notion of integration. Yet there is a symbolic dimension both to the process of creating the works of art within the Nuevos Ministerios station and to the content of the paintings themselves – a dimension that exists independently of (or co-dependently/relatively autonomously with) the material fact of corporate sponsorship. In any case, the fact that Metro de Madrid may have taken the initiative and even sponsored this cannot fully determine the significance of Trazos Singulares either as public display (the social process of artistic production) or as completed exhibition (the paintings as finished artistic products). In the gap between sponsorship and artistic product, and in the gaps between the existence of that which is represented, the act of representation itself, and the apparently reified, finished image, there is a liminal (and oppositional) space reserved for "creative activity, art and knowledge … symbolism, the imaginary and play" (Lefebvre 1996: 147). This space may be shaped in part by corporate sponsorship, but it is the nature of art and of signification to resist any one systematic determination of its meaning.

What happens when the Trazos Singulares exhibit is viewed as more than just a showy form of corporate outreach? What happens if we admit that, as Leslie G. Roman puts so well in the essay "Disability Arts and Culture as Public Pedagogy," "inclusion and equity are mighty tasks that require artful social imagination and the commitment of material resources" (2009a: 61)? That is, what exactly is the opportunity for which the material resources of Metro de Madrid have provided? First, Trazos Singulares reflects an intent to disalienate people with disabilities from the urban landscape over which they have little control, in that it encourages their presence in a specific station (Nuevos Ministerios) and encourages also, through the discourse of art, their perspective on a range of Madrid's most traversed urban spaces. Second (in content and in artistic form), the exhibit's paintings allude symbolically to a world in which people with disabilities play a role in (re)imagining those spaces. As per Lefebvre, creative activity, art, symbolism, the imaginary, and play are important ways of responding to capital's entrenched control over city-space, even if such activities may not currently influence the decisions made by city planners, architects, and the "bourgeois science" (Lefebvre 2003) of urban design.

What is so intriguing about the paintings included in the exhibit is that many of them incorporate both photographs of the existing spaces (train stations and their constituent parts: trains, elevators, staircases, ticket machines …) and paper drawings made by the artists themselves. Such mixed-media images highlight plurality through their strongly "mixed" construction, but more importantly, they effect a curious fusion of "objective" and "subjective" views of the city and its built environment for transportation through the materiality of iconic/indexical signification. In effect, these iconic/indexical representations of the city as imagined by disabled producers (photographs, drawings, tracings, colourings, elaborations) symbolically enter into dialogue with the city as it has been historically conceived and produced by urban planners and architects. Some of the most intriguing examples of this type of mixed image show, respectively, the drawn Banco de España station sign with a ground-level low-angle photograph of a nearby building, a low-angle shot/drawing situated in the Plaza de España, and a number of metro station interiors. In many of the mixed-media images included in the exhibit, it is difficult to see where the photographs end and where the drawings/paintings begin – such that, symbolically and artistically, the city as iconically imagined by disabled producers is as important in the artwork as the city infrastructure as it has been designed and built. In other images in the exhibit, the artists have included no such photographic images (or collages of photos) and instead have elaborated a completely subjective vision of the train-car itself – as a moving organism, or as a malleable/expanding space depicted simultaneously from both objective and subjective viewpoints. Still others highlight the power of subjective visions of the city through clear appropriations of Cubist style that present the city as fragmented and necessarily dependent on an active act of viewing that might suture together its disparate parts. For individuals within the discourse of art, these images are a means to reimagine the city and its transportation infrastructure – the artists with cognitive disabilities participating in the exhibit are artistically and symbolically exercising their right to the city. This includes their right to represent the city, to (re)imagine its spaces, and, symbolically, to contribute to the future development of urban infrastructures.

Overall, throughout the exhibit aesthetic representation mixes subjective and objective perspectives, iconic/indexical and symbolic signification, to fashion a vision of the city that is collective in design. It must not be overlooked that, as Siebers notes, "aesthetics is pertinent to the struggle to create a built environment accessible to people with disabilities" (2010: 58). Although this notion of the importance of aesthetics may have been explored more often in relation to aesthetic/artistic images depicting people with disabilities (e.g., see Ware 2008; Siebers 2010: 100–20, ch. 5, on "trauma art"), it might also be taken to mean the artistic images produced by people with disabilities whether they depict disability explicitly or not. Equally, the notion of an accessible built environment might be taken to mean access not merely in a physical sense but also in a social sense, and moreover, in the sense that disabled and able-bodied/cognitively abled urbanites alike might have more control over the production of urban spaces.[17]

Third, however – and this is one of the most important outcomes of the exhibit – there is the brute fact of the visibility of the disabled artists themselves. The traces of importance are not the Singular Traces likely referred to in the exhibit's title – that is, they are not the two-dimensional products of art themselves – but rather the traces of the embodied activity of artistic production. That is, the sixty paintings produced on site testify not merely to a previous artistic activity but more specifically to the fact that this activity was carried out *in the Nuevos Ministerios metro station by the disabled artists themselves*. The visual representations produced are traces of that embodied and public performance. The importance and even the relative novelty of this event can be fully understood by referring to the recent UN Convention on the Rights of People with Disabilities (from 2006; opened for signature in 2007; entered into force in 2008).

Of the fifty rights detailed in the UN Convention, several are of particular relevance to the Trazos Singulares exhibit. In a general sense, Article 19, "Derecho a ser incluido en la comunidad" (The Right to Be Included in the Community) – which was also dramatized in one of the televised spots mentioned earlier – is also relevant here, in that the event has symbolically and physically provided a space for disabled artists in one of the most traversed areas of the city's transportation infrastructure. Of arguably greater importance, however, are Article 29, "Participación en la vida política y pública" (Participation in Political and Public Life), and Article 30, "Participación en la vida cultural" (Participation in Cultural life). Article 29 seeks

> promover activamente un entorno en el que las personas con discapacidad puedan participar plena y efectivamente en la dirección de los asuntos públicos sin discriminación y en igualdad de condiciones con las demás, y fomentar su participación en los asuntos públicos. (To actively promote an environment in which people with disabilities might participate fully and effectively in the management of public matters without discrimination and in equal conditions to others, and foment their participation in public matters.) (Art. 29, "Convención" 2010: 160)

In addition, Article 30 seeks the adoption of appropriate measures

> para que las personas con discapacidad puedan desarrollar y utilizar su potencial creativo, artístico e intelectual no sólo en su propio beneficio sino también para el enriquecimiento de la sociedad. (so that people with disabilities might develop and use their creative, artistic, and intellectual potential not merely for their own benefit but moreover for the betterment of society.) (Art. 30, "Convención" 2010: 163)

Trazos Singulares ultimately provides a much-needed outlet for a certain degree of (symbolic) input into public matters; at the same time, it emphasizes the relationship between the creative potential of people with disabilities and the larger Spanish society for which the Metro functions, in this case, as a synecdoche. While the event is perhaps a far cry from placing people with disabilities on transportation governance boards or giving populations with disabilities decision-making capability in Metro de Madrid – both of which would be welcome opportunities in line with the spirit of the UN Convention but that might not account for severe impairments in populations with cognitive disabilities – it nonetheless might serve as a complement to such improvements and most definitely invites questioning of the sort that would lead to those changes.

Moreover, though access to art by disabled populations is something that has been discussed by scholars (Taylor 2005: 325; see also Lige 2011), what is so interesting here is that the works produced by disabled artists should be so directly relevant to their own perceptions of city-space. Operating, in Lefebvrian terms, at the intersection of urban space both as perceived (photographs) and as imagined (drawing/painting), and complemented by the embodied production of works carried out by artists with IDD *in situ*, the exhibit foregrounds the interaction of disabled residents of Madrid with city-space as it is *lived*. Here, importantly, the iconic nature of visual art – the iconic representations of specific locations in the city's railway system, for example – is a key material link between the aesthetic realm and the social one. Recalling what Tanya Titchkosky has identified in a related context as the notion of "disability as a collision between imagination and desire, reflecting the meaningfulness of our bodies in everyday life" (Titchkosky 2009: 83), here we see what happens when disability comes to embody yet another mediation – an artistic tension between the iconic, indexical, and symbolic city representation as it has been (re)produced over time by able-bodied/cognitively abled urban planners and as it has been (re)imagined by artists with cognitive disabilities.

Lest readers assume that this exhibit is not without its own problems, it is important, finally, to dwell for a moment on the extent to which it might be considered insufficient. As Licia Carlson notes – drawing upon Henri Stiker's book *The History of Disability* – it is often more revealing to examine the method of including or integrating disabled populations in society than it is to examine the fact of their exclusion (Carlson 2010: 3). That is, we must examine the specific conditions under which disabled people are encouraged to take part in public discourse. For example, are they allowed to participate fully or only in a limited capacity? Are they given access to central and privileged discourses of great social significance or only to spheres of peripheral importance? In this case, it is tempting and indeed possible to devalue the exhibit – both its ephemeral integration of disabled producers and its enduring mixed-media images – by arguing that, for example, Metro de Madrid is taking an easy and showy route to merely symbolically integrating disabled populations into the built environment, perhaps even exclaiming that "Oh, but works of art will never change society." Although the former response may be true, the latter is clearly misguided, and reflects a curious division of contemporary daily life into autonomous spheres where each has little impact on the others. That is, there is a common tendency to see aesthetic matters as a world of their own, a world of little or no immediate relevance to matters of broader social or political importance.

Yet as Lefebvre's urban theory articulates, particularly in *The Urban Revolution* (2003) but also in *The Production of Space* (1991a), this misguided notion that the sphere of artistic production bears little relevance to social and political struggles – a notion that is pervasive in today's alienated urban environments – is surely yet another consequence of an alienating view of contemporary urban life. To let the meaning of the exhibit be determined by the intention or mere involvement of the Metro de Madrid corporation is to allow this alienated view to remain operational and unquestioned; in a sense, this aestheticized/aestheticizing view of the exhibit recapitulates the contemporary view of urban planners who have equally approached the city as an aesthetic object, one somehow divorced from the political and social discourses that were articulated as part of urban theory's nineteenth-century (utopian) socialist history.[18]

Still, aesthetics and culture – even in this problematic case – provide an opportunity for populations with cognitive disabilities that may be much more difficult to replicate in other areas of social life. To see in Trazos Singulares the potential for a much more radical project pushing for the full inclusion of people with IDD into Madrid's urban fabric and future decisions (political, social, and economic) is to recover the revolutionary potential of all artistic production – even, and especially, if this potential has not yet been realized. Envisioning the event simultaneously from both a disability studies perspective and a Lefebvrian perspective on urban studies allows us to glimpse how the city is ultimately a product of spaces not only as conceived but also as perceived and actually lived. Lefebvre's urban critique teaches us that art and creative activity may function as a key momentary disruption of the exclusionary logic of urban design, and also that the act of transforming space – even if ephemerally – is necessary if that spatial logic is to be challenged. Similarly, disability scholars note that that "the art of theorizing, the art of telling a new story," can be a "moment of disruptive provocation" (Titchkosky 2009: 83). In the future linking of these two insights there may be a recipe for mobilizing aesthetics and culture to enact lasting social change for people with disabilities, IDD or otherwise, who live in contemporary cities.

Setting aside the sponsorship by Metro de Madrid, Trazos Singulares points to the radical potential of future events that might similarly encourage disabled artists to occupy privileged city-spaces and to use those spaces as a pretext for (re)imagining both their city and the circumstances of their inclusion or exclusion in urbanized societies. In *Disability Aesthetics*, Siebers makes a prescient remark concerning the underappreciated connection between the need for an accessible (material) built environment and the need for improvements regarding less tangible, social and political mechanisms of exclusion:

> The debate in architecture has so far focused more on the fundamental problem of whether buildings and landscapes should be universally accessible than on the aesthetic symbolism by which the built environment mirrors its potential inhabitants. While universal access must remain the ambition of the disability community, a broad understanding of disability aesthetics reveals the hidden inhibitions and defense mechanisms that work against advances in universal design and undercut the political and social participation of people with disabilities. It also shows that aesthetic disgust with disability extends beyond individual disabled bodies to the symbolic presence of disability in the built environment. (Siebers 2010: 58)

Siebers's artful transition from the question of physical access in the context of the built environment to the way in which aesthetic and symbolic forms reflect deeply rooted social ideologies should not be overlooked. Moreover, the implication is precisely that the built environment of the city reflects the social and political conditions under which it has been produced. In disability studies just as in the Lefebvrian tradition of urban studies, it is important to highlight that the production of space is a social process involving space as conceived, perceived, and lived; as both material and mental; and that such space is a shifting territory on which urban citizens must persistently struggle to exercise their right to the city. In any case, as disability scholars have pursued with vigour and as Lefebvre's urban theory suggests once it has been applied to the themes of disability studies, art remains an accessible and potentially transformational discourse, certainly one of many important links between disabled populations and their greater potential and future influence over the larger able-bodied/cognitively abled urban society in which they live.

In conclusion, despite some clear drawbacks, Trazos Singulares contains the seed of a potentially radical social and even political change. This artistic exhibition – which poses important questions regarding inclusion and the social visibility of disability, questions that are all too infrequently raised in this kind of a public forum – may not have succeeded as a catalyst for social change for people with cognitive disabilities, and it clearly was not even designed as such. Yet it remains an innovative, welcome, and powerfully symbolic reminder of what might be accomplished in the future. Perhaps the component that was lacking was the inclusion of disability theorists working alongside the disabled artists. Leslie G. Roman writes about a series of events held in Vancouver, Canada, called "The Unruly Salon" where "the combination of disability scholars and disabled artists worked!" (2009b: 6; also 2009a). Perhaps future collaborations can continue to emphasize how the right to the city might be reclaimed for populations with cognitive disabilities.

María Gallardo and Miguel Gallardo's *María cumple 20 años* (2015)

The graphic novel *María cumple 20 años* also helps us think more carefully about the benefits of collaboration when considering populations with severe cognitive disabilities. Born in 1955 in Lleida, Catalunya, Miguel Gallardo is a professional graphic artist who collaborated on a number of visual projects associated with La Movida. La Movida – concisely defined as an explosion of cultural activity following the death of Spanish dictator Francisco Franco in 1975 – intensified during the late 1970s and 1980s and led to the international recognition of, among others, director Pedro Almodóvar.[19] Even before the twenty-first century began, Gallardo had produced an extensive *oeuvre* including series, publications, monographs, catalogues, illustrations, animations, and television work. It is significant that some of the work for which he is best known has involved collaborations: his co-creation of the pioneering graphic magazine *El Víbora*, and his co-authorship of the comics character Makoki, for example.[20] His earlier publications unfolded in the context of a vital counterculture that embraced themes of sexuality, drug use, and popular music previously denigrated as transgressive by the dictatorship. The publication of the comics text *María y yo* (2007), however, reflected the development of a more personal creative mode for Gallardo, in terms of both content and style. As indicated in the eponymous documentary film *María y yo* (2010), directed by Félix Fernández de Castro, Miguel found that he was beginning to draw different kinds of pictures for his daughter to enjoy. As he drew for María, he developed a visual style that was more rapid, more fluid, and simply more iconic than he had used in his previous professional work.[21] He engaged in this process continually and over the years was able to fill notebook after notebook with iconic representations of the real people who were part of María's life. As this section explores, Gallardo's more recent work involving his daughter – whether one regards it as personal or autobiographical – is decidedly collaborative both in its context and in its execution.

My point of departure, given the significant impact that María has had on her father's artistic content as well as his graphic style, is to recognize *María cumple 20 años* as a collaboration between two co-authors that exposes the neurotypical misunderstandings of autism. Readers will note that both volumes, *María y yo* and *María cumple 20 años*, list their authors as "María Gallardo and Miguel Gallardo," in that order. It may be tempting for readers to see this instance of co-authorship as a mere conceit, fashioned in response to the fact that, as Ian Hacking has written, "autism narrative is a boom industry" (2010: 261).[22] Nevertheless, such a reaction is not appropriate in this case, for reasons I outline in the remainder of this chapter. That is, I do not see this instance of co-authorship as an intentional conceit, but instead as an organic collaboration. My choice to use the word collaboration is supported by specific stylistic and thematic aspects of the volume, discussed below. It is also important for readers to acknowledge the larger context of what collaboration may mean for populations with severe cognitive impairments. That is, my previous analysis of *María y yo* appealed to readers familiar with the work of internationally known autistic celebrity professor, speaker, and author Temple Grandin as a point of entry in order to emphasize the importance of visuality for her and for others like her.[23] Here, however, it makes more sense to draw a contrast with Grandin that is relevant to the present book's focus on the invisibility of cognitive difference and its concomitant acknowledgment of the topic of impairment. Grandin, like all academics and all authors – whether society sees them as able-bodied, able-minded, or disabled – has necessarily benefited from the assistance of editors and from the attention afforded her work by the publishing industry.[24] Unlike María, however, Grandin – being more verbal – is in more of a position to tell her own story in the conventional ways outlined by ableist and individualistic imaginaries.[25] Yet while María may not be in a position to tell her own story with respect to these normative expectations, Miguel and María can in fact tell their shared story together.[26]

In the previous graphic novel and documentary film, readers and viewers alike were introduced to a young María through visual representations of everyday experiences of autism; in contrast, *María cumple 20 años* portrays its co-protagonist now as an adult. This more recent volume continues its forerunner's hallmark themes and formal strategies, which are once again worthy of exploration in their own right. Thus this section focuses first on this sequel graphic novel's general depiction of the experience of autism as a visual contribution to dialogues on neurodiversity. Given the circumstances discussed above, I regard this not as María's individual experience of autism, but rather as an experience of autism intimately shared by a team of father–daughter co-authors. Second, it traces the comic's embrace of a more collaborative model of representation than was evidenced in the original. Finally, it explores the wider significance of this kind of collaborative model of cognitive disability representations in cultural production, returning to this chapter's epigraph written by Michael Bérubé. Ultimately, an awareness of the benefits of attending to nuances of cognitive impairment, as opposed to a notion of physical impairment that has largely been eschewed in disability studies research in the humanities, prompts the need for a more collaborative approach to the production of and participation in cognitive disability representations.

The shared experience of autism represented in *María cumple 20 años* functions as an autobiography of two people. Miguel purposely draws himself into the unnumbered pages of the story[27] from the beginning and does not engage in the abstraction that would be required of a narrative purporting to focus solely on María at the expense of her interdependent connections with others. The comic starts with the page title "19 de julio de 2014" (19 July 2014) (2015: 2) and chronicles Miguel's yearly trip to visit María in Canarias, with the understanding that from there the pair will embark on what is routinely a month-and-a-half-long vacation together (2015: 5). The text immediately draws attention to traits shared by father and daughter: "Tenemos un montón de manías comunes los dos" (we both have a ton of common manias), including anticipation, not wanting to get rid of anything, and the need to order the world (2015: 2). The first two examples of these manias depict Miguel arriving early to the airport and a shirt he has refused to part with for fourteen years; the third is a margin-spanning panel applying to both father and daughter. This panel highlights four sets of circumstances through discrete visual reference points under the heading "¡... Orden en el mundo!" (... Order in the world!): "Papelitos / Los dos iPad juntos / ¡Hay migas en el suelo! / Ese vaso fuera de sitio" (Scraps of paper / Our two iPads together / There are crumbs on the floor! That glass out of place) (2015: 2). These visual depictions are accompanied by the word-specific combinations of text and images (McCloud 1994: 153) that constitute the bulk of the comic's style. Through its visual form this single panel also suggests that these concerns apply equally to father and daughter. In particular, the shift from a more traditional panel structure to a wide panel lacking any sort of internal partition conveys an expansiveness – and thus a sense of connectedness and overlap – that readers can apply to reinforce the notion of shared traits. Also emphasizing their shared relationship, the subsequent first four panels on the next page depict Miguel and María sharing the panel frames (2015: 3) – looking at each other or talking in the same direction. Following embedded images of the front covers of the original Spanish and translated Russian versions of the comic *María y yo* is the statement that "En el año 2009 nos dieron el premio nacional de cómic de Cataluña ¡a los dos!" (In 2009 they gave us the national comic award – to the two of us together!). This recognition in the text that both María and Miguel received the national comic award is further indication that the work constitutes a collaboration and can be taken implicitly as a prompt to recognize how experiences of severe cognitive impairment cannot be considered outside of collaborative social relationships.

This sequel returns to the hallmark themes of *María y yo*: not only travel, but also favourite activities and behaviours, the everyday value of pictograms, social marginalization, and the strength of relationships with friends and family. In reference to a travel scene prominently situated at the beginning of both the previous graphic novel and the documentary film of the same name, the text notes that as an adult, María now "se comporta en el avión" (behaves herself on the plane) (2015: 6), likely a result of consistent behavioural reinforcement and modification therapy seen in the documentary but not so visible in the earlier graphic novel. After arriving in Barcelona with Miguel, María "se va flechada a su cuarto a comprobar si todavía están las dos cajas llenas de dibujos que le he ido haciendo estos años" (goes straight to her room to see if the two boxes of drawings I have been doing for her over the years are still there) (2015: 7). The fact that the image spans a full page indicates the importance of this event in the life of María. Since space equals time in the comics (see McCloud 1994: 100), the full-page panel also suggests the quantity of time she routinely spends looking through these drawings. Evidence that this is one of her preferred behaviours can also be seen in the visual abundance depicted through the numerous notebooks and papers strewn across both the floor and bed of the image (2015: 7).

Like all of us, María at times expresses her dislike of certain situations. One of her most common reactions is to scream – a theme that appears numerous times in the comic (2015: 25–6, 28; see also 51). While it is common for neurotypical explanations to describe people with autism as being easily overwhelmed by excess sensory stimulation, it is interesting that *María cumple 20 años* does not take this route. Instead, as noted above, it frames María's dislike of unfamiliar situations as a trait she shares with her father ("anticipación" [anticipation] above, 2015: 2). Regarding this point, the text here prefers to represent her behaviour without recourse to the clinical point of view that was more common in Fernández de Castro's documentary film about María. Using an everyday explanation, a page titled "¿Qué pasará?" (What's next?) (2015: 9) notes for readers that "María se pone nerviosa porque le cuestan las transiciones de un sitio a otro" (María gets nervous because transitions from one place to another are difficult for her) (2015: 10). One practice that can help María feel less nervous is the use of pictograms. Readers of the earlier comic and, especially, viewers of the documentary film were introduced to the value of pictograms in María's everyday life. These images help María anticipate what will happen during a given day; they also help her shape her expectations accordingly, "para que no se pierda con las actividades diarias" (so that she does not become lost [in the sequence of] daily activities) (2015: 11).[28] Pictograms were an increasingly prevalent part of the later parts of the earlier comic and the documentary film; thus the fact that readers see an example of a pictogram so soon in *María cumple 20 años* is a significant shift (2015: 11, see also 18–19). This is another example of how the sequel graphic novel illustrates the enduring collaborative value of consistent behavioural reinforcement introduced in previous cultural products. Here, the format of the pictograms is used not merely to indicate María's anticipation of the day's events, but also to reflect on daily activities and preferred routines (2015: 12–13, 36) – even with the passage of time, she insists on repeating specific activities that she and her father enjoyed in the past (2015: 39).

The text suggests that one of the behaviours that can prove problematic is María's enjoyment of pinching people: something she does to strangers as well as people she knows. The sustained appearance of this behaviour on six pages of *María cumple 20 años* (2015: 4, 14, 15, 16, 17, 18) conveys to readers that there has been much discussion and consideration of the motivations and consequences of this activity in the life shared by Miguel and María. Significantly, in one of the father-and-daughter "Preguntas y respuestas" (Questions and Answers) panel sequences, whose form will be familiar to readers of *María y yo*, the father asks his daughter, "¿Pero María, por qué pellizcas a las personas que te gustan?" (But María, why do you pinch the people you like?) (2015: 15). To this question, María responds, "Para que me hagan caso" (So that they pay attention to me) (2015: 15, see also 14). The inclusion of a narrative-voice caption under this latter image – which reads "¿No es lo que queremos todos?" (Isn't that what we all want?) – might be taken as an acknowledgment of didactic value for readers less knowledgeable about autism. The text does not take a clinical or medical approach to autism, but it still attempts to deliver a message about autism to readers who may be less likely to acknowledge similarities between themselves and María (2015: 15). The next two pages make clear that the meaning of María's pinching changes with the circumstances. For her, it is a form of communication. Thus, while she uses pinching to express love for her grandmother in Barcelona (2015: 14), she at times may pinch strangers, whose reactions may not be as welcome (2015: 16), and she may sometimes even use pinching as a threat or a form of aggression (2015: 17). Consistent with the topic of behaviour modification more generally, two pages (2015: 18–19) chart out how pictograms are being used to help María reduce her use of pinching – they serve as substitutes when she communicates, and she is rewarded for using them with activities she likes. Importantly, the last two of María's preferred activities depicted are both labelled "dibujar" (drawing): in one panel, Miguel draws as María looks on; in the other, María draws on her own without Miguel sharing the frame (2015: 19).

As included in the earlier comic and as dramatized in the documentary film, María continues to be fond of music: "María cuenta además con un oído absoluto para la música, una vez entra una melodía en su cabeza, a veces de una forma obsesiva, nunca más se va" (María possesses a perfect ear for music, once a melody enters her head, sometimes in an obsessive way, it never leaves) (2015: 20). She has efficiently and intuitively developed an ability to use her iPad to listen to music, such that Miguel remarks she is a talented DJ (2015: 20). A full-page panel illustrates María listening to music on her iPad while sitting on her bed, occupying the bottom half of the image (2015: 21). The empty space in the top half of the image and surrounding the outline of her body in the bottom half contains twenty-one song titles paired with their corresponding artists and drawn in either black script, blue script, bold black script, or bold blue script. The two-tone script represents a barrage of music, with quick transitions from song to song,[29] while the space occupied on the full-panel page suggests that María listens to songs or song fragments obsessively for extended periods of time (2015: 21).[30] Viewers of the 2010 documentary film will remember how, in a specific scene combining noise from various sources (the television, a steaming coffee pot on the stove, traffic heard through an open window …), received sound was used as a metaphor for the way in which autistics experience sensory stimulation as overwhelming.[31] In *María cumple 20 años*, however, self-modulated, received sound is treated simply as something María enjoys, in the process testifying to her ability to master technology. So it is significant that this sequel shifts back towards the emphasis of the original comic and away from the documentary film's tendency to represent María as isolated and alone.[32] *María cumple 20 años* thus portrays María's behaviours in everyday terms as practices she enjoys, instead of taking a more clinical or even didactic approach.[33] The way the musical groups and song titles are arranged in the page's empty space suggests a spatial metaphor for how María is able to organize her environment; this implies that she is developing an autonomy associated with adulthood as well as the confidence that comes with mastery of digital tools.

If we are attending to the notion of cognitive impairment, however, there are still times when María's inability to communicate with others on their terms becomes frustrating, both for her and for others. An interesting example of this is the enigmatic case of "Nonuyus" (2015: 22), which continues the theme of music as one of María's favourite hobbies. Four panels narrate María's persistent requests for May to play

4.1: "Nonoyus" sequence from *María cumple 20 años* (Gallardo and Gallardo, 2015), 22.

"Nonuyus" for her, a request her mother does not understand. María requests this mysterious song during the day and at night, even during dinner – at all hours of the day (2015: 22). There is a certain humour, born of frustration, that builds through the sequence. This stems not only from the repetition of the request, but also from an image of the globe featured in the third panel criss-crossed by the reverberating sound of the word "Nonuyus," suggesting that María's request is echoing around the world. The use of both blue and black-and-white tones in the drawings here maximizes the visual contrast of the images and thus amplifies the scene's persistent emotional tension.[34] Also, panels two and four are subdivided into four mini-panels that quicken the action, and this intensifies the reader's engagement with the sequence. One day, as captured in the fourth panel, María's mother May happens to put on Stevie Wonder's song "I Just Called" – which includes the words "No New Year's Day …" (a phrase that María had been voicing as "Nonuyus") – and María happily borrows May's iPad to continue listening to the song by herself (2015: 22). The nine-panel sequence on the following page features another misunderstanding, one that also concerns music as one of María's preferred activities (2015: 23). In the case of "Nonuyus" María was expressing something her mother did not understand; here, another family member expresses something that she takes too literally. One day her grandfather says "Me voy con la música a otra parte" (I'm going to take the music elsewhere), which prompts María's inconsolable sadness as well as frustrated speculation on what has caused this to happen (2015: 23).[35] One way of interpreting this sequence is to recognize that when family members use access to music as a way of encouraging good behaviours in María, there can be a down side.

Both the earlier graphic novel and this more recent sequel critique patterns of social marginalization involving those who experience autism in society, and once again *María cumple 20 años* chooses to emphasize the ways that others look at María. In a two-page sequence titled "Miradas" (Looks), the comic artfully blends narrative-voice text, dialogue bubbles, the characteristic stare-arrows readers saw throughout *María y yo*, and strategies mobilizing the colour blue against the black-and-white background composition for increased emotional impact. The narrative-voice text is worthy of citation:

> Paseamos por la calle con María / y la … / gente … / mira… / Las miradas se concentran / A veces las siento en el mismísimo cogote / Dan ganas de girar la cabeza como la niña del exorcista y / … largar un discursito / y pasarme un poco de la raya / En las pelis queda muy bien, pero en la vida real no es tan fácil … / Las miradas son una asignatura pendiente que arrastro desde hace tiempo / Todavía es algo que me ataca y me da rabia / Sé que es algo difícil de cambiar y que es más un problema mío que los demás / Se me hace un nudo en el estómago y no puedo desatarlo / Aunque a María en realidad, le importa un pimiento / Agradezco las sonrisas de las abuelas de vez en cuando / y los niños descarados que

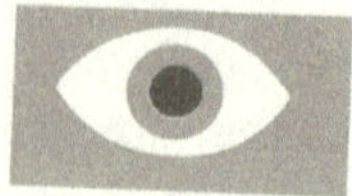

4.2: "Miradas" sequence from *María cumple 20 años* (Gallardo and Gallardo, 2015), 30–1.

LAS MIRADAS SON UNA ASIGNATURA PENDIENTE QUE ARRASTRO DESDE HACE TIEMPO

TODAVÍA ES ALGO QUE ME ATACA Y ME DA RABIA
MIRADAS

SÉ QUE ES ALGO DIFÍCIL DE CAMBIAR Y QUE ES MÁS UN PROBLEMA MÍO QUE DE LOS DEMÁS

SE ME HACE UN NUDO EN EL ESTÓMAGO Y NO PUEDO DESATARLO...

AUNQUE A MARÍA, EN REALIDAD, LE IMPORTA UN PIMIENTO...
BE water MY FRIEND
POM POTROM
POTROM

AGRADEZCO LAS SONRISAS DE LAS ABUELAS DE VEZ EN CUANDO
¡ QUÉ GUAPA !

Y LOS NIÑOS DESCARADOS QUE PREGUNTAN...
¿ POR QUÉ CAMINA ASÍ LA CHICA, SEÑOR?

ME GUSTARÍA HABLARLES A TODOS Y EXPLICARLES CÓMO ES MARÍA... PERO SON DEMASIADOS...

...DECIRLES LAS COSAS SORPRENDENTES QUE TIENE MARÍA, POR EJEMPLO... SU MEMORIA

> preguntan … / Me gustaría hablarles a todos y explicarles cómo es María … Pero son demasiados … / Decirles las cosas sorprendentes que tiene María, por ejemplo, su memoria.
>
> When we walk outside with María / the people … / stare … / at her … / Their looks are concentrated on her / Sometimes I feel them on the back of my neck / They make me want to turn my head around like the girl in *The Exorcist* and / … rattle off a speech / and even cross the line a little / In the movies that tends to work, but in real life it isn't that easy … / These looks are an unresolved matter I have long carried with me / It is something that angers and infuriates me / I know it's something difficult to change and that it is more of a problem for me than it is for others / I get a knot in my stomach and I can't undo it … / Even though María couldn't care less … / I am grateful for the smiles of grandmothers once in a while / and for the impertinent questions of children … / I'd like to talk to all of them and explain what María is like … But there are too many of them … / To tell them the things about María that would surprise them, for example … her memory. (2015: 30–1)

The formal features employed here are significant in their own right and add meaning and nuance to the text. Throughout this sequence the strategic use of the colour blue adds a dynamic dimension to the standard black-and-white style; it also adds an emotional depth to the panels in different ways. At various points, blue overlays are used to highlight different aspects of the visual field, including the following list: onlookers who are staring at María, as a reflection of their charged emotional state; María and the back of Miguel's neck, as the objects of the questionable emotions of the onlookers who are staring; Miguel when he imagines crossing a line in his speech delivered to these onlookers, reflecting his own charged emotional response; the image of a smiling grandmother, suggesting a sense of warmth; and the final image in the sequence, which depicts a smiling María, suggesting the outward radiation of what the narration frames as her surprising qualities. Most of this two-page sequence employs word-specific combinations, but there are intriguing exceptions. A few of the panel combinations can be considered duo-specific, with the words and the images contributing something their complement lacks. Such is the case, for example, with one panel where the image depicts María walking away. Note that to understand the specificity of this image one needs to take into account the panel featuring the questioning child two panels later, whose dialogue references María's specific form of walking depicted here. Another example is the panel reading "Todavía es algo que me ataca y me da rabia" (It is something that angers and infuriates me), which expresses two distinct but complementary emotions. The words express the intensity of Miguel's anger, while the image – the large word "MIRADAS" (Stares) in blue weighing down on his head and neck, also in blue – suggests that he is frustrated, overwhelmed, and (judging from the look on his face) perhaps even sad. In addition, a number of panels employ image-specific combinations, such as the first five panels depicting the gaze of onlookers, where the image says everything readers need to know and the text is superfluous. What is interesting in this sequence is the way in which both text and image foreground Miguel's experience of these stares. Note that he appears in eight panels, while María appears only in four – and only in one of the panels, the last one mentioned above, do we see her face, which is smiling. This imbalance in visual presentation of course reinforces the text's insistence that this is more of a problem for Miguel than for others (perhaps also including María). This is a clear representation of how Miguel shares in the social experience of cognitive disability with his daughter – theirs is a collective experience of autism, and the social marginalization of this disability experience is thus also shared.

Given that this reading of *María cumple 20 años* is focused on the notion of collaboration, its most interesting aspect is the way in which the comic emphasizes community and relationships through family and friends. The main vehicle for expressing this emphasis is the iconic representation that characterizes visual representations in particular. *María y yo*, in both its graphic novel and documentary film versions, had emphasized María's prodigious memory for people she has known for even a short time. Readers and viewers saw how the iconic drawings that Miguel created for María became a way not merely of documenting their shared relationships with others but also of communicating. A full-page panel titled "Dibujar" (Drawing) shows María suggesting the names of people she knows to Miguel, who draws them in a notebook (here: "Emilio, Biel, Judith, Joseluis, Pilar, Bhavna"). As the father draws for his daughter, the narrative text reminds readers of the significance of this activity:

> Cuando empieza el verano, comienzo a dibujar para María, un trabajo que me llevará todas las vacaciones. Hace muchos años que dibujo para ella y se ha convertido en un medio de comunicación entre los dos. María me hace los pedidos a partir de su asombrosa memoria para las personas y los

> sucesos. (When the summer begins, I start to draw for María, a task that I carry out during the entirety of our time together. I've been drawing for her for many years, and it has become a way of communicating between the two of us. María makes her requests of me based on her amazing memory for people and events.) (2015: 32)

As did the original comic, this sequel features a number of pages dedicated to iconic representations of people as an illustration of the material basis of the pair's communicational method. One page features sixteen faces, each labelled with a name, that represent a particular group of related persons (2015: 34); in another full-page panel, María and Miguel sit at a table with eight other labelled invited guests (2015: 35); yet another page shows six named people in bed on account of an accident or illness (2015: 37). These are the faces and names of people who constitute what the volume terms María's "red de cariño" (network of love and support) (2015: 56).[36] The text specifies who these people are in a nine-panel-spanning narration that begins thus:

> Para este camino que tenemos por delante, necesitamos a las personas que nos rodean … la gente que nos ha acompañado hasta aquí y la gente que conocerá María a partir de ahora … las personas que están en sus listas, no solo su familia cercana, sino también amigos y conocidos que han descubierto a María y han aprendido a quererla. (For the road we have ahead of us, we need the people around us … the people who have accompanied us up until now and the people that María will meet from now on … the people who are on her lists, not merely her close family, but also friends and acquaintances who have discovered María and have learned to love her.) (2015: 56)

Readers will note here, too, that the subtle but important use of the first person plural ("we" and "us" in English translation) frames María's social network as inclusive and ever-expanding.

María cumple 20 años goes beyond the original comic in that for the first time it incorporates the drawings of others besides Miguel. Importantly, it also presents the activity of drawing as a communal everyday practice in which anyone can engage – in principle then, as a practice through which anyone can get to know and communicate with María, and through which María can get to know and communicate with anyone. There is a full page devoted to drawings for María made by Marta, who "la acompaña casi todas las tardes en Canarias" (accompanies her almost every afternoon in Canarias) (2015: 40). There is another full page containing the drawings for María made by Laia, who "la acompaña algunos días en Sa Riera en verano" (accompanies her some days in Sa Riera during the summer) (2015: 41). Even though the styles vary depending on the person doing the drawing, the basic principles of iconic representation are present in both examples (one or more of the following: hair shape, hair length, height, outfit/dress), and each person depicted is accompanied by a written name in close proximity to the representation – a reference to the style of practical iconic drawing expressly developed by Miguel as a communication with his daughter. The text makes clear that María herself "ha logrado convencer a muchos adultos que están a su lado para que lo hagan" (has managed to convince many adults around her to do it [draw for her]) (2015: 40). Significantly, María herself has taken up the practice of drawing (2015: 42–3, 44–5, 47; including also the inside front and back covers). Narration in the comic book makes clear that over many years Miguel has engaged María through assisted drawing, guiding her hand and creating basic human figures (2015: 42). At first, Miguel's narration indicates that he suspected the drawings she started to make on her own two years prior to *María cumple 20 años* were angry birds (2015: 44), but then his good friend Marco – "que es un aspi (síndrome de Asperger)" (who is an Aspy [person with Asperger's syndrome]) – discovered that they were not birds but instead people with their mouths open (2015: 45). We see a whole page devoted to María's artistic process (2015: 43), and on numerous pages we see images actually drawn by María herself. These appear in the book, taking up both full pages (2015: 44, 47) and parts of pages (2015: 42, 45), and contribute to the book's multivocal composition.

The story of how María began to draw is simultaneously a story of her active engagement with the world. It illustrates the significance of her relationships with other people as well as her desire to communicate with others. It is an expression of her love for her father, but also of the bonds she has been able to form with people like Marta and Laia. It is an outlet that serves multiple functions. As the text puts it:

> La decisión de María de ponerse a dibujar ha sido importante para ella, le ha dado autonomía, ya no depende tanto de mí para hacer sus listas y el dibujo le sirve para expresarse y delimitar las cosas que le gustan y que le preocupan. Ahora María tiene dos intereses en su vida que le ayudan a

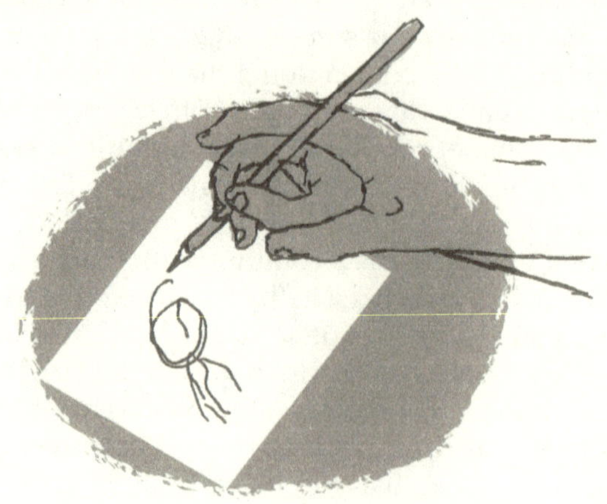

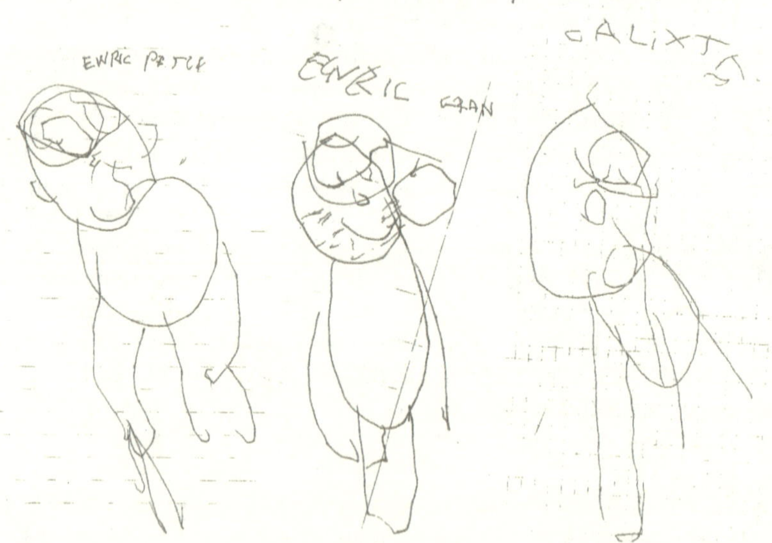

4.3: María's iconic drawings from *María cumple 20 años* (Gallardo and Gallardo, 2015), 42–3.

MARÍA DIBUJA

HACE DOS AÑOS QUE MARÍA SE HA PUESTO A DIBUJAR COMO UNA ILUMINADA, DE PRONTO SE HA ENCONTRADO CON EL DIBUJO Y ESO HA SIDO UN DESCUBRIMIENTO IMPORTANTE. MARÍA DIBUJA CARAS, LAS CARAS DE SUS LISTAS.

> comunicarse con los demás y con el mundo exterior: el dibujo y la música. (María's decision to devote herself to drawing has been important for her, it has given her autonomy, she no longer depends as much on me to create her lists and drawing allows her to express herself and to define what she likes and what bothers her. Now María has two interests in her life that help her to communicate with others and with the exterior world: drawing and music.) (2015: 47)

It may be important to underscore that María has come to drawing in the same way as artists who may not experience cognitive disability – through time, opportunity, practice, support, and ultimately the benefit of an artistic community that connects her with others. Through the publication of *María cumple 20 años*, readers of the graphic novel can also form part of María's artistic community. (Interestingly, she is already recognized as a cultural celebrity of sorts, as indicated on 2015: 3). The inside front and back covers of the volume are key to understanding how this comic's core is constituted by María's drawing – and also to the interpretation of María's drawing. The faces she draws are featured on the front and back inside covers, but only on the back inside cover do names accompany each face. In this way, the composition of the volume as a whole stages for readers the insight that Marco, above, has regarding her drawings (2015: 35). Seeing the front inside cover, readers may not understand what the images are; but on completing the graphic novel and seeing the back inside cover, they participate in a "reveal" that recapitulates Marco's hermeneutic discovery of the meaning of the drawings. Together, these inside front and back covers convey the progression from unknown to known, or put another way, they present the story of the discovery of María's engagement with iconic representation as both an engagement with others in a common activity and more specifically as a form of communication.

In the most recent comics text authored by María Gallardo and Miguel Gallardo, it is iconic drawing that serves as the explicit link between people. Artistic production thus stands as a symbol of the potential of collaboration, as well as testament to the power of collective acts and collective imaginaries to bring people together. This chapter has explored two very different contexts in which cultural and artistic production has been linked, whether more or less effectively, to deeply rooted patterns of social marginalization surrounding cognitive disability. One of these testified to the limitations and the potential of large-scale events to address the social and urban marginalization of developmental disability, and the other explored a small-scale cultural product focused on the value of art as a way of building family and community connections supportive of experiences of developmental disability. Both of these attempts centre on the notion of visibility, and both underscore the value of collaboration for populations with severe cognitive impairments. Returning to this chapter's epigraph penned by Michael Bérubé, we must remember that "the dynamics of disability compel us to recognize that there will always be among us people who cannot represent themselves and must be represented" (2005: 572).[37] *Cognitive Disability Aesthetics* is a call for disability scholars in general to recognize something they may have been slow to acknowledge – that not all people with disability can represent themselves in the ways required by ableist norms of individualism and ability. That said, I believe that the contexts explored in this chapter suggest another option outside of the represent-or-be-represented binary. Understanding the collaborative potential of visual artistic representations may open a pathway towards understanding the experience of cognitive disability in an ableist society, critiquing at once both the individualistic myth that requires every artistic producer to work "on their own" and the falsehood that disability resides purely in the body or the mind. Both the Trazos Singulares exhibit and *María cumple 20 años* allow for the material reality of cognitive impairment while mobilizing the aesthetic/cultural field as a corrective to disabling social conditions.

5 Sequencing Alzheimer's Dementia: Paco Roca's Graphic Novel *Arrugas* (Wrinkles) (2008)

"One of the most encouraging signs in recent years is that at last people with dementia are being recognized as having true subjectivity."

– Tom Kitwood (2011: 70)

Any approach to the cultural representation of Alzheimer's must appreciate the way in which "the emergence of Alzheimer's disease (AD) in epidemic proportions toward the end of the twentieth century is the product of biomedical discourse; it is an attribution that signifies the biomedicalisation of dementia in the elderly" (Burke 2008a: 63). In the Introduction to *Thinking about Dementia* (2006), Lawrence Cohen warns of the political, cultural, and economic shifts that have prompted an "aging public" to consume "Alzheimer's narratives as a form of dependency anxiety"; he also signals the dangers of uncritically accepting the medical model of disability related to Alzheimer's and reminds us of the need to go beyond the discourse of disease to understand the broader cultural significance of "the stigma of physical and economic frailty" (Cohen 2006: 7). These are crucial guidelines for any discussion of Alzheimer's, and the latter comment is more broadly relevant to disability studies approaches in general. With this in mind, chapter 5 of *Cognitive Disability Aesthetics* analyses the visual representation of Alzheimer's disease in *Arrugas*, an award-winning graphic novel created by Paco Roca (2008).

Born in 1969, Valencian artist Francisco Martínez Roca began his artistic career in the 1990s working on historically important comics projects like *Comix Kiss Comix* and *El Víbora*.[1] Creating a point of contrast with *Arrugas*, the content of these earlier and more flashy publications was driven by the culture of excess, sex, drugs, and rock'n'roll that some would equate with the legacy of the 1980s cultural movement in Spain called La Movida.[2] The 2000s saw a clear development in Roca's reputation and his production of a growing list of graphic novels showcasing his artistic and thematic versatility: *Gog* (La Cúpula, 2000), *El Faro* (Astiberri, 2004), *Hijos de la Alhambra* (Planeta, 2007), *Las calles de arena* (Astiberri, 2009), *Emotional World Tour* (with Miguel Gallardo; Astiberri, 2009), *El invierno del dibujante* (Astiberri, 2010), *Memorias de un hombre en pijama* (Astiberri, 2011), *La metamorphosis* (texts by Franz Kafka, illustrated book; Astiberri, 2011) and *El juego lúgubre* (Astiberri, 2012). Against this body of work, *Arrugas* – which by 2012 was in its eighth edition – stands out as a much more mature piece, as well as a stunning example of how the everyday experience of aging can be represented in graphic narrative.

First published by the French publishing house Guy Delcourt as *Rides*, *Arrugas* was subsequently printed by Astiberri Ediciones in Bilbao, País Vasco, to critical acclaim. In France it had been recognized as one of the top twenty graphic novels of the year, and in Spain it received two awards at the prestigious Salón del Cómic de Barcelona: the prize for Best Script, and the prize for Best Work by a Spanish Author. It has since been translated into Japanese (Sohakukan Shueisha Productions, 2011), Dutch (Silvester, 2009), Finnish (Wsoy, 2009), and Italian (Tunué, 2008). It has won the award for Best Album at Expo Cómic, Madrid, the Premio Nacional de Cómic 2008, the award for Best Album at the festivals of Lucca and Rome, and the prize of the Ministry of Culture in Japan.

The many intriguing visual elements of *Arrugas* are in a way signalled by its title, which points to a visual metonym for senescence. Wrinkles are the most visible sign of old age, a coarse surface that accompanies the aging process. As such, the graphic novel's title emphasizes the physical consequences of aging, a material process whose effects also begin to impact the brain, and through it, the mind. *Arrugas* gains its verisimilitude from being based in part on true stories. This visual representation of Alzheimer's disease reflects the graphic artist's own experiences. At the end of the work, in two unnumbered pages that function as a coda of sorts, Roca reflects on specific people he met who inspired the characters in his text. Readers learn that the artist began the project by gathering anecdotes from friends who had elderly parents. Thus, Emilio was inspired by "the real Emilio" who had Alzheimer's, and who was the father of a friend named Diego (2008:

102–3). Other characters in *Arrugas* were also inspired by true anecdotes, such as those concerning Salva's aunt, who feared abduction by aliens; and Ismael and Hugo's mother, who would stockpile mundane items to give as gifts to her sons when they came to visit her. Roca also spent time visiting residences for the elderly, where he met Pellicer, a medal-winning athlete; and Dolores, who always held the hand of her husband with Alzheimer's – both these people inspired characters in *Arrugas*.

Locating Roca's comic within a wider tradition of visual narrative, it is important to recognize that representations of intellectual disabilities have enjoyed a special place in recent Spanish cinema.[3] Films such as *Yo, también* (2009), *León y Olvido* (2004), *María y yo* (2010), *¿Qué tienes debajo del sombrero?* (2006), and *Más allá del espejo* (2007) have brought representations of Down syndrome, autism, and alexia/agnosia into the cinematic spotlight. This serves as a corrective for the observation that portrayals of physical disabilities have often overshadowed those of cognitive disabilities in now-classic films such as *El cochecito* (1960), *Acción mutante* (1993), *Carne trémula* (1997), and *Mar adentro* (2004).[4] Moreover, Roca's *Arrugas* is part of a cultural moment in which visual representations of Alzheimer's dementia are exceeding past patterns established in cultural production. Looking at recent years only, the number of films touching on this form of cognitive disability has increased substantially: *Volver a Villoro* (2006), *¿Y tú quién eres?* (2007), *Bucarest: la memòria perduda* (2008), *My Way* (2007), *Amanecer de un sueño* (2008), *Bicicleta, cullera, poma* (2010), *La mitad de Óscar* (2010), *La mosquitera* (2010), *Cuidadores* (2010), *Las voces de la memoria* (2011), and, finally, the 2011 film version of *Arrugas* itself (dir. Ignacio Ferreras). Yet whereas many of these films do indeed deserve to be taken as manifestations of the "dependency anxiety" identified by Cohen,[5] I do not think it is fair to identify Roca's original graphic novel as part of this trend.[6]

Intellectual disabilities and even Alzheimer's itself have been increasingly represented on the silver screen in Spain. It is much more rare that contemporary graphic novels have touched on the subject using an everyday and non-spectacular approach – in either the Spanish-language or the Anglophone tradition. Speaking generally, only recently have experiences of disability figured into analyses of comics, as evidenced by Margaret Fink Berman's 2010 article on disability in the comics of Chris Ware, José Alaniz's 2014 book *Death, Disability, and the Superhero: The Silver Age and Beyond*, and the 2016 volume *Disability in Comic Books and Graphic Narratives*, edited by Chris Foss, Jonathan W. Gray, and Zach Whalen. In addition, Spanish-language comics continue to be understudied in Anglophone contexts. While the graphic novel in Europe has received some significant attention (e.g., Beaty's *Unpopular Culture: Transforming the European Comic Book in the 1990s*), graphic novels and comics from Spain have not enjoyed the attention in English publications that has been given to, for example, the Franco-Belgian and German contexts. That said, comics and graphic novels published in Spain are figuring into an increasing number of works published in Spanish (e.g., Alary; Dopico; García; Gasca; Merino), and work published in English has built upon this tradition.

Arrugas stands out as a privileged text that speaks to the imbrication of comics art with wider circuits of visual art. As an artistic product the graphic novel should not be seen as entirely distinct from visual art in general; even so, it deserves special treatment as a unique genre. As this chapter explores, Roca's comic masterfully exploits formal aspects of the medium of the graphic novel (closure, the gutter, word/image combinations, and more) while delivering a vision of life with Alzheimer's-related dementia (ADRD) that emphasizes textures of the everyday over the spectacle of loss. The protagonist of *Arrugas* is Emilio, an elderly man experiencing ADRD whose son and daughter-in-law feel they can no longer care for him at home. The story begins as they decide to move him into a transitional care facility, where he meets a cast of characters and finds a dear friend in his new roommate, Miguel. *Arrugas* blends various types of narrative sequences in a rich visual presentation that oscillates among various points of view. Along with the frequent and seemingly objective presentation of everyday scenes set in the residents' rooms and in the facility's cafeteria, hallways, reading room, and outdoor areas, there are subjective memories, which are presented directly (e.g., flashbacks of the younger days of Emilio and of the facility's other residents). Blurring the boundaries between subjective and objective viewpoints, *Arrugas* features semi-subjective scenes that fuse an individual character's subjective experience of his or her present with the third-person point of view of that very same present in interesting ways. It goes beyond the concerns of its central character, addressing not only Emilio's experiences but also those of his peers in the facility. Emilio is more than just the protagonist; he also provides a central point around which to organize all manner of insights into the subjective experience of the aging process in general and ADRD in particular.

This chapter's first section, "Senescence, (Inter)Dependency, and Aging," concisely rehearses the theoretical framework of interdependence as articulated by Eva Feder Kittay and Licia Carlson. It also engages with specific research in the health fields regarding the experience of ADRD as a means to document the viability of Roca's visual representations, which are analysed in subsequent sections. The second section, "Diagnosis, Staging, Symptoms, and Transition," explores the form and content of Roca's original comics text in detail, focusing on the significance of memory, motor skills, friendship, and support systems for patients experiencing ADRD. Particularly important here is the image of a stairway, which appears and reappears as a metaphor for aging and senescence. The concluding section, "The Semi-Subjective, Interdependence, and Collective Narration," turns towards narrative's power to connect us all, both through the shared experience of aging and through the reader's participation in sequential art. From the perspective of collaboration, the semi-subjective is important because it is inclusive of multiple points of view. Whether those points of view are taken to relate to different characters or to more abstract contrasts involving subjective and objective data, the semi-subjective thus necessarily foregrounds the social framework within which individual consciousness takes shape; it also provides a visual affirmation of interdependency approaches to cognitive disability. To the extent that readers are able to link semi-subjective formal strategies with multiple points of view – and thus with the notion of an interdependent shared collectivity – an implicit and artistic denunciation of the individualist ideology feeds our dependency anxiety. Throughout, the emphasis is on a close reading of the relationship between *Arrugas*'s form and its content.

Senescence, (Inter)Dependency, and Aging

Arrugas does not focus directly on issues related to inadequate care, state policies, or institutional circumstances, but rather on the subjective experience of someone living with Alzheimer's-related dementia. The present chapter thus examines the subjective experience of senescence and ADRD in *Arrugas* specifically from a perspective that is just as attentive to artistic form as it is to the content of disability as a represented theme.[7] This requires first that we address how concerns relating to both senescence and disability studies overlap in the graphic novel. Making sense of this overlapping finds ground in previous scholarly work linking dependency, care, aging, disability, and the human experience. It is also important to identify how clinical and non-clinical research into Alzheimer's disease can help us understand how *Arrugas* contributes to our understanding the effects of dementia. These effects need to be approached from a perspective that acknowledges the individual symptoms of ADRD while also taking into account the way these effects are experienced collectively by families, friends, and loved ones. These explorations end by prioritizing temporality as it relates to the issues that accompany ADRD *and* to the complex narrative structure of *Arrugas*. The analysis of cultural production that follows examines the representation of temporality as a primary theme in the story-world of Roca's text and also the way in which its formal strategies foreground its themes through temporal processes. *Arrugas*'s structure destabilizes the univocal understanding of time, and in addition, the reader actively constructs the meaning of the visual text through an interactive process that unfolds over time.

Seen both in its wider context and as a pathbreaking representation of Alzheimer's in comics art in Spain, *Arrugas* speaks to the increasing representation of senescence and disability in visual art more generally.[8] The success of this particular graphic novel in other languages confirms that Spain is not alone in facing the issues raised by an increasingly aging population: the matter of Alzheimer's disease has global resonance. But while it is devoted to representing specific effects of the disease, *Arrugas* is not an issue-based work. That is, it does not concern itself with the likely prospect that there will soon be a shortage of beds in transitional care facilities (see Anon 2011), nor does it explore what it would mean for Emilio's family to care for him outside of an institution. It begins with the moment of Emilio's arrival at a transitional care facility, glossing over the decisions that children of aging family members must face – difficult economic, social, and familial decisions. This is not to say there are no institutional critiques to be made in an interpretation of *Arrugas* – merely that the growing literature on quality of life in a global sense as it relates to people with intellectual disabilities more generally is what is relevant here.[9]

The value of *Arrugas* is that it explores, at a personal scale, how current institutional placements come to be experienced subjectively by aging populations. In this way it resonates with Tom Kitwood's remarkable work as part of the Bradford Dementia Group, which, for example, sought to affirm personhood by acknowledging the unique subjectivity of the person with dementia, thus validating the reality of their experience and their feelings. *Arrugas* provides visual echoes of these concepts, not necessarily in the institutional setting itself but through the form of the graphic novel.[10] Adapting the scholarship of Lucy Burke to the present analysis, one could say that *Arrugas* "departs from the deficit thinking that dominates medical models of disability" precisely by exploring "the lived and shared experience of disease" and emphasizing "relational models of subjectivity" (2008a: 68).[11] The approach employed here has been to use the story as a starting point from which to emphasize the interdependency of all members of human societies. This perspective necessarily contains dimensions that are sociocultural, political, and economic; it also indicates the ties between lifelong health, aging, and general well-being.[12]

The analysis of *Arrugas* that follows draws from a theoretical frame that has contextualized senescence within a disability studies perspective. The theorists who have best articulated this linkage between aging and disability are Carlson and Kittay. In focusing specifically on issues of cognitive ability, they seek to establish a wide philosophical framework that approaches dependency as the basis for the human experience rather than as a lack of normal functioning (see also Sedgwick 2002: 23). In a sense, they confront more directly than some disability studies scholars a deeply rooted ideology – that is, an individualist ideology that allows the discourse of disability, and other colonizing discourses, to become to a certain degree naturalized or automatic within society. This pervasive social discourse that frames dependency, and with it disability, as a deviation from the norm is supported by what Kittay, Jennings, and Wasunna call "the myth of the independent, unembodied subject – not born, not developing, not ill, not disabled, and never growing old" (2005: 445). In truth, we are all dependent, or interdependent. In critiquing the above myth, Kittay cites Marx, who acknowledged that we are "a species being"; and she asks, "Who in any complex society is not dependent on others, for the production of our food, for our mobility, for a multitude of tasks that make it possible for each of us to function in our work and daily living?" (Kittay et al. 2005: 445; Kittay 2001: 570; see also Kittay 1999). Though we might pretend otherwise, all human beings are "inevitably dependent" in certain ways throughout the course of our lives (Kittay et al., 2005: 443). For her part, Carlson draws attention to the prejudicial perspective of cognitive ableism, itself a socially constructed and culturally negotiated discourse: "a prejudice or attitude of bias in favor of the interests of individuals who possess certain cognitive abilities (or the *potential* for them) against those who are believed not to actually or potentially possess them" (Carlson 2001: 140, original emphasis; see also Carlson 2010). From this perspective, populations with Alzheimer's disease or other forms of cognitive disability are not marginal groups but rather groups that express the fragile and interdependent nature of the human experience in the widest sense. The opportunity here is to see Alzheimer's dementia as one point where the discourses of aging and disability converge.

The volume *Cognitive Disability and Its Challenge to Moral Philosophy* (2010), co-edited by Carlson and Kittay, features a number of chapters with the word dementia in the title and more still that are relevant to the questions raised by ADRD as a category of disability that arises with old age (see also Carlson and Kittay, "Introduction"). Hilda Lindemann's "Holding One Another (Well, Wrongly, Clumsily) in a Time of Dementia" emphasizes the role of family members in what she calls "identity maintenance": she writes that "because strangers cannot well provide this kind of care, I argue that family members have a special responsibility to hold on to the person's identity for her" (2010: 163 and 162 respectively). In *Arrugas* it is the absence of stories, of family narratives, that is most apparent – given the relative absence of family members within the graphic novel's emplotment – although Emilio's new friend and roommate in the transitional care facility, Miguel, becomes a kind of substitute for a traditional notion of family. In addition, as Lindemann notes, "it's not only other people who hold us in our identities. Familiar places and things, beloved objects, pets, cherished rituals, one's own bed or favorite shirt, can and do help us to maintain our sense of self" (2010: 163). The spaces that would have been familiar to Emilio prior to entering the facility do not figure into the plot; however, the graphic novel replicates this distinction between familiar and unfamiliar spaces through a spatial contrast internal to the building. The first floor provides a newly familiar living space for Emilio; the second floor – to which residents transition as they require more regularized care toward end-of-life – represents the loss of a newly acquired home and the loss of newly familiar things. The second floor becomes increasingly important in Emilio's life, just as it will become increasingly important for the analysis that follows.

Bruce Jennings's chapter from Carlson and Kittay's volume titled "Agency and Moral Relationship in Dementia" raises similar concerns about how individual identities are in truth not as individual as they may seem. Instead, our identities are always necessarily sustained by a social group or a collectivity. Jennings calls for "a special conception that I am calling memorial personhood; 'memorial' because it falls to others to sustain continuity of the demented self over time by recalling the self that has been when the individual cannot do that alone. But then, who among us can really do that alone?" (2010: 171, also 176). Key to Jennings's approach is the concept of "re-minding": "Re-minding is changing the environment and the external support system that surrounds the person so that *different* abilities do not become the *absence of* abilities. Re-minding, as the play on words suggests, is remembering who one is, most fundamentally – as a relational human subject, person, agent – a maker and a[n] interpreter of meaning" (Jennings 2010: 173, original emphasis). The author also stresses the importance of what he calls hedonic or satisfaction conceptions. In *Arrugas* these conceptions are embodied by Emilio's friend, Miguel, who seeks to bring satisfaction and pleasure to Emilio's daily life: "These accounts identify quality of life with states of awareness, consciousness, or experience of the individual. Happiness or pleasure, however those terms are precisely to be defined, are the sine qua non of quality of life" (Jennings 2010: 177).[13] Miguel seeks out and provides adventure for Emilio on a daily basis, including – at the extreme – an unauthorized trip in a car that, sadly, ends in disaster and injuries (Roca 2008: 74–80).[14] As the chapters by Lindemann and Jennings imply, and as *Arrugas* dramatizes, even when the chronic or acute care necessitated by dementia is absent, senescence in itself is at best still a journey into infirmity that renders new and continuing forms of human interdependency more visible than they might previously have been.

Though it does not discuss graphic novels, Hispanic studies scholar Matthew Marr's monograph *The Politics of Age and Disability in Contemporary Spanish Film* explores these kinds of theoretical concerns in the visual context of Spanish cinema specifically. The key contribution of his book is that it emphasizes "an ideational linkage of adolescence, senescence, and disability," which "are often experienced – and customarily screened as – subject positions linked to self-estrangement" (2013: 6). The chapters of his book that he devotes to the films *Justino, un asesino de la tercera edad* (1994) and *Elsa y Fred* (2004) draw on Simone de Beauvoir's *The Coming of Age* and Betty Friedan's *The Fountain of Age* in ways that tie senescence and disability together: "Old age, after all, stands distinctively apart from other categories of social marginalization in view of its distinctive potential for universality, that is, its all-inclusive eligibility as a pejoratively construed, bittersweet Other into which dramatically more individuals than ever will eventually morph" (2013: 63). The context Marr provides of Spain's increasing elderly population since 1950 is particularly valuable (2013: 68), but the topic of dementia is not specifically foregrounded in the films under discussion there. Marr does well in noting that "agedness [...] is a relative construct like childhood or adolescence" (2013: 69), but it is arguably in the topic of elderly dementia that the links between senescence and disability are most clearly expressed. What it is important to see is that dementia is a way of reconciling the potential conceptual gap between old age and disability by finding common ground across social and health science perspectives.

The subjective experience of Alzheimer's-related dementia must be approached simultaneously from one perspective that is clinical and another that might be called qualitative or humanistic; both are key to understanding *Arrugas*. Research into the disease and its symptoms has pointed to a set of general characteristics that can prove instructive. Clinical investigators have traced "the role of global cognitive decline" (Amanzio et al. 2008: 2), the "breakdown in episodic memory performance," and the "breakdown in semantic memory structures" that accompany the disease (Balota et al. 1999: 361, 362); as well as the imperfect relationship that exists for those with Alzheimer's between recognition of faces, objects, and colours, on one hand, and names and qualities on the other (Brennen et al. 1996; Nielsen et al. 2004). In addition to these issues of memory and cognition, which Alzheimer's may share with other forms of dementia (Orsini 1988; Reilly et al. 2010; Saffran and Branch Coslett 1996; Westmacott et al. 2004), other investigators have assessed the links between motor skills and remembering (Masumoto et al. 2004: 300)[15] and have identified what might be called "Alzheimer's speech" (Ramanathan 2008: 1) as well as the effects of the disease as expressed in writing (Venneri, Pestell, and Caffarra 2002). These hallmark characteristics of Alzheimer's as noted in clinical research do, in fact, figure into the content of *Arrugas*, as will be examined in greater detail below, though this aspect of the work is arguably complemented by its non-spectacular, everyday approach, which ultimately emphasizes the human and social dimensions of ADRD over insights provided by the clinical paradigm.

Non-clinical research is equally important in making sense of the represented world of *Arrugas* and has several contributions to make to the present interpretation. Linguistic research into the speech of Alzheimer's dementia patients has argued for the significance of non-verbal communication, which may even come to be predominant "in late-stage dementia patients who have lost most or all of their ability to speak coherently" (Ridge, Makoni, and Ridge 2003: 153). The notion of narrative is also important, given that it can be meaningfully applied both to the person living with Alzheimer's and to family and friends who tell themselves stories about their loved ones and who participate in what, as we have seen, Jennings calls "re-minding."[16] One researcher has even used the notion of "narrative as self-portrait" as a particularly convincing way of exploring what might be called the incompleteness or implicitness of verbal narratives of Alzheimer's. As we will see, *Arrugas* offers ample opportunity to reconsider this supposition in light of the fact that narratives can themselves be visual (Hamilton 2008). Moving further on to cultural and literary terrain, previous research has investigated Alzheimer's disease as represented in fiction and film[17] – though it is no easy task to identify previous work taking on graphic novels and ADRD.

The importance of narrative for understanding how Alzheimer's dementia is represented in *Arrugas* might be generalized further in terms of the importance of time – as narratives may exist only through time. It is significant that the themes of memory and motor skills, and of reading, speech, and writing as they relate to Alzheimer's disease, all have a temporal aspect. As Anne Davis Basting explains,

> people with ADRD lose the ability to comprehend the chronological time systems that orient so much of global culture that it is nearly impossible for them to function without someone who can translate that world for them. Severe short-term memory loss can bring disorientation and paranoia: Who is this person coming into my room? What is this room? Gradually, the forgetting of details grows into the loss of concepts. One does not just forget where one put the keys. One cannot comprehend the *meaning* of a key. (Basting 2001: 79)[18]

In *Arrugas*, then, Emilio's fading sense of self and his accompanying lack of familiarity with the people and things around him raise a variety of concerns. Readers can see, in his experience as dramatized on the page, the marginalization and self-estrangement of senescence in general as explored by Marr. They stand as witnesses to a social attempt to sustain his personhood that squares with what is discussed by Lindemann and Jennings. And also evident is the expressive presentation of the disorientation and conceptual loss indicated in the quotation above by Basting. What is most important is the way in which these losses are unified in the graphic novel's visual and narrative presentation of ADRD, which prioritizes its social context and human dimensions. This presentation translates Emilio's experience into visual forms of communication that viewers will well comprehend as metaphors for non-visual human experiences connected with aging. In addition, the graphic novel's narrative complexity – its necessary emphasis on temporality through visual narrative – emphasizes the theme of chronological and contemporary time, which proves to be so difficult for those with Alzheimer's to grasp, as both a negative and potentially positive experience. *Arrugas* problematizes and humanizes the Alzheimer's experience of temporality by going beyond the notion that time is simply lost to suggest that time is also regained in a sense. As discussed further below, the significance and the meaning of such regained time, in the graphic novel, is dependent on the individual characters, who tend to experience it in positive ways. The analysis of *Arrugas* that follows builds on the theoretical links between senescence, disability, and interdependence; it also looks at the ways in which notions of time and narrative are foregrounded in the graphic novel's presentation of dementia.

Diagnosis, Staging, Symptoms, and Transition

Importantly, the link between senescence and Alzheimer's disease and old age is made directly in the text in a sequence where Roca allows a doctor to explain the disease to Emilio and thus simultaneously to the readers. Roughly halfway through the work (2008: 56–8), Emilio has begun to suspect that he has Alzheimer's, and he asks the doctor whether he takes the same medication as another resident named Modesto. The doctor states things directly – "Emilio, usted sufre de Alzheimer [Emilio, you suffer from Alzheimer's]" – before describing the disease for him:

> El Alzheimer es una forma de demencia senil. La demencia es la pérdida de las funciones mentales, memoria, lenguaje, capacidad de razonar ... Se altera la conducta y la vida social. Y lo de senil se usa porque suele ser más habitual en edades avanzadas. Es muy característica la pérdida de memoria reciente, sin embargo, la memoria pasada sigue funcionando bien. En parte es por eso por lo que los mayores hablan sólo del pasado. Pero ahora bien ... El Alzheimer es un tipo concreto de demencia, la más frecuente. Alrededor del 60% de las demencias son tipo Alzheimer. Además de la

> memoria reciente, con el tiempo se destruye la memoria pasada, la orientación, el lenguaje, la capacidad del enfermo para cuidarse y dirigir sus actos por sí mismo ... Es duro decirlo, Emilio ... Está usted en los primeros pasos del Alzheimer. Es una enfermedad degenerativa, progresiva e irreversible. Es muy duro para quien lo padece y para su familia.
>
> Alzheimer's is a form of elderly dementia. Dementia refers to the loss of mental functions, memory, language, the ability to reason ... One's behaviour and social life are affected. The word elderly is used here because it tends to become more common with advanced age. The loss of recent memory is very characteristic, however, long-term memory continues to function well. In part it is for this reason that the elderly talk only about the past. Nonetheless ... Alzheimer's is a specific type of dementia, and the most frequent. Around 60 per cent of dementias are of the Alzheimer's type. Beyond recent memory, with time it also destroys long-term memory, awareness, language, the ability of patients to take care of themselves and accomplish what they need to on their own ... It is a difficult thing to say, Emilio ... You are in the first stages of Alzheimer's. It is a degenerative, progressive, and irreversible disease. It is very difficult on the person who suffers from it and on their family. (2008: 56–7)

This clinical perspective serves a valuable instructional or educational purpose for readers who might not be familiar with Alzheimer's disease. The informational definition articulated by the doctor – who, it must be stressed, is a minor character in *Arrugas* – orients readers to the general symptoms and effects of ADRD. Note, however, that although the clinical perspective is important for our understanding Emilio's situation and for the graphic novel as a whole, the artist chooses not to construct the graphic novel around the medical understanding of the disease, but rather to contextualize that medical view within the everyday lives of people living with it. In this way, even while presenting a health sciences perspective on the material reality of cognitive impairment, he socializes and humanizes ADRD. From this perspective, perhaps more interesting are the events that prompt Emilio's question to the doctor and the visual presentation of how he receives this information. Each of these will be discussed in turn.

Emilio's awareness that he has Alzheimer's develops over time; this is reflected in the strategic pacing and narrative structure of *Arrugas*. Once interned in the transitional care facility, he meets Dolores and Modesto, who are always found sitting next to each other. As did the real person who inspired her character, Dolores always holds her husband's hand, even as she feeds him or gives him his pills. At the cafeteria table, Emilio is often in a position to watch the two interact, and at one point, Miguel leans over to him and says about Modesto, "Tiene Alzheimer [He has Alzheimer's]" (2008: 38). Here what is most striking is the portrayal of this important moment within two extended frames that function as if they were a cinematic shot–counter shot. Also, there is a curious parallel construction that adds meaning to our reception of the scene as readers. There is a parallel between the characters of Modesto and Emilio that is portrayed visually. Two long panels sit one over the other: in the first, Emilio is on the right, his friend and helper Miguel on the left; below that, Modesto is on the right, his wife and helper Dolores on the left. The two panels simulate shot–counter shot from Emilio's point of view; their parallel positioning within the frame suggests a parallel life trajectory.

In a later scene that returns to the familiar set of the cafeteria table, when Emilio and Modesto receive each other's medicine by mistake, the nurse says: "Bueno. Da igual ... Modesto y tú tenéis la misma medicación. [Oh well. It doesn't matter ... Modesto and you both have the same medication]" (2008: 55). At this time, during a moment of clarity, Emilio understands what this really means – that he, like Modesto, has Alzheimer's – and for two frames his eyes open more widely than has been their custom. There is a key difference between the two frames: in the second one, as his eyes look up from his medication to glance at Dolores giving pills to Modesto, the drab beige paint on the background wall of the cafeteria behind him suddenly becomes uncharacteristically bright yellow. This exploits the graphic property through which background environments in comics art become expressive of subjectivities.[19] The sharp change in the background speaks to a sharp change in Emilio's mental state. The next frame, of Dolores giving Modesto his medicine while they hold hands, functions as a point-of-view shot: the paint on the wall has returned to its original beige, as if to help contrast the banal, everyday nature of life as it unfolds in the facility with the exceptionality of Emilio's realization.

Throughout *Arrugas*, Roca exploits the formal properties of sequential art in order to portray Emilio's subjective experience and emotional response. In the very next sequence, in fact, we see the discussion between Emilio and his doctor. The formal properties of this sequence – including the drastic cut or narrative transition to the doctor's explanation of Alzheimer's – emphasize for readers the emotional weight

5.1: Parallel life trajectory of Emilio and Modesto from *Arrugas* (Roca, 2008), 23.

5.2: Emilio at a crossroads, from *Arrugas* (Roca, 2008), 20.

5.3: Iconic modulation from *Arrugas* (Roca, 2008), 96.

that Emilio's surprising realization has placed on him. His reaction to the news that he has Alzheimer's is shown to us indirectly, through seven successive point-of-view panels spanning three rows on the page, in which we see only Emilio's legs and feet against the monotonous beige of the laminated floor. Roca uses seven separate panels (rather than an extended or single panel) to emphasize how immobilized this information has made Emilio; in doing so, the graphic artist is maximizing a primary representational property of comics – iconic redundancy – so as to underscore Emilio's reluctance or even inability to accept this bad news. The position of his legs and feet remains unchanged throughout the sequence, further communicating the moment of shock he is experiencing while the conversation unfolds (2008: 57–8). As the two panels that function as bookends for this sequence show – by giving us similar mid-shots of the downward tilt of his head – he is having a hard time accepting this diagnosis and is struggling to maintain his former understanding of his situation. Overall, the repetitive graphic presentation of the panel content and the formal strategy of using multiple distinct panels serve to accentuate the reader's understanding that his emotional state is flat-lining. His final question to the doctor in this sequence – "¿Y con el tiempo acabaré en el piso de arriba? [And with time will I end up on the second floor?]" – is met with the doctor's stunned silence. A cut then leads into a sequence where he and Miguel contemplate the stairs to the second floor (2008: 58–61) – a symbol of the future that awaits him in the later stages of Alzheimer's.

The development of these later stages, and Emilio's increasing frustration over them, are the motor that drives the storyline forward in *Arrugas*. Note that the graphic novel does not clearly present the progression of chronological time; instead, it shows time's passing indirectly through the change in seasons and the disappearances (presumed deaths) of other residents in the facility. In another sense, through the repetition of familiar scenes at regular intervals, time seems to stand still in the facility. At one point, a two-page spread (2008: 46–7) drives home the monotony of the facility with eleven panels whose composition is remarkably similar and devoid of words. In a few we see only empty chairs; but in others the residents suddenly appear to us, seated and seemingly napping while sitting up. They are all stationary, in chairs against a wall under a clock. We know intellectually that time is passing because of the movement of the clock's hands from one panel to the next, and also because of the sunlight and eventually the darkness entering the room from an unseen window off-panel to the right of the frame. The only movement appears when a nurse rolls a resident in a wheelchair towards our left – but the clock times and appearances and disappearances of the residents seem to be somewhat out of joint. In this scene, Roca has seemingly placed us in the position of the residents: we do not experience time's passing as a fluid movement – an intimation that some patients with Alzheimer's have trouble fully grasping the motion of chronological time.

In a much wider sense, however, the passing of time in *Arrugas* is most clearly marked through the development of Emilio's Alzheimer's symptoms. For example, he "loses" his watch early in the novel (2008: 25), "loses" his wallet and his money at its midpoint (2008: 51), and further on "loses" his black socks (2008: 87). Once Emilio has been transferred to the second floor for a greater level of assistance with his everyday activities, Miguel finds these items in a box that Emilio kept under his mattress (2008: 94). It seems that Emilio was keeping them in a safe place but, due to the progression of Alzheimer's, was unable to remember where he had put them. This forgetting causes all manner of misunderstandings, most notably the notion that Miguel has been stealing items from Emilio. The regular pacing of these events throughout the graphic novel mimics the steady progression of the disease. This organizational structure of the narrative is, of course, combined with other clues that his disease is progressing and also paired with parallel storylines of other characters.[20]

As Emilio tries to grasp the doctor's news that he will inevitably progress towards the later stages of Alzheimer's, he becomes more interested in contemplating his likely future on the second floor. Earlier, when he had first entered the residence, during the tour Miguel gave him, an abrupt close-up panel showed him asking "¿Y esa escalera adónde va? [And where does that stairway go?]" (2008: 19). Miguel's explanation distinguished between those "válidos [able-bodied residents]" living on the first floor and the "asistidos [residents requiring assistance]" on the second. The use of an intriguing text–image combination in the five-panel page that follows Emilio's question (2008: 20) reinforces the theme of *Arrugas* and gives us insight into the inner experience of its protagonist. The first row on the page consists of two panels that provide readers with Miguel's explanation of the major detail of the facility's floor plan, but the second and third rows are more interesting, visually speaking. The second row consists of a single panel that spans the width of the page, depicting a span of approximately five steps in a stairwell in relative close-up. The effects of hallway lighting create a diagonal shadow on the left side of the image that runs top to bottom, artistically replicating the use of chiaroscuro staging in cinema and thus speaking to the symbolism evoked through sharp contrast. Here the use of contrast summons for readers the distinctions between young and old, relative independence and increasing dependence, able-bodied and disabled; and, by logical extension, between the opposing forces of life and death. Superimposed on this image, in three connected speech bubbles that run top to bottom as they move left to right diagonally down the page, are the words Miguel voices to Emilio: "Allí arriba van a parar los que ya no pueden valerse por sí mismos ... los que han perdido la razón, los que tienen algún tipo de demencia, como Alzheimer ... No me gustaría acabar ahí arriba [That's where those who can't take care of themselves end up ... those who have lost their mind, those who have some type of dementia, like Alzheimer's ... I wouldn't want to end up there]." This left-to-right diagonal text placement cuts across the right-to-left diagonal shadow line mentioned above, schematically forming an "X".

The compositional and formal significance of this "X" pattern can be seen as reflecting the notion that Emilio is at a crossroads – most immediately in his visual contemplation of the second floor, and also speaking of the trajectory of his life, given his recent placement in the transitional care facility. The extension of the second-row panel from page margin to page margin reads as the intersection point of this "X" or the nexus of this metaphorical crossroads. Its extended spatial width calls for readers to invest more time contemplating the stairs, and thus contemplating Emilio's possible future as he does. After all, this second-row image we see of the stairs is in part a point-of-view image from Emilio's perspective, something that will be repeated after Emilio speaks with his doctor. In a simple sense, the "'X" constituted by this second row creates an interesting visual symmetry in the image that prompts readers to linger on and sympathize with Emilio's inner doubts and concerns. In a formal sense, however, the "X" within this panel contrasts text-line to shadow-line, and thus word to text. In this way, the diagonal downward positioning of Miguel's successive statements serves an additional function. While the stairs visually lead to the second floor, the descending direction of the written text reminds us that this potential movement upward is in fact a downward marker of deterioration. There is, here, an interesting and inverse relationship between words and images: as language deteriorates over time as one of the effects of Alzheimer's, the visual world becomes more immediate and perhaps for that reason more important. This contrast is thus particularly poignant in that it represents Emilio's material experience of the progression of ADRD: downward text maps to progressive issues regarding expressive language; stairs and shadow leading the eye upward map to an uncertain future whose details are unknown.

The third row's return from one to two panels contributes to the symmetrical composition of the page. Echoing the identical formal expression of the first row, it scales up the "X" figure (with an extended nexus) by rounding out the two feet of the letter. In this way it brings a sense of partial closure both to the scene and to Emilio's unvocalized and visually implied thoughts on his own future and mortality. The page functions as a relatively autonomous unit, even if this encounter will repeat later on in the graphic novel. In contrast to the panels on the first row, which were drawn from a first-floor point of view, both of the third-row panels are drawn from a perspective rooted at the top of the stairway. As readers we look down at Emilio and Miguel. In the first third-row panel we see Miguel walking off to the left, stating "Prefiero no enseñártelo. Me deprime subir ahí [I'd prefer not to show it to you. Going up there depresses me]," and in the second Emilio is now alone. In contrast to Miguel's movement, Emilio remains immobilized, briefcase in his right hand, still as can be and still looking upward – at the second floor, at his future, and directly at us as readers. This time our point of view as readers puts us in the very same shadow that Emilio had contemplated from below just a moment ago, and the vertical downward-facing angle of each third-row panel composition makes him seem powerless and insignificant. In symbolic terms, we now occupy the position of Emilio's future – a point of view that prompts us to anticipate both his diagnosis of Alzheimer's and his eventual passing to the assisted-living floor of the transitional facility.

As mentioned earlier – and in line with the graphic novel's narrative structure – this scene at the stairway reappears after Emilio has spoken with the doctor about his diagnosis. Given the metaphorical and symbolic value of the stairway scene discussed above, this repetition prompts a return to those deeper forms of lucid contemplation that had been communicated only visually. The start of this more lengthy sequence (2008: 58–61) thrusts the reader back into a deeper contemplation of Emilio's doubts, concerns, and future through the use of two page-width-spanning panels. The first depicts Emilio in close-up, against the beige background, with no other details save some shadows at the left side of the panel. The voice of Miguel, in off, asks him, "¿Estás seguro que quieres subir ahí? [Are you sure that you want to go up there?]" (2008: 58). There is an emptiness to the image caused by a deliberate lack of represented detail. This lack of detail together with the extended width of the panel brings us closer to sympathizing with Emilio's thoughts, as the few shadows at the left side of the image bring back the theme of aging, infirmity, and death as implied in the previous sequence (2008: 20). In a sense, he may as well not even be standing in the hallway of the facility – place is minimized and at the extreme unimportant, as the formal composition of the panel encourages identification with the protagonist's doubts and concerns.

The second panel (2008: 59) also spans the page and presents the same daunting image of the stairway as we saw before (2008: 20). Here the image is depicted from more of a long shot, which allows us to see a slightly greater number of stairs (just over six), as well as the banister on the left of the frame, which, along with the familiar shadow line, leads upward. What is different here is that, aware of what awaits Emilio, both he and Miguel decide to venture up to the second floor. The relative lack of text (2008: 59) reflects the solemnity of the occasion and the worry, fear, and trepidation Emilio is experiencing when faced with his uncertain future. Once upstairs, the two men pass through a set of doors into the second-floor cafeteria, where they walk through an overwhelming scene. An elderly woman hurriedly approaches them, asking whether they have seen her parents; other residents are sleeping, crying, screaming, and on the whole not communicating with one another. The scene is all the more overwhelming for the contrast established between the silent and prolonged approach up the stairs and the overuse of text once in the cafeteria. As they walk back down the stairs, a lone panel with no text is followed by a lucid statement from Emilio to Miguel: "No voy a acabar ahí, Miguel. Haré todo lo posible para no acabar ahí [I am not going to end up there, Miguel. I'll do everything possible not to end up there]" (2008: 61). From here on, through the actions of its protagonist, *Arrugas* gives us a valuable opportunity to experience the frustration some people diagnosed with Alzheimer's can feel.

Now that Emilio understands that he is at risk of being moved to the second floor, he asks Miguel to help him. At first Miguel suggests reading to maintain his mental acuity – something that Emilio finds too frustrating because he cannot remember what he has just read (2008: 62). Next he suggests a more elaborate plan that involves tricking the nurses and the doctor (2008: 63). The pair work collaboratively to hide

Emilio's growing memory problems, which on a number of occasions saves him from being exposed in front of the facility staff: for example, when Emilio mistakes a spoon for a knife in the cafeteria (2008: 65–6). Miguel also instructs Emilio about the value of dressing well, as staff members can note signs of disease progression by the way a resident is dressed (2008: 69). When Emilio is next scheduled for an examination with the doctor, Miguel makes sure he has the answers to predictable questions written down on his arm, even though in the end Emilio has problems reading them and is saved by the actions of another resident, whose obvious escape attempt receives urgent attention from the staff (2008: 70). Ultimately, of course, the material effects of the progression of Emilio's Alzheimer's are too powerful to be kept in check by Miguel's suggestions. In spite of the labels Miguel affixes to his clothing to help him remember the names of the items he wears (2008: 86), Emilio's memory and behaviour worsen: he asks to be taken to the city as he believes he is expected at work (2008: 81).[21]

Fitting with the everyday perspective of the graphic novel, Emilio's unavoidable move to the second floor is not romanticized in *Arrugas*. In fact this event is not depicted at all – it just happens. The narration selectively leaves this moment out of the story's emplotment. In a touching scene, after it is more than clear that Emilio will very soon be unable to take care of himself, Miguel helps him button his shirt (2008: 89). The single-page sequence consists of eight panels and a final white blank space where the ninth panel should be, marking this event as one of the last times the two roommates will interact in the space they have shared for so long. The first row of panels depicts Emilio's frustration through what might be compared to a series of cinematic jump-cuts. With the transition from each panel to the next, Roca varies the distance and focal point of each image, giving readers the disorienting sense that the passing of chronological time here is just as unclear for us as it likely is for Emilio. From a close-up of Emilio's hands on the buttons we cut to a long shot of the same action, and finally to a close-up of his face looking down, presumably watching the ineffective actions of his hands. An eyeline-match panel begins the second row and shows us Miguel as a witness to Emilio's frustration: he is seated on his bed with a worried look on his face. Another long shot of Emilio alone, which would have fit in with the panels of the first row, is followed by a long shot of Miguel buttoning Emilio's shirt for him, and then a close-up. The eighth panel is a close-up of Emilio alone, smiling, relieved that his frustration has passed and still looking down as if unable to fully grasp that it is Miguel who has helped him. After the white non-panel, which implies Emilio's transition to the second floor, we see a sequence depicting Miguel eating in the cafeteria next to an empty chair (2008: 90), and we must actively construct for ourselves that Emilio's transition to the assisted living floor must have occurred in the interim. This can perhaps be understood as a key choice made by the graphic artist to avoid spectacularizing ADRD as loss and to instead focus on its more routine experience in everyday life.

It is necessary to point out, of course, that in charting the progressive effects of Alzheimer's disease – both in Emilio and in the other characters – *Arrugas* also focuses on positive aspects of its characters' lives in the transitional care facility. Beyond the care and treatment residents receive – whether on the first floor or the second – the graphic novel also represents tender moments between residents, friends, and family. Family visits are a source not only of disconnection but also of connection, and Emilio in particular seems happy when he sees his family (2008: 52–3). Even despite his occasional deception of other residents to acquire money, Miguel's hedonic support of Emilio and others is a consistent part of the storyline of *Arrugas*: he helps a woman make a phone call to her family, provides residents with everyday items they need, and consistently tries to keep everyone's spirits high. In addition, the importance of motor skill development for patients with Alzheimer's disease is foregrounded in an impressive sequence that combines activity, humour, and an interesting narrative flourish of its own.[22] One of the most important aspects of *Arrugas*'s presentation of Alzheimer's dementia, however, may not be the content and formal strategies mentioned above, but rather its use of the semi-subjective, which suggests a social commitment to collective responsibility for the material experience of disability.

The Semi-Subjective, Interdependence, and Collective Narration

In cinema, "semi-subjective" refers to a visual perspective that represents neither a third-person or "objective" shot nor a first-person or "subjective" point-of-view shot. Instead, the semi-subjective bridges the objective and subjective camera positions in a subtle way. One example provided by the work of director and cinema theorist Pier Paolo Pasolini is that of a shot where, capturing a child in movement back and forth on a swing, the camera moves also from side to side with the motion of the swing. In this case, we are talking neither about the point-of-view perspective of an identified or unidentified onlooker nor about an objective treatment that would be implied in a stationary camera. This use of the semi-subjective thus creates a *sympathy* between the spectator and the subject of the camera, all while leaving its point of view in a state of indeterminacy. As a strategy of narration – perhaps akin to the complex strategies of shifting prose narration Mikhail Bakhtin identified in the nineteenth-century Russian novel – the semi-subjective visually brings viewers' attention to confront the existence of a narratological perspective and even to question its authority. What is so compelling about the presentation of Alzheimer's-related dementia as we experience it in *Arrugas* is Roca's use of this same semi-subjective strategy, now transposed onto the unique medium of comics art to prompt us to sympathize with its characters. The effect of this strategy is that readers appreciate the subjective experience of Alzheimer's disease from a perspective that is more humanistic than clinical.

From the first scene – a thirteen-panel sequence that unfolds over two pages (2008: 7–8) – *Arrugas* foregrounds the way consciousness is affected by physical changes to the brain rooted in the progression of Alzheimer's. In the first panel of the graphic novel, readers see an establishing scene of a bank interior. Bank customers are lined up in three queues leading to teller stations on the left border of the panel. Unobstructed by those waiting their turn is a view of a back office where a man is seated behind a desk. Facing us as readers, even if he is only distantly visible, the man (Emilio) counsels a couple through what he clearly understands to be bad news. Each of the first three panels spans the full page width, and readers successively read the delivery piece by piece, first in an establishing shot as above, next in a medium close-up of the bank loan officer from a relatively high angle, and finally in a medium close-up of the couple from a relatively low angle. From this point on, as the couple reacts to the bad news, the panel width is reduced from one page-spanning panel to two panels, and subsequently two rows of three panels. This use of form quickens the pace of reading, inducing an emotional intensity in readers that is heightened by the sudden revelation that the bank officer is not at work at all, but instead at home in bed, experiencing a moment of spatio-temporal confusion rooted in deep memories that are relatively disconnected from the present moment. The juxtaposition of high and low angles prefigures this shift, subtly undermining the position of social power from which the loan officer speaks. Notably, in the third panel of the sequence, the word balloon emanates from the bottom of the frame, further adding to the feeling that the bank employee has a lower status than he realizes.

As the sequence plays out, readers witness several drastic changes in selected panel details that together prompt a shift from semi-subjective to objective reality that can be identified as such through retroactive determination. At first, the couple and the loan officer seem to merely be present in the same space of the bank building. But in truth, the space they share is not that of a bank office but that of a bedroom in a private residence. Emilio is actively remembering and even enacting his role at the bank, but his scenario is not shared. In the row comprising panels 9–10–11, readers see that the couple are not sitting down at a desk in the bank office but instead are standing up over Emilio's bed. Interestingly, they are wearing the same clothes in both the bank scene and the bedroom scene. Both before and after the shift in perspective, Emilio's son wears the same red collared-shirt and white undershirt, and his son's wife the same green-toned sweater. Emilio's appearance, however, is quite distinct in each place. At the bank he is a younger, black-haired man with suit and tie, while in the private residence he has white hair and wears a bathrobe. As we soon realize, the scene in which we have been participating as readers corresponds to Emilio's subjective mental world and not to the reality that the couple have been perceiving. It is important to recognize that we initially see the world from a point of view that is simultaneously his yet not solely his own. The consistency of the couple's clothes and appearance, and their consistent positioning within the represented space, indicate that objective details nonetheless find their way into the mental space that Emilio enacts. The fact that his appearance is the only one to change accentuates the notion that this is his journey alone. This visually manifests the emotional shock and disorientation Emilio must feel transitioning from the space and time he routinely imagines back to the space and time of the immediate present from which he is progressively distanced. This shock is translated into the comics medium through two punctuating panels (10 and 11) with a high degree of iconic redundancy whose effect underscores Emilio's white hair and a close-up of his emotional reaction. In the end both Emilio's self-image and the perceived *mise en scène* are revealed to be the product of a memorialized selfhood whose connection with the present has been severed.

Particularly effective in this regard is the game of representational presence and absence as presented through the sequence's formal properties. This game speaks immediately to the experience of ADRD as panels reveal the sudden presence of a bed tray with a glass of water, a bowl of soup, and a soup spoon. The sudden appearance of objects that have not previously been present to Emilio's consciousness dramatizes the inverse of the loss described earlier by Basting.[23] If this process of drawing Emilio back to the immediate present is a social enactment of the "reminding" that Jennings writes about, here it is experienced neither as comforting nor as reassuring by Emilio and his family. Instead, there is a certain violence to this transition towards lucidity, to this abrupt reorientation – a violence that soon manifests itself in the frustration Emilio expresses by throwing his soup bowl and bed-table tray to the floor. The return to panels of page-spanning width at the close of this sequence illustrates Emilio's resigned adaptation to the objective reality he shares with his housemates. The final panel's relative lack of details – it shows only his son being drenched with soup against a large amount of grey wall – communicates self-estrangement, and the fact that Emilio's word balloon once again emanates from the bottom of the frame illustrates a downward turn in his feelings.

This entire sequence and its culminating image dramatize what Tom Kitwood, implicitly blending clinical and non-clinical perspectives, has called "dementia as a form of bereavement": here, Emilio has "to face two kinds of loss simultaneously – the loss of mental powers, and the loss of a familiar way of life" (2011: 29). The strategy of semi-subjectively representing the internal realities of other individual characters who are experiencing what is plausibly also ADRD is repeated during the graphic novel, giving visual representation to established tenets that for decades have validated the unique subjectivities of each person with dementia (see Kitwood 2011: 70–1). While outside of art "it is impossible … to enter fully into the experiential frame of another person, simply because each person is unique" (2011: 71), in its own way *Arrugas* stages that possibility for us – it is a prompt for our empathetic identification with the subjective experience of dementia.[24]

Arrugas moves on to present other examples of the semi-subjective image in a range of characters. When we experience another semi-subjective portrayal of Emilio's ADRD late in the graphic novel, for example, there is a similar relative disconnection from the present, one that is held in tension with his incomplete awareness of his immediate surroundings. In a sense, the manifestation of these shared visual or spatial elements in Emilio's subjective world is linked to the fact that his Alzheimer's has not progressed far enough to completely disconnect him from the present. In this later scene (2008: 44–5), Emilio stands at the bathroom mirror shaving with an electric razor. Once again his hair is black and his face devoid of wrinkles, intimating that his mental representation of himself has shifted back in time to an earlier period – his middle-aged years, when he worked at the bank. It is night, and in the contrasting panel on the left we can see Miguel asleep in the room (2008: 44). When Miguel wakes up and walks into the bathroom, we see both an elderly Miguel and a middle-aged Emilio in the same mirror image. Emilio states that he must go to work, to which Miguel replies that it is three in the morning (2008: 45). Emilio's shock at hearing this is reflected in the use of an extended panel width. Having heard the correct time, he turns to look at his friend – and thus also at us as readers – and at once becomes white-haired in both reflection and reality. In each of these two uses of the semi-subjective, we are seeing the world through Emilio's mind's eye, but we are never completely disconnected from his immediate context. And importantly, up until now, neither is he completely disconnected. Compared to other characters in the graphic novel, his is a relative disorientation that selectively incorporates aspects of the visible world around him.

This is not as strongly the case with other characters in *Arrugas*: Félix, Carmencita, or Modesto, for example. Félix's inner mental world is revealed to the readers visually even as Miguel and Emilio participate in it without realizing. In the comics version of *Arrugas*, we see a young Félix, perhaps twenty to thirty years old and in military garb, smoking a cigarette on a break while at a desert military base (2008: 33). As Miguel and Emilio walk by, we see them in the same military garb worn by Félix, who now stands up to salute. Within this semi-subjective portrayal of the young officer's subjective world, the uniforms worn by the pair of white-haired elderly gentlemen become a visual marker of the power of Félix's dementia to recast the existing world according to its own logic. This is a visual logic of memories rooted in the past, memories that now surge forth to change a character's image of the present – and as readers we are able to participate in that change. When Miguel remarks to Emilio that he wonders what goes on in Félix's head (2008: 33), we recognize that we are participating in a memory to which not all characters in the story-world have access. The two friends have no idea how Félix sees them. We also have access, for example, to Carmencita's disoriented inner world, when she hallucinates a group of aliens on the grounds of the residence, who lean casually against their spaceship, smiling. Other characters are present in the scene, but only Carmencita and the graphic novel's readers know it when one of the aliens speaks, saying "Ya te quedarás sola, ya … (Now you will be alone forever …)" (2008: 44). These examples are interesting precisely because of the way that iconic signification is decoupled from a single viewpoint. The representations we witness are collective in origin, and in the case of such semi-subjective portrayals, the border between one perspective and another is elusive.

The case of Modesto is perhaps more indicative of the possibility for the progression of ADRD to bring about an extreme disconnection from the present, but also the possibility for this temporal disconnection to have a positive aspect. In a sequence that unfolds within the objective space of the facility cafeteria, Dolores is feeding Modesto, as she customarily does, when Antonia asks Dolores what she whispers to her husband that routinely makes Modesto smile (2008: 66–8; see also 24). Dolores responds with an answer that is later unpacked in a visual sequence spanning two full pages: "tramposo [tricky]" (2008: 66). The sequence that follows is best understood as a hybrid event. Earlier in the graphic novel, Roca had presented a sequence that was in truth a flashback, where Emilio remembered the fear and trepidation he experienced on a particular day as a child when he was overwhelmed by the everyday act of attending school (2008: 11). Here, the sequence in question is, at least in part, a flashback to Modesto's childhood. We hear the word "tramposo" in one panel; the next panel portrays Modesto as a young child, occupying the same position within the frame as in the previous panel. In the mini-narrative that unfolds, we are in the mountain village of Modesto's youth as he asks a younger Dolores if she will be his girlfriend. In front of her laughing friends she replies, "Sólo si me traes una nube [Only if you bring me a cloud]" (2008: 67) – a seemingly impossible request. He then takes her up to the church bell tower, where the young couple watch a cloud approaching them with the wind and passing over them and through the bell tower, much to their delight. In this intercalated story, the scene ends with the young Dolores smiling and calling Modesto "tramposo" (2008: 68), after which we see the book-end panel image of an elderly Modesto smiling. Even here there are parallels between the subjective world and the objective world as in other semi-subjective sequences – not only the use of the word "tramposo," but in particular, Dolores's positioning to Modesto's right both within the subjective memory-world and in the objective cafeteria-world. At the same time, however, this sequence potentially involves a shared memory – one that involves two people who met when they were young. The likelihood is that Dolores knows precisely that she is invoking the memory of their shared childhood experience in the church. Even so, what the reader has witnessed here is a scene that is simultaneously memory and almost complete disconnection from the immediate present entangled with the complications of ADRD – an example of Jennings's "re-minding" that remains effective only because it references a memory long-established in the individual's early life. What is clear is that, because of their long history, Dolores and Modesto can share in this re-minding activity in a way that is impossible for the other characters in *Arrugas* – a fact that evokes the emotional connections and social relationships at the heart of the graphic novel.

Though it is not an example of the semi-subjective but rather a related example of a more subjective experience of "becoming Alzheimer's," a key sequence towards the end of *Arrugas* stages for us the experience of losing the ability to recognize faces. The simple term recognition, of course, is best understood as shorthand for a variety of sub-tasks that may not all come into play in the graphic novel.[25] In a general sense, however, the lack of facial recognition that accompanies the progression of Emilio's Alzheimer's disease becomes a visual metaphor for impaired cognition, which may include the simultaneous erosion of semantic access and naming (Brennen et al. 1996: 106). The sequence in question occurs after Emilio has been transferred to the second floor. Miguel goes upstairs to visit him and to continue in the support role he has increasingly adopted while witnessing the cognitive decline of his roommate. The second-floor cafeteria is loud and overwhelming, just as it was when the two friends ventured upstairs to take a look. Now, however, Emilio is distanced enough from his immediate present that he seems to take no notice. While Miguel feeds Emilio using a spoon – the bib around the latter's neck serving as a visual reminder of the advanced stage of his ADRD – we see some panels that can be seen as alternating point-of-view shots. First there is Miguel's view of Emilio in mid-close-up; three subsequent views of Miguel follow at a similar distance, one right after the other. Tracing the development of these panels can clarify just how Roca immerses us in a more direct experience of the effects of ADRD.

In the first-panel view of Miguel the outline of his face is visible and part of an ear, just as is the smallest portion of white hair atop his head; notably, though, his face has no features – no eyes, eyebrows, nose, or mouth. No wrinkles. In the next panel, there is a bit more hair, part of a mouth, and some rudimentary hints of eyes and a nose. In the third panel we see Miguel as we have seen him before throughout the graphic novel: all of his facial features are clearly visible, and pronounced wrinkles show on his forehead, by his eyes, and near his mouth. Over the course of these three views, Roca modulates the level of iconicity of his drawing as a way of simulating Emilio's struggle to make sense of this person in front of him. The last image on the page (2008: 95) shifts back to showing us Emilio's face – his mouth is no longer agape, and he does not look worried, but neither does he look happy. As readers, we must question whether he recognizes Miguel. On the next page (2008: 96), from Emilio's point of view, Miguel's features begin to disappear and once again become more iconic than we have become accustomed to in Roca's graphic novel. The depiction of Miguel in the wide panel in the centre of the page is drastically without skin pigment and even lacks the colours of his shirt and jacket. The bottom third of the page extends this erosion of specificity and of colour by eschewing the representation of a panel altogether and relying on the white background of the page and gutter. This image on the verso page (2008: 96), which sits parallel to the image of the train smoke on the visible recto page (2008: 97), makes clear through visual metaphor that Emilio no longer remembers who Miguel is. In the end, Emilio cannot visually recognize his friend. By following Roca's deft visual metaphor of his now severe Alzheimer's symptoms, in a sense we have gained an appreciation of his struggle through a metaphor for cognition made visible on the page.

The final example of the semi-subjective in *Arrugas*, and perhaps the one that is richest with symbolism, is the recurring self-image sustained by Señora Rosario. This same semi-subjective scene appears numerous times throughout the novel (2008: 18–19, 52, 97) and even on the cover of the book's eighth edition. Our introduction to Rosario is prompted by a comment Emilio makes on his initial tour of the facility: "¿No hay nadie despierto en la residencia? [Is nobody awake in the residence?]," he asks, at once incredulous and wary of the situation he is being thrust into (2008: 18). As a consequence of this question, Miguel introduces Emilio to Rosario, who is one of the facility's more disoriented residents. The next image is a panel spanning the width of the page that shows a train passing over a mountain bridge. Seen from a low angle, with clouds in the background and a tree in the foreground, the composition of the train scene connotes a sense of serenity. We see a young woman in a chair whose surrounding *mise en scène* is that of a train compartment. The woman's expensive fur coat, along with the comfortable chair, elegant curtain, and side-table lamp, gives us to understand that this traveller is well-off and vacationing in the first-class car. When Miguel says hello, Rosario responds "¿Ustedes también van a Estambul? [Are you also going to Istanbul?]," and Miguel's answer is no, that he and Emilio are getting off at the next stop (2008: 18). The elderly gentlemen Miguel and Emilio appear as they objectively are in the sequence, but the door Miguel touches is not the door of the residence but rather the French door of an expensive train compartment; this signals that here too we are seeing the characters from a point of view that approximates Rosario's almost complete disconnection from her present. The final image of the sequence brings us out of this semi-subjective and back into the objective reality of the transitional care facility. From this point of view, we see an elderly Señora Rosario seated, not on a train in the first-class car, but in a wheelchair next to a window at the residence. She seemingly stares out the window of the residential facility, but in her reality, of course, she is still staring out the window of a train car – at a beautiful mountain pass that maps back to another time in her distant memory. It is of interest that when her family comes to visit we see them once again from a semi-subjective perspective in her train compartment as she talks about visiting her husband in an Istanbul hotel (2008: 52). This use of the semi-subjective strategy in a sequence where all other characters' family visits are portrayed objectively and visually indicates to readers and viewers the severity of her Alzheimer's symptoms while engaging iconic signification as a collective representation.

At the end of the graphic novel, Antonia uses her walker to move herself over to the window, where she sits down by Rosario. Here, *Arrugas* uses the semi-subjective to push us even further into Rosario's world, in effect to have us see things from her point of view. In previous depictions of Rosario's inner experience the characters entering her train car retained their own clothing; here, once Antonia sits down beside Rosario, we see her too at a much younger age. There is an element of sympathy here that works on two levels. Antonia – one of the more lucid elderly residents in the facility, whose frustrations are more familial and social than they are related to problems of memory or language loss – seems to be willingly participating in Rosario's world. When Rosario asks her "¿Usted también va a Estambul? [Are you also going to Istanbul?]," Antonia surprisingly says, "Sí. [Yes]," clearly playing along (2008: 97). Yet if Antonia is playing along, it is unclear whether the younger version of herself that we see is her own self-representation or an interpretation on the part of Rosario. If it is the latter, then the visual narration of the graphic novel is bringing us further than it has before into the inner experience of Rosario's subjective consciousness. The images of Rosario's train car were never portrayed in such a subjective style – there were always obvious indicators of the objective reality that escaped her perception, even if these were limited to the presence of newcomers. Antonia may be reliving a previous experience or at least a previous youthful mental state in order to sympathize and relate to her co-resident – but it is important that in this case we are notably seeing a unique fusion of two consciousnesses on the page: Antonia's image of herself and Rosario's image of herself at once. No matter the interpretation one chooses, one must admit that there has, in fact, been a collective expansion of iconic representation in our experience of these semi-subjective visual portrayals throughout *Arrugas*. We ourselves, as its readers, have been able to sympathize with Roca's characters throughout the novel – we have been the ones sharing their world and sharing in their subjective experiences visually.

To a significant degree, *Arrugas* has given both readers and viewers the opportunity to reconcile the subjective memories of various characters with the objective story-world in which they are immersed first-hand. Awareness of this narratological layering leads us to recognize, also, our own reconciliation of the world Roca has represented for us with our own objective world as readers of his graphic novel. The smoke that emerges from Rosario's train on the mountain pass (2008: 97) and that subsequently dissolves the border between panel and gutter in truth blends the panel image with the blank surrounding margin of the book we are reading. I prefer to consider this smoke as a cloud, in order to square with the intercalated story of Dolores and Modesto's childhood experience in the church bell tower related above. Clouds are used as a recurring symbol in the graphic novel as a way of evoking the transitory nature of the human mind in the widest possible sense – and also the uncertainty engendered by the cognitive impairment associated with ADRD.[26] The semi-subjective – to the extent that it is inclusive of multiple points of view, whether of different characters or of both subjective and objective data – foregrounds the social framework within which the individual consciousness takes shape. As regards ADRD in particular, this social framework means above all else that we are all interdependent: in our daily lives, in our youth, and in our old age. *Arrugas* makes clear that – able-bodied or able-minded, disabled physically or cognitively – in the end it is this social framework and this interdependency that gives our lives meaning.

As a complex graphic novel that exploits the rich representational possibilities of sequential art in various ways, *Arrugas* can get us thinking about narrative on various levels at once. For example, we may begin to contemplate, more or less intensively, the notion of "narrative as self-portrait" (Hamilton 2008) in a way that prioritizes the visual modality of storytelling. Roca's graphic novel is compelling not only because of the details he represents in these visual narratives, but also because of the gutter, which allows readers opportunities to actively construct the story-world through the gaps that are so crucial to the structure of sequential art. At an even more basic level, narrative is another way of saying that we organize our experience: "Indeed, it has been said that life comes to us in the form of stories – we do not have unmediated access to our lives, but rather we know them through stories. Narrative is an integral feature of experience, not merely a conduit for representing it" (Gubrium 1986: 21). We use stories to tell ourselves who we are, to tell others who we are, and to tell others who they are. *Arrugas* shows how this process of storytelling is always a collective act.[27] We rely on others to tell our own stories when we can no longer do so; but what we experience visually in *Arrugas* is the idea that even those who seem unable to tell stories are narrating themselves long after many suppose they have stopped doing so. The visual medium of comics art then seems apt for this purpose of portraying caregiving stories ... and it might even be said that the reader of Paco Roca's graphic novel becomes a caregiver in a visual sense.[28] Ultimately, the unique aesthetic aspects of visual narrative allow us to understand the material experience of ADRD within a collective and social framework that folds the clinical back into the non-clinical, everyday, social experience of cognitive disability.

6 Screening Schizophrenia: Documentary Cinema, Cognitive Disability, and Abel García Roure's *Una cierta verdad* (A Certain Truth) (2008)

"Research on media representations of mental illness is burgeoning; however, the intersection of disability with mental illness is an area that has not received due scholarly attention ... At a time when twenty-five percent of the global population can expect to struggle with a mental disorder in their lifetime, and ten percent struggle with a disability, more sophisticated and nuanced representations are well overdue."

– Valerie Palmer-Mehta (2013: 362)

In the popular imagination, as in the professional judgment of many white-robed health care providers, a thin line separates the "mentally disabled" from the "mentally ill." There may very well be a legal distinction between these terms, just as there may be a medical distinction. But I regard any such distinctions as a thin white line. In the present context of analyses of visual texts in the humanities, I employ the term "the thin white line" in order to animate the spirit of sceptical inquiry implied by the documentary and fiction films *The Thin Blue Line* (1988), directed by Erroll Morris, and *The Thin Red Line* (1998), directed by Terrence Malick. In the most general sense, this chapter's scepticism regarding psychiatric/medical practice can be tied to similar critical judgments on law/order and war suggested by these two above films. This is a scepticism regarding structures of social and state power and their uneven and decidedly harmful impact on individual lives. Here I am also concerned with the blurry nature of theoretical distinctions between illness and disorder, on one hand, and disability, on the other. The notion of cognitive impairment discussed in earlier chapters of *Cognitive Disability Aesthetics* introduces another level of disciplinary critique to this endeavour that some may find discomfiting. I believe this is necessary if we are to think through how disciplinary knowledge may itself function as a power structure that itself marginalizes certain material experiences of disability.

A social model of cognitive disability is sorely needed in the twenty-first century, and I am sensitive to the fact that the present approach is not wholly satisfying. The effort to integrate issues of psychiatric illness into the social model of disability that has informed decades of humanities scholarship is not wholly satisfying. But I believe it has a strong potential. Applying a disability studies perspective to issues of cognition heretofore underexplored by the discipline allows humanists to reclaim the study of cognitive disabilities from the health and medical sciences. This in itself could be empowering. In ceding discursive control of cognitive disabilities to more quantitative and scientific fields, disability studies scholars in the humanities have collectively privileged a cognitively abled perspective. In focusing largely on physical disabilities and on critiques of pervasive able-bodied norms, these scholars have left out many individuals and groups. In its current formulation, the strong social model of disability in the humanities tends to ignore impairment, especially as it relates to cognition, and even as it engages psychiatric illness.

Some may rightly fear that the notion of psychiatric impairment is not cleanly compatible with such a social model. Yet ignoring it completely is just as frightening if the result is that we ignore the material experiences of severe cognitive disability. At the risk of repetition, I take very seriously the suggestion by David T. Mitchell and Sharon L. Snyder that it may be time for a return to impairment (2015: 1, 160; 2010: 199; see also Bérubé 2016: 56–7). I intend this to be not the final word, but rather a call for others to think more intensely about cognitive disability and the challenges it presents for largely physical modes of thinking about disability. Such modes have disproportionately dominated the academic field, impeding more careful and sustained consideration of cognitive difference.

The first section of this chapter, "Asylums, Community-Based Care, and the Clinical Gaze," introduces readers to past scholarship on mental illess and to contemporary debates over its appropriate treatment. Each of the terms in the section title is of great importance for understanding the form and content of Abel García Roure's documentary film *Una cierta verdad* (A Certain Truth) (2008), discussed in the chapter's second section. In the first section, however, I turn to the work of

Michel Foucault (*History of Madness* and *The Birth of the Clinic*) to chart a move away from dialogic approaches to infirmity towards a modern clinical model that prioritizes the immediately visual world over the depth offered by narrative. I argue that this paradigm shift has brought new precision to the clinical treatment of some physical conditions even while simultaneously ensuring that the treatment of mental illness remain imprecise. This section closes with a brief analysis of another Spanish documentary film directed by Ione Hernández and produced by Julio Medem – *1% esquizofrenia* (1% Schizophrenia) (2006). Hernández's film engages key tropes and visual metaphors of the clinical gaze and thus serves as a point of contrast with García Roure's more complex film.

The chapter's second section, "Representing Schizophrenia in *Una cierta verdad* (2008)," explores a documentary filmed in Barcelona by García Roure, a critically acclaimed director and student of Joaquim Jordà. I pursue close readings that are attentive to connections between film form and the artistic properties of the documentary, on one hand, and the film's content and message, on the other. Ultimately, the film's disability representations stage encounters with schizophrenia that are more attentive to questions of cognitively abled power, of autonomy and self-management, and of the political commitment of art than they are to the spectacular discourse of psychiatric illness. This chapter – perhaps even more provocatively than in chapter 5's discussion of Alzheimer's dementia – is a call for scholars in the humanities to continue to think through how the social and medical paradigms of disability fit together.

Asylums, Community-Based Care, and the Clinical Gaze

The distance between the much-criticized asylum model or institutional model of psychiatric care and largely inadequate community-based psychiatric care is an implicit point of reference for understanding García Roure's documentary film on schizophrenia. As a way of exploring this distance in distilled form, I turn to a review essay titled "Under Lock & Key: How Long?," published in *The New York Review of Books* on 17 December 2015. Written by Aryeh Neier and David J. Rothman, that essay examines the legacy and the space of the asylum in general terms. It passes judgment both on the asylum's generalized historical role and on its current place in society and in medicine. It foregrounds the wider inconsistency whereby some mental health issues are considered disabilities and others are not – an inconsistency that happens to be quite relevant for scholars of disability studies in the humanities. This is a tall order, and one that is perhaps too complicated to explore in a form as concise as a *NYRB* review. That said, the professional standing of the co-authors is notable: Neier has been executive director of both Human Rights Watch and the American Civil Liberties Union; Rothman is the Bernard Schoenberg Professor of Social Medicine and History at the Columbia College of Physicians and Surgeons and president of the Institute on Medicine as a Profession (2015: 5). Given their complementary blending of medical expertise and social advocacy, the pair might at first glance seem to represent a unified voice regarding what those seeking mental health services need. Such a first impression, however, would be misleading.

There is no question that explorations of the contemporary call for a "return to the asylum" (2015: 70) need to be nuanced, a position on which I agree with the essay's authors. As Neier and Rothman make clear, asylums have a "bleak history," one that dates back to the nineteenth century in the American context (2015: 70). Regarding the processes of deinstitutionalization that have unfolded since the 1960s, they write that "there is no denying that despite the best efforts of lawyers and advocates, dollars and services have not generally followed patients released from institutions into community facilities" (2015: 71). What is more interesting than the data provided and the positions taken by the authors – even more interesting than their final word, perhaps[1] – is how the mentally disabled and the mentally ill are regarded as separate populations. Statements such as the following one employ word choices that implicitly engage the marketplace rhetoric of competition and that overstate the distinction between these populations from a point of view that tacitly accepts the normative position of ableist society and its classificatory schemes:

> The mentally disabled have fared better than the mentally ill, first because parents have been relentless supporters of the rights and needs of their children. They discover the handicap of their child soon after the birth and become ardent advocates for programs and services. Second, Medicaid funding for the mentally disabled – but not for the mentally ill – is increasingly available to encourage release from institutions and the phasing out of the institutions themselves. (2015: 71)

Here it is necessary to point out that the uncritical use of the term "handicap" – which appears twice on the same page of the essay – conveys a lack of understanding regarding the social approaches to disability that have unfolded since the 1960s in the American context. More significant, however, the distinction between "mentally disabled" and "mentally ill" is never convincingly or directly explained for readers.[2]

The essay suggests, as evidenced in the above quotation, that "mentally disabled" refers only to children or to disabilities that are present from birth. One must wonder, are these cognitive disabilities developmental in nature? And if so, why would the authors exclude cognitive disabilities that occur *after* birth from their discussion? Are these naturally to be categorized as illness and not disability? Are they making the assumption that a disability lasts for one's entire life, from birth until death, whereas an illness is temporary? This sort of argument, while not clearly articulated in the essay, would lead one to the misguided notion that there is a "cure" for mental illness but not for mental disability. Such a misguided logic might assert that, if they are present from birth, disabilities can never be cured or treated, whereas illnesses, if stemming from events after birth, can be cured, treated, or at the least managed. This distinction cannot be convincing either for disability studies scholars or for disability activists because it subtly affirms ableism as the central norm of human societies.[3] Several questions are worth asking here: What forms of social power are invested in these discourses? Who benefits from the imprecise use of terms such as "mental disability" and "mental illness"? What interest is served by contrasting temporary disabilities with lifelong ones? These are questions that Neier and Rothman seem not to have asked.

In the letters section of the subsequent issue of *NYRB* (26 February 2015), Dominic Sisti and Emanuel Ezekiel take issue with Neier and Rothman. In particular, they question the simplistic judgment that obtains therein, by which all possible forms of the asylum are suspect, and from which it seems to follow that all possible states of community-based support are preferable. As Sisti and Ezekiel rightly point out, this is a false dichotomy:

> The past horrors of some shuttered institutions are undeniable, but we must also recognize the disturbing realities of the present. There are over one million individuals who have serious mental illness warehoused in our nation's jails and prisons – many committed nonviolent crimes. A quarter-million more are homeless. Some of these individuals – and others – cannot care for themselves, they deny or are unaware of the severity of their illness, or they present a danger to themselves and others. In the

> *Journal of the American Medical Association*, we argued that for some of these seriously ill patients psychiatric asylum is warranted. (2016: 41)

The interplay between the perspectives of Neier and Rothman (2015), on one side, and Sisti and Ezekiel (2016), on the other, is interesting precisely because they are both right, in a sense. If we are willing to see the asylum not as a present-day manifestation of past horrors but instead as a space where intensive support can be provided to those whose needs cannot be met in the community, and if we are willing to admit that community-based programs are not always sufficiently supported, then there is no reason to have to choose one approach over the other. But Neier and Rothman ask us to do just this, asserting that community support – even if insufficient and plagued by systemic issues that have not been addressed – is always preferable to the intensive support that an asylum can provide.

Clearly, the two pairs of commentators seem to be focusing on two divergent populations while believing they are discussing the same issue. This is a discursive microcosm of how discussions about disability tend to unfold. Those with psychiatric health issues are not a homogeneous population for whom placement in either "the asylum" or "the community" can be recommended wholesale. These terms themselves are also constructs. How can one discuss the asylum or the community without knowledge of how personnel, resources, support, oversight, and methods of operation play into the experience of living in one place or the other? The asylum may be a historically questionable institution, but that does not mean that community services are sufficient to provide adequate care to all people living with psychiatric disability, which takes various forms and has various degrees of severity. In arguing over two polarized options without uncovering the social, spatial, and clinical relationships implicit in these terms, popular discourse and professional debate both fail to address the *material experience* of psychiatric disability and the *social construction* of psychiatric disability. Assuming that everyone can have their needs met in the community is just as problematic as assuming that everyone cannot. Of the populations who need either community-based or institution-based supports centred on psychiatric care, only the most able-minded populations – in addition to those with the most family and monetary supports – would clearly be able to exercise more of a choice. Not everyone has these advantages. In the current systems, some needs are unlikely to be met in the community without sufficient regulation and support through extensive health programming. Neier and Rothman's argument against the asylum is welcome to the extent that the institutional model has been forced even on those who would thrive with more autonomy in a community-based model. But the exaggerated form this argument takes in the article implies that the only populations worth considering in the asylum-versus-community debate tend to be more able-minded, on one hand, or more socially privileged, on the other.[4] From the perspective of a social model of disability that admits discussion of impairment as part of explorations of the material reality of cognitive disability experiences, there is no need to exclude any populations with psychiatric needs from consideration.

Understanding these general dynamics associated with models of both institutional and community-based care is important, for these issues are at the core of Abel García Roure's documentary film. Beyond these large-scale matters, *Una cierta verdad* also emphasizes the small-scale interactions between patients and providers. Specifically, the film illustrates the inadequacy of the clinical gaze when confronting health problems whose cause is not immediately visible. To chart how cognitive disabilities associated with the term madness have been historically invisible, we must turn to the work of Michel Foucault. There is perhaps no work as significant on the general topic as Foucault's labyrinthine *History of Madness* (2006),[5] which – together with *The Birth of the Clinic* (1994 [1972]), of course – traces the distinction between madness and reason as progressively produced through historical developments, discursive and material power structures, and both tangible and less tangible social institutions. Both *The Birth of the Clinic* and *The History of Madness* focus on the visibility of illness as well as the role played by vision in the modern clinical gaze; both also illustrate how this visible model has often ignored cognition completely. This has not meant that the experience of cognitive disability has enjoyed relative autonomy from ableist frameworks and patterns of medicalization. Instead, this transition towards a visible model of clinical practice has continued to influence our collective understanding of cognitive difference. It has done so by encouraging the primacy of the cognitively abled gaze and the essentialization of cognitive difference as an individual and not a collective problem.

In chapter 7 of *The Birth of the Clinic*, "Seeing and Knowing," Foucault writes about the historical shift from a linguistic (technical/aural) to a sensory (aesthetic/visual) form of clinical practice. This shift diminished the need for observation through language, through dialogue, through time and understanding, and replaced it with the possibility of a more immediate discovery of a truth that lay visible in the material world. Dialogue with the patient still had a place in the newer observational paradigm, but it was the visual that became primary with the arrival of the concept of pathological anatomy that came to displace dialogue. As Foucault explains, these historical developments

> freed medical perception from the play of essence and symptoms, and from the less ambiguous play of species and individuals: the figure disappeared by which the visible and invisible were pivoted in accordance with the principle that the patient both conceals and reveals the specificity of his disease. A domain of clear visibility was opened up to the gaze. (1994: 105)

Before this "domain of clear visibility was opened up to the gaze," interaction between the clinician and the patient was centred on narrative, exchange, touch, language, and the time needed for the "play of essence and symptoms" to unfold. Foucault suggests that this was a dialogic relationship where the visible and the invisible provided meaning in tandem and over time. The rise of the clinical gaze discussed and critiqued by Foucault is one where time was flattened into space, where sight substituted imperfectly for sound, and where the invisible was severed from its visible counterpart. In this paradigm, cognition was subjected to a paradigm of direct observation that was not favourable either to its nuance or to temporal unfolding.

Foucault elaborates on the questions that originally drove the clinical paradigm's transition from auditory and dialogic narrative towards visual and spatial observation:

> The theoretical and practical problem confronting the clinicians was to know whether it would be possible to introduce into a spatially legible and conceptually coherent representation that element in the disease that belongs to a visible symptomatology and that which belongs to a verbal analysis. The problem was revealed in a technical difficulty that was very revealing of the demands of clinical thinking: the *picture*. Is it possible to integrate into a picture, that is, into a structure that is at the same time visible and legible, spatial and verbal, that which is perceived on the surface of the body by the clinician's eye, and that which is heard by that same clinician in the essential language of the disease? (1994: 112, original emphasis)

As Foucault goes on to remark, however, there was little possibility of integrating the spatial and the verbal into a coherent picture. This balance between the visible and the legible, the spatial and the verbal, is a precarious one, for observation will always tip the scale towards what can be instantly seen. "The correlative of observation is never the invisible, but always the immediately visible," he writes (1994: 107). Clinical experience thus begins to attune itself more to "the visible and the expressible" (1994: 196) than to the invisible.[6]

Note that this historical and clinical shift towards the visible developed along with a push to make clinical practice more coherent and systematized. The portion of *History of Madness* subtitled "Doctors and Patients" (part 2, section IV) in particular engages that persistent, elusive, and ever-so-blurry notion of a "cure" for madness. At the same time, it explores the chaos and disorganization that were so central to an important prehistory of our modern clinical approaches and institutions. Therein Foucault writes:

> Medical thought and practice in the seventeenth and eighteenth centuries do not have the unity or at least the coherence that we presently associate with them. The world of the cure is organised along principles which are in a certain sense peculiar to it, and which medical theory, physiological analysis and even the observation of symptoms do not always control perfectly. We saw earlier how hospitalisation and internment were independent of medicine, but even within medicine itself, theory and therapy only communicate in an imperfect reciprocity. (2006: 297)

Even in this brief quotation there are a number of points of great relevance to contemporary representations of schizophrenia. Foucault highlights the inability of seventeenth- and eighteenth-century medicine to synthesize observable phenomena with knowledge. Historically speaking, there were gaps between theory and practice, just as "hospitalisation and internment were independent of medicine." The communication between these pairs was "imperfect," in Foucault's wording, and thus, one could also say, insufficient. In this context, the notion of a "cure" can be seen as a manifestation of the dream of a precision that clinical practice itself is lacking, the idea of establishing a link between theory and therapy. One can argue that, still in contemporary times, the notion of a "cure" for madness is a discursive mirror for the inadequacy of the priority given to the visible world by the clinical gaze to impact treatment of less visible cognitive impairments.[7]

The questions posed by aesthetic/cultural representations of schizophrenia in disability cinema resonate with contemporary studies of psychiatric disability and have the potential to reveal just as much about our disabling social environment as do other areas of this growing interdisciplinary field. Since 2000, significant work on cognitive disability has indeed been published.[8] Yet on the whole, the literature on psychiatric disability written from a disability studies perspective – that is, understanding the latter as a paradigm that prioritizes the disabling character of the social environment – has tended to be eclipsed by medical approaches that essentialize disability and situate it ontologically inside the disabled body (and here, simultaneously within the disabled mind). At the same time that scholars in Anglophone disability studies have been calling for a more global and international approach (Mitchell and Snyder 2010; Murray and Barker 2010), studies of disability cinema in Spain have been steadily expanding as if in response to that call. With regard to disability studies centring on Spain, there is a long-standing filmic tradition of disabled characters in cinema, but those films have yet to be analysed from a disability studies perspective.[9] *Una cierta verdad* is not the only twenty-first-century film to address disability in Spain, of course, but since its debut in 2008, its message has yet to be fully appreciated. Notably, though interviews with the director abound and though the film is sporadically mentioned in research of a wider scope, not a single scholarly article has explored *Una cierta verdad* in depth.

Before analysing García Roure's film, let us briefly consider other representations of schizophrenia that have received attention in Spain. In particular, it will be helpful to think through how schizophrenia was presented in an informational documentary in order to understand just what *Una cierta verdad* achieves with greater artistry. In some sense tied to the explanatory and didactic impulse prevalent in both documentary and fiction films centring on disability (see Mitchell and Snyder 2016: 22), *1% esquizofrenia* (2006) by Ione Hernández was widely screened in Spain. Not insignificantly, noted filmmaker Julio Medem is also listed as a director, and the film's production company is Alicia Produce, named after Medem's daughter, who has Down syndrome. I use the term informational to describe this film because it is not a narrative documentary of the sort that follows one or more characters through their everyday activities, but rather a series of interviews strung together, all focusing on the topic of schizophrenia.

Given the relative invisibility of cognitive disability, the general public might well benefit from being introduced to people who are faced with it. Claudia Merlo responds precisely to the need to correct for this social invisibility when she writes of the documentary that

> su merito está en invitar al espectador a un acercamiento hacia un tema, velado muchas veces por el misterio y lo desconocido, superando estigmas y prejuicios y ofreciendo la posibilidad de compartir las experiencias dolorosas y profundamente humanas de las personas que presentan este trastorno mental.

> Its merit lies in inviting the spectator to move closer toward a theme that is many times clouded in mystery and the unknown, overcoming stigmas and prejudices, offering the possibility of sharing in the painful and profoundly human experiences of the persons who exhibit this mental disorder. (2009: 80)

Over the course of more than an hour, the densely compacted interview segments of *1% esquizofrenia* frame the question of schizophrenia from biological/genetic, clinical/psychological, and social/environmental perspectives. A number of the interviews bring attention to and criticize the social marginality associated with experiences of schizophrenia. Ione Hernández herself has been quoted as saying that if persons with schizophrenia are ill, "entonces yo llamaría enfermos a todos los que habitamos en este planeta [I would then call all of us living on this planet ill]" (qtd in Quintanilla 2007).[10] Clearly, the documentary's intention is to move beyond merely rendering experiences of schizophrenia visible and to advocate strongly for the social acceptance and understanding of schizophrenia. In a certain sense, it succeeds. Yet what is ultimately lacking in the film is an artistic sensibility that would reinforce the trenchant critiques voiced by some of its interviewees and render its message with greater coherence. Such an artistic sensibility would provide a clear path for viewers seeking to make sense of the wide variety of opinions expressed in the film, some of which trend too far towards the purely medical/clinical pole and do not acknowledge the importance of both defining schizophrenia and supporting experiences of it in societal terms.

The film is structured according to themes rather than an overarching narrative. This allows the presentation of a wide range of views on interconnected subjects: "miedo [fear]" (6:38); "muros invisibles [invisible walls]" (9:57); "familia [family]" (12:09); "drogas [drugs]" (20:20); "delirio [delirium]" (24:00); "flüidos [fluids]" (31:46); "agresión [agression]" (35:32); "ingreso [admission]"; (37:26)" "suicidio [suicide]" (41:18); "arte y locura [art and madness]"; "tratamiento [treatment]" (49:25); "tiempo [time]" (55:52); "psicoterapia [psychotherapy]" (58:12); "esperanza [hope]" (1:01:48); "mañana [tomorrow]" (1:04:33); "el uno por ciento [the one percent]" (1:05:57). The basic frame composition of *1% esquizofrenia* sets up a battle of voices in rather stark and binary terms: when viewers see segments of interviews with doctors, clinicians, therapists, family members, and allies and advocates, these figures are located on the left side of the screen, while the segments of interviews with schizophrenics tend to be screened with those figures positioned on the right side of the screen. This simplistic set-up is problematic for two reasons: first, it tends to visually isolate those with schizophrenia from their support systems and allies, thus formally recapitulating the social isolation associated with experiences of disability in an ableist society; and second, this dichotomy obscures the vast differences of opinion reflected in the heterogeneous messages of those placed on the left side. This group includes those who talk about "curing" schizophrenia (see 1:02:00–1:03:00); those who unapologetically embrace a strictly biochemical and/or pharmacological approach, in the process denigrating the value of psycho/social approaches; those who accept that pharmacology has a role in treatment but who criticize how it is employed and overemphasized; those who debunk the myth that overstates the risk and reality of schizophrenic violence; and those who strongly critique patterns of social marginalization as well as the lack of social and community supports available to schizophrenic patients.[11] The strong medical standpoint, for example, is expressed by a white-robed clinician (50:18) who insists that mental illness will be cured biochemically or pharmacologically. But another interviewee positioned on the left complains that pharmacology only makes symptoms go away and critiques society for thinking it is solving a problem by merely getting rid of symptoms it sees as undesirable (52:00). Some viewers may be disappointed that the distance between these two viewpoints is not definitively resolved in the film either through the content of the interviews or by their arrangement during post-production editing. In effect, the intent to express a variety of opinions has outweighed the need for a more consistent critique of the purely medicalized approach to treating schizophrenia.

While the film is strongly centred on the verbal content and emotive expression of interviews conducted during the filmic process, the impact of decisions made regarding artistic images and music during post-production cannot be ignored. It is fair to say that these decisions contribute to the film's lack of a clear point of view regarding the social treatment of schizophrenia. The film's background music, largely consisting of strings and piano, is variously haunting, disturbing, and moving – dramatically expressing dark feelings, depression, resignation, transcendence, and even hope. Early in the film, this music is used mostly across interview transitions, but as the film advances, and particularly as it reaches its conclusion, it is increasingly used during interview segments. With its dynamic crescendos and emotional weight, the music contributes to a spectacular image of schizophrenia, exceptionalizing it and marking it as non-normative rather than underscoring the everyday experience of those who live with it. In addition, highly evocative visual images of questionable relevance are used intermittently throughout the film. Though this may not be the director's intention, these images effectively "other" experiences of schizophrenia in that they provide loaded visual metaphors for risks and dangers, emotional peaks and valleys, mystery and enigma – all of which reflect how the ableist imagination typically perceives mental disorder.

For example, the film's first image is a blurry one of a curtain blowing with the breeze through an open window and featuring this quotation: "Nos hemos dado cuenta de que hay unos muros invisibles, no son las tapias del manicomio, pero metafóricamente es un muro más sutil y por tanto mucho más difícil de romper [We have realized that there are invisible walls, they are not the walls of the mental institution, but metaphorically it is a much more subtle wall and therefore it is much more difficult to break]" (0:08). Walls, windows, and doors become the film's key metaphors of isolation. These suggest restricted access to another world; they also essentialize the normative distinction between experiences of schizophrenia and experiences of able-mindedness, even when their use creates a friction with interview content launching a strong critique of clinical practice.

Beginning with the very first image, then, visual and architectural references to the space of the mental institution become primary symbols in the aesthetics of *1% esquizofrenia*. Through their visual excess and recurrent abundance, these images of walls, windows, and doors metonymically recall imagined and/or real experiences of the asylum. We see a number of shots and zooms involving windows (0:02:40, 3:13, 4:28, 1:01:48, 1:02:18, 1:03:00, 1:03:29), mobile frames capturing hallways and doors (4:46, 5:06, 6:38, 7:16, 7:53, 24:00), and pans of institutional rooms (37:21, 38:11, 38:56; 40:43), as well as hospital gurneys in movement (42:10, 42:54). Though the film's images may soon transition to exteriors – buildings, playgrounds, and the like (9:16, 9:58, 11:40, 12:09, 15:54) – it is significant that those exteriors include ambulance rides (41:24, 41:48) and dark tunnels (26:40, 27:15, 27:50) or symbols of danger or clouded thought – lightning strikes seen at a great distance (21:45, 22:57, 23:11), or clouds (55:50, 56:28, 1:05:57). These image selections convey an impulse to treat the topic dynamically. Given their metaphorical weight, however – that is, the sense of isolation conveyed by walls and windows, or the danger and enigma implied by lightning, clouds, and darkness – they also ground viewer expectations in the architectural logic of the institution, in the imprecision of the clinical gaze, in the archaeological symbolism of excavation and discovery, and thus also in the transcendent yet mythic finality of light and revelation – and thus also of "cure." When we do see a human figure it is either a partial or a fragmented view – as in the close-ups of a person's forehead (29:00, 29:34; 30:58) or of a person's eye (1:06:04, 1:07:05, 1:07:23, 1:07:47, 1:07:54, 1:08:13). This fragments the individual visually and subjects his or her form to metaphorical violence through cinematic language.[12]

It is easy to see how these images reaffirm the sort of conclusion that Neier and Rothman make all too easily in their *NYRB* essay. The documentary film's haunting music, the stock architectural images that symbolize the asylum, the gradual progression from interior to exterior worlds, and ultimately the appearance of a street scene teeming with people, function together to implicitly launch an aesthetic critique of the historical conditions associated with confinement in a mental institution. Yet just as it is in Neier and Rothman's article, this argument is facile because it grapples only with the issue of confinement and not with the issue of social and community supports. This more nuanced question regarding the tension between coercive institutional power and inadequate community-based support is precisely what takes centre stage in García Roure's film, discussed in the next section.

For some viewers of *1% esquizofrenia*, there is a risk that the admittedly dramatic aesthetic decisions discussed above may come to obscure issues most worthy of exploration. At stake here is the conflict evident in Foucault's history of clinical practice, where he charts the decline of narrative as a primary way of approaching illness. As one of the film's schizophrenic interviewees states matter-of-factly: "Es más fácil dar una pastilla y anularte que estar una hora contigo hablando intendando saber cuál es el problema que tienes, ¿no? [It is easier to give you a pill and knock you out than it is to spend an hour talking with you, trying to find out what the problem is, you know?]" (53:03). It is important that early in the film, one of the interviewees delivers a concise defence of a patient-centred point of view – "Los que mejor conocen nuestra enfermedad somos nosotros mismos [We are the ones who best know our illness]" (2:55) – and an advocate affirms a central tenet of the social approach – "Más de personas enfermas son personas vulnerables [Rather than ill people they are vulnerable people]" (4:42).[13] But these positions are gradually complicated as clinical and medical points of view compete for the viewer's attention with social approaches to schizophrenia. The film's overly conventional and facile critique of the horrors of institutions and the ills of forcibly interning schizophrenic patients in hospitals (39:00) have to contend with white-robed voices of clinical power who affirm schizophrenia as the "prototipo de lo que se llama loco [prototype of what is termed crazy]" (4:00) and with those who advocate biochemical and pharmacological "cures" for schizophrenia – and all this in a situation where, as one interviewee puts it, "no sabemos todavía lo que es [we still do not know what it (schizophrenia) is]" (4:58). In the end, even though *1% esquizofrenia* is a welcome attempt to bring greater social visibility to experiences of schizophrenia, its engagement with traditional associations – the tropes of mystery and enigma in particular, as highlighted in Claudia Merlo's comment – risks playing into heavily circulated representations of schizophrenia in popular culture.[14] By contrast, Abel García Roure's film stakes out a much more nuanced position and is thus better able to recognize the material reality of cognitive impairment while sustaining a focus on cognitive disability as expressing a social relationship.

Representing Schizophrenia in *Una cierta verdad* (A Certain Truth) (2008)

A compelling portrayal of the individual experience of schizophrenia, a denunciation of the brutality that systematically accompanies its medical treatment, and perhaps something of an apology for our collective failure to bridge the distance between the cognitively abled and those living with this psychiatric disability – Abel García Roure's *Una cierta verdad* (A Certain Truth) (2008) is all of these things. What García Roure does so well in the film – something that was counteracted in *1% esquizofrenia* by its aesthetic decisions, from music and visuals to editing and post-production – is acknowledge the reality of severe cognitive impairment without spectacularizing schizophrenia.

Director Abel García Roure (Barcelona, 1975) studied filmmaking with Joaquim Jordà at the Universitat Pompeu Fabra de Barcelona. Among his other accomplishments, he was assistant director on the films *En construcción* (Work in Progress) (2000, dir. José Luis Guerín) and *El cielo gira* (The Sky Turns) (2004, dir. Mercedes Álvarez). *Una cierta verdad*, his first long-form cinematic product, is a highly nuanced documentary prioritizing the interplay between the film's two privileged groups: providers and patients. The battle of voices we watch unfold on-screen, then, is not constituted by the medicalized self-talk of the person with schizophrenia;[15] rather, it is constituted by a social dialogue between these two polarized groups of actors.

This dialogue – one that is simultaneously clinical and social – is pushed forward by two sets of goals that differ so strongly that conflict is unavoidable. To put this into terms that are far too stark to match the director's perspective, but that illustrate the crux of the matter nonetheless: providers focus on the disease, abstracting it from the patient, who becomes a mere residue or afterthought; whereas patients yearn for a quality of life whose elusiveness is frequently compounded by the imprecise doses or debilitating effects of the medications they are forced to suffer. The potential resolution of this conflict seemingly lies outside of the clinical institutions into which we are drawn along with these necessarily social actors. The film suggests that the clinical paradigm's low tolerance for nuance and lack of precise tools is what perpetuates this ongoing battle of voices. The resulting picture emphasizes that schizophrenia is a psychiatric disability experience involving biological/material elements that must be understood simultaneously in social terms. All of this foregrounds the need for medical and social models of disability to find a common ground.

The release of *Una cierta verdad* in 2008 is best understood as part of a longer history of attempts to draw attention to the needs of people with schizophrenia. *1% esquizofrenia* was a high-profile attempt to draw attention to this psychiatric disability and to the social dynamics implicated in its post-Transition treatment. But it is equally important to acknowledge that contributions to that longer history have also come from the psycho-social and clinical-medical spheres. The Transition towards democracy in Spain that followed the death of dictator Francisco Franco on 20 November 1975 offered new opportunities to address mental health issues through community frameworks, but it also created new hurdles:

> The development of a system of comprehensive community services and the deinstitutionalization process started in Barcelona at the beginning of the 1980s ... Before deinstitutionalization, patients with severe schizophrenia lived in hospitals and most of their basic needs were met by the institutions. Nowadays in Spain, with admission to long-stay inpatient units very uncommon, patients live in the community. (Ochoa et al. 2003: 201, 202)

Another highly relevant study from 2001 found that patients in Catalonia continued to face insufficient access to community-based psychiatric services (Duñó et al. 2001: 688).[16] In addition, it must be considered that people with schizophrenia living in the community have needs that are not always seen in the same way by the patients themselves and by outpatient program staff. Help with symptoms of psychosis was the most frequent need identified by patients taking part in the above study (Ochoa et al. 2003: 206). Yet patients and staff reported only the relatively low rating of "fair agreement" on needs regarding drugs and psychotic symptoms (Ochoa et al. 2003: 205).[17] Another Spanish research study validated the concerns expressed by some that antipsychotic drugs carry additional health risks that are not fully understood (Bobes et al. 2007: 171).[18] Cultural products have worked to bring these interrelated issues concerning treatment for schizophrenia to the forefront of public discourse. Such discourse – inclusive of García Roure's film and contrasted with specialized research articles – has the benefit of reaching a much wider audience.

Compared to Hernández and Medem's film, *Una cierta verdad* is a much more challenging cinematic text. This is, in part, because it raises important questions regarding the role patients take in directing their treatment – the social inequity that compels them, through threat of violence and in fact through brute force, to accept medications with debilitating side effects whose risks are not completely understood. More importantly, given the significance of aesthetics/culture when approaching cognitive disabilities, which have tended to be invisible in society, *Una cierta verdad*'s artistic composition and narrative structure require more of viewers. Though García Roure's film is a documentary, the shots captured, camera positions, editing and pacing, costuming, and prop symbolism all play a role in emphasizing the limitations of a contemporary clinical paradigm whose current approach to schizophrenia relies more on power than on knowledge, more on force than on precision.

As a way of underscoring *Una cierta verdad*'s contribution to a "new disability documentary cinema" (Snyder and Mitchell 2010) – a cinema whose value, I argue, lies in part in that it focuses through iconic/indexical signification on "real people" as a way of rendering cognitive disability visible – I want to spend time introducing readers to its major characters and enduring patient–provider conflicts. Along the way, I ask readers to keep in mind wider issues already discussed, not merely the historical separation between madness and reason but also the global turn in disability studies and the representation of cognitive disability in Iberian film. I emphasize García Roure's social commitment, introduce the documentary's major protagonists, and continue to assert the imprecision of psychiatric clinical practice as a major theme. Next I prioritize the visual narrative's spatial dimensions. The Parc Taulí hospital in Sabadell (Barcelona) is portrayed as the site of an emanating material and discursive power that impacts patients far beyond its walls. Finally, I return to the film's title and to its closing sequence, which drives home the central insight and social commitment of the director's captivating cinematic essay.

Whether we understand schizophrenia as mental illness, a cognitive disability, or both at once, Foucault's work on madness and the clinic (discussed in the previous section) can shed light on *Una cierta verdad*'s critique of contemporary clinical practice. Foucault's description of what readers may want to see as a historical age gone by seems to echo visually throughout the documentary. For example, the first set of images in the film encapsulates its central critique: that the clinical gaze is imprecise. From 0:00:02 until 0:00:43 – after a fade-in from black – a blurry security-camera monitor displays patients seated in the hospital waiting area (see also 0:16:14–0:16:31; 1:05:16–1:05:20; 1:05:35–1:05:43). Horizontal two-tone bars obscure their images at the same time that they mediate those images for us. Simultaneously, for viewers, this enacts a connection and a distancing. Almost as a reminder of the Foucauldian critique of the medical gaze, these and the other monitor-images that reoccur throughout the documentary become powerful symbols of the persisting imprecise nature of contemporary clinical thought and practice, which relies all too much on what is immediately visible.

García Roure also uses this blurry display monitor as a way of symbolizing the thin line between reason and madness – certainly a hallmark theme of cultural production in Spain going back to the Quijote.[19] It can be difficult to distinguish, for example, just who is mad and who

6.1: Blurry monitor feed from *Una cierta verdad* (2008), Evohé Films, S.L., Corporació Catalana de Mitjans Àudiovisuals, S.A. y Vértice Cine, S.L.

is sane when both are caught up in complicating social power struggles. In social reality, as with Cervantes's protagonists, both the patients and the providers in *Una cierta verdad* are well-matched counterparts: though it is possible for patients with severe impairments to suffer infrequent episodes of psychosis with consequences for themselves and for others, they seek the better quality of life they experience when not taking imprecisely dosed meds that force them into slumber.[20] Though some providers may have the best interests of patients at heart,[21] these frequently conflict with the best interests of society or of clinical practice, which prefers patient slumber and turns all too easily towards the use of brute force. These options are extreme ones, to be sure, but admitting that treatment for severe psychiatric illness must extend beyond the walls of the institution for those living in the community, contemporary clinical practice has struggled to find sustainable social solutions outside of this polarized conundrum. Beyond merely symbolizing social distance and hazy solutions, then, the decision to draw viewer attention to the monitor feed additionally signals that social and medical power only moves in one direction: the patient is the object of clinical observation, itself an imprecise instrument.

The inevitable result of imprecise observation is that the provider's intent to arrive at the "truth" of disease leads intermittently to the blunt instrument of forced medication (see Valverde 2010: 8). Hovering over the patients we see in the documentary is the threat of force, marshalled by social institutions and meted out in imprecise doses. One key difference between the historical context explored by Foucault in *History of Madness* and *The Birth of the Clinic*, on one hand, and its restaging in contemporary form, on the other, seems to be the integration of the hospital and medicine, or rather, the complication regarding or even the collapse of their independence. If we follow the director's suggestion, the contemporary hospital as an institution has not brought control, unity, or organization to the treatment of madness but instead additional chaos, confusion, and imperfection. A primary concern of *Una cierta verdad*, then, is to represent this imperfection and the impact it has on the lives of the patients García Roure followed for two years while making the film.

As viewers should expect, *Una cierta verdad* functions as a decidedly non-spectacular window onto the textures of everyday experience for people living with schizophrenia.[22] The director has stated that his intention was to provide a more even treatment of the theme of psychosis than one usually finds in media representations:

> He partido de la idea de que hay un estigma muy fuerte respecto al tema; tras analizar la aproximación que se ha hecho desde el cine a la psicosis [trastorno mental en el que se incluye la esquizofrenia y la paranoia], o bien excesivamente romántica, o bien marcadamente antipsiquiátrica, he tratado de iluminar el tema desde la experiencia real del enfermo, de su relación con la enfermedad, explicar su sufrimiento, y contar las distintas evoluciones que puede tener. (de la Rosa 2007)

> I began with the idea that there is a very strong stigma about it; after analyzing how cinema has approached psychosis (a type of mental disturbance that includes schizophrenia and paranoia) either from an excessively romanticized or a markedly anti-psychiatric viewpoint, I tried to shed light on the topic from the real experience of the patients, of their relation with the illness, to explain their suffering, and to portray the different paths it can take.

In another interview, García Roure describes his own perspective as "humana [human]," "cotidiana [everyday]," and "íntima [intimate]"

(Vázquez 2009: 18). There is, of course, a strong link between the clinical paradigm and the cinema – both are grounded in the practice of observation. The cinematic window provided by the director, however, is midway between that of clinical observation and that of patient experience, regarding which the film remains neither fully committed nor fully dismissive.[23]

Because it presents both aural and visual data, cinema here is a perfect vehicle for exploring the superimposition of two historical stages in the evolution of the clinical paradigm as captured by Foucault. As mentioned earlier, *The Birth of the Clinic* explores the historical shift from a linguistic (technical/aural) to a sensory (aesthetic/visual) form of clinical practice, cataloguing how a "domain of clear visibility was opened up to the gaze" (1994: 105). In this new domain the relative importance of dialogue with the patient was reduced and the visual became primary. These historical developments in pathological anatomy diminished the need for observation through language, through dialogue, through time and understanding, and replaced it with the possibility of a more immediate discovery of a truth, one that was visible in the material world. As a film very much concerned with a psychiatric illness whose expression is still not immediately visible, *Una cierta verdad* screens the inadequacies of the modern practice of psychiatry as it tries to navigate the superimposed paradigms of linguistic/discursive/temporal and visible/sensory/spatial truth. Unable to ground itself purely in the "domain of clear visibility" opened up by the modern clinical gaze, its investigation of the relatively invisible realm of the mind must rely more on an older model of spoken probing, a questioning of the patient through dialogue, rather than on newer forms of clinical practice that potentially unite the visible and the expressible.[24] The film works to draw attention to and even renew (through film form) this central character of psychiatric practice – that it is a narrative and dialogic art just as much as it is a science. García Roure draws us into the interplay of language and power at the heart of this clinical practice, staging for us the sustained and battling voices with which any provider and patient are familiar. While the providers use the clinical gaze to assess their patients, we as viewers of the documentary film are able to engage what Rosemarie Garland-Thomson (2009) calls the generative potential of staring by spending significant time with them.

The film's setting is a teaching hospital, not a mental institution in the classical sense, so unlike the protagonists of Jordà's *Monos como Becky* (1999), for example, *Una cierta verdad*'s social actors are community members who require intermittent rather than continual observation. It is tempting here, as with many documentaries, to presume that there is no point of view – that this documentary film is merely an objective window onto human experience.[25] But make no mistake: here, too – just as in the films of García Roure's mentor Jordà – we have an expressly social commitment on the part of the director.[26] One scholar has indicated that the film is implicated in a tradition of cultural production dedicated to "elimina[ndo] los tabúes existentes y la imagen siniestra de la enfermedad [eliminating the existing taboos and the sinister image of the illness]" (Real-Najarro 2011: 184). This commitment is expressed through attempts to push viewers to adopt a different subjective experience of the world than their own.[27] The frequency of camerawork that lingers on windows and doorways, combined with footage of security monitors, reinforces this theme of *how* we look – of what and who we see when we observe (stare at) people with mental illness. Together with the persistent appearance of the interstitial institutional corridors we traverse with the camera crew and hospital staff, this emphasis suggests the importance of positioning and perspective – where it is we look *from*, and how viewers who might tend to be both cognitively abled and relatively unfamiliar with health care institutions will access these patient stories, and whether some level of understanding can be reached through visual representation.

Perhaps the key protagonist of the film is Javier Sánchez (age fifty-eight), who lives on his own in the community. Javier receives visits from Josep Manel Santos, a psychologist with the hospital's PSI (Plan de Seguimiento Individualizado [Plan of Individualized Support]) outpatient program. Their discussions range over topics of personal, artistic, philosophical, intellectual, and medical interest – and over the indoor spaces of his apartment and various outdoor spaces presumably near his residence – in the course of which a struggle gradually emerges as the pair's opinions increasingly diverge concerning the downside of imprecisely prescribed medication and the value of the energy, creativity, and autonomy Javier enjoys when not on his currently prescribed dosage. Eventually, Javier is forcibly interned for observation. Viewers watch as he is abruptly brought by police from his apartment to the Parc Taulí, the teaching hospital of the Universitat Autònoma de Barcelona. Another key patient, Rosario Hernández Manzano, insists that she is bewitched and that she is only able to speak of the voice in her head when receiving prescriptions at her hospital appointment. Javier's scenes are dialogic and conversational; Rosario's filmed appearances tend more towards confessional monologues. In their appearances in the documentary, Javier and Rosario show clear symptoms of schizophrenia and paranoia; a third protagonist, Bernat Pérez Acero, is more lucid and thus provides a third, less immediately turbulent model of patient–provider interactions.[28]

We never learn much about one of the film's patient-protagonists. Alberto is the first to appear after the opening sequences and is systematically distanced from viewing audiences beginning with his arrival at the emergency clinic at the Taulí. But he is crucial to the film's message nonetheless. He hardly speaks when questioned by Dr Agustín, and when he does speak, it is in short phrases delivered in a volume barely above a whisper (0:04:31–0:04:58; 0:05:30–0:06:24; 0:06:39–0:07:00).[29] We never clearly see his face. Instead, the camera shoots him from behind when in the same room or from the hallway when outside a room; he is regularly captured shrouded in his hoodie, isolating himself in the sounds emanating from his earphones (e.g., in a long shot where passers-by obstruct our view of him from 0:09:16–0:09:21; see also 0:56:19). In one particularly uncomfortable scene, viewers are embedded with five hospital staff, who step into what viewers may reasonably presume is Alberto's room to force his meds on him. With hoodie over his head and earphones plugged in, he stares out of a window. The event's efficiency and brutality follow logically from the inadequate dialogue between the provider and the patient. During the operation, which is over as quickly as it begins, the camera hovers in the hallway, peering into the room as it captures the interned patient in a long shot that reaffirms his simultaneously medical and social marginalization.

The fact that we have no early or sustained access to Alberto's face[30] is a clear expression of the director's vision, which is to move gradually from a medicalized to a social view of schizophrenia. It has been observed elsewhere that the film's narrative arc is structured by two moments: in the first, the doctors are privileged and the patients are marginalized; in the second, the focus shifts away from the doctors towards humanizing the patients:

> En este primer segmento de la película, los protagonistas son indiscutiblemente los médicos (o más bien, la institución médica), puesto que Roure les confiere un rostro y una presencia definida, mientras que los pacientes son presentados como grupo, no con como individuos, desprovistos de un rostro que los singularice ... Este primer planteamiento de la película se disipa al iniciarse el segundo segmento puesto que Roure empieza a

> introducirnos en las historias personales de tres pacientes que padecen diversos grados de psicosis (esquizofrenia, paranoia, etc.). En esta parte los enfermos empiezan a tener rostro, a ser visibles, y a singularizarse delante de la cámara. (Petrus 2009)
>
> In this first segment of the film, the protagonists are unquestioningly the doctors (or better said, the medical institution), given that Roure gives them a face and a defined presence, while the patients are presented as a group, not as individuals, deprived of a face that might individualize them ... This [character of the] first part of the film evaporates with the beginning of the second segment given that Roure begins to introduce us to the personal histories of three patients who suffer varying degrees of psychosis (schizophrenia, paranoia, etc.). In this part the patients begin to have a face, to become visible, and to individualize themselves before the camera.

The director clearly prefers to represent each side of this social battle through a multiplicity of voices, such that the effect is one of two competing "teams," each with its own set of messages.[31] These teams – of doctors on one side and patients on the other – are placed in dialogue with each other throughout the film, even up through the beginning of the end credits. Interestingly, the editing of the film privileges the cut, using cross-cutting as a pervasive technique[32] to emphasize the dialogic nature of the clinical enterprise and often as a way of breaking these dialogues up strategically. In one case, as Javier's logic becomes recognizably schizophrenic, the film cuts to a psychiatrist's concise description of the disease; in another case, the cut comes just as Javier has made a lucid critique of the forced and imprecise medicalization of people with schizophrenia, potentially emphasizing the power of this words.[33] As the film makes clear, there is an inequity in how the distance between patients and providers is resolved socially.

Note that *Una cierta verdad*'s gradual shift towards privileging patient experiences (the progression towards patient narration identified above) occurs along with a clear shift in the spatial exposition of the film. The primary anchor for the film's often competing and certainly overlapping perspectives is the physical and clinical environment of the Taulí. The hospital appears as an exterior in *Una cierta verdad*'s first scene, one that is echoed throughout the film as we repeatedly cross the building's threshold (e.g. 0:55:44; 1:41:32); it is captured from within in the first of the two cinematic movements identified above; and it is progressively overshadowed as the director spends more time with patients in the community during the second half of the film.

The disparity in how patients and providers enter the Taulí becomes a metaphor for access to power. Patients are brought in by ambulance, or they enter through the emergency waiting room, where the camera and editing repeatedly frame them as outsiders with little access to the power structure represented by the inner core of the hospital. As patients wait in the entry area, we routinely observe them from inside the provider area; we peer out at them through automated glass doorways and glass walls via long shots that identify them with the outside and ensure that their figures are small on the screen, as if a metaphor for their lack of both clinical and social power. Also significant is how both doctors and patients are shot in the film in relation to the hospital space. While the film's main patient-protagonists are shot both inside and outside the hospital (Rosario, walking during the day, riding the bus, walking at dusk; Javier at a variety of times and in numerous settings), its doctors are shot purely inside the walls of the Taulí. Thus they appear to us as manifestations of its material environment or internal architecture, and become synonymous with the clinical gaze. They are unable to observe the patients in their own environments, and by implication they may be less likely to imagine the patients as autonomous human beings. The exception is the liminal figure Josep Manel, whom we see both inside and outside the hospital. At around the 0:22:11-minute mark, a figure that appears to be Josep enters the Taulí through what comes off as a secret passage into the very heart of the hospital. The use of a tracking shot for this method of entry is in marked contrast to the cut-based transitions from exterior to interior scenes usually employed in the documentary. That is, we never visually accompany protagonists such as the patients Javier and Rosario as they enter or exit the hospital; in this way, the film effects a separation between the treatment they are able to receive in the community and what goes on inside the Taulí.

Javier's story is by far the most compelling in *Una cierta verdad*, and the considerable time he spends in or near his own apartment speaking with Josep is the film's emotional and critical core. Their conversations form a thin connecting thread linking the discursive and material power of the hospital with the lives of people with schizophrenia living in the community. As the film traces that thread, it illustrates both the reach of clinical power and the limits of its reasoning. At one crucial point, an interesting use of editing connects the extramural interactions between Javier and Josep with a cinematic metaphor. After

Javier expounds his "ideas sobre la cohesión de la material [ideas on the cohesion of matter]" (0:37:21), showing Josep two pieces of art he has made that illustrate vectors emanating from a cube and a sphere, the editing cuts from interactions in Javier's home to shots of information travelling through a pneumatic tube in the hospital (0:38:27–0:38:43). These shots are static, and capture the parcel at various moments during its passage through the pneumatic tubing. The editing between the cuts is such that the relationship between each static shot and the next obscures any sense of directionality or of the totality of the tubing system. As viewers we cannot connect one section of tubing with any of the others.

There is a dual meaning to the cut that takes us from this patient's home to the hospital. The criss-crossing sections of pneumatic tubing can be seen as a clear clinical metaphor for signals in the brain of a schizophrenic patient that are disrupted and prone to crisis.[34] But this sequence is also a clear metaphor for the imprecision of clinical observation – the information of the pneumatic tube system that viewers glean visually from these shots is necessarily incomplete. One cannot form an impression of how the complete system works solely from vision. Both these possible interpretations exist simultaneously, reinforcing the theme of polarized actors who appear as battling voices. The dual message is this: Javier's psychiatric disability creates symptoms that need to be addressed, and the imprecision of clinical observation and the blunt instrument of medication cannot take the place of more sustainable social solutions.

What the extramural conversations between Josep and Javier reveal most, as they take up a greater part of the film's duration in the second half, is the ineffectiveness of the communication between the two. Within a concise period of time, Javier makes a number of important declarations to his assigned outreach psychiatry contact that are, in reality, repetitions of previous conversations. Javier expresses the importance of his attempt to get better and says that his life would be more meaningful if he only had time to do some drawings (1:15:20). He worries about the side effects of medications, stating the possibility that patients can be prescribed meds that can cause a stroke (1:15:50). Josep crafts and sustains clunky metaphors for Javier's need to submit to internment despite the fact that he has not done anything (e.g., to paraphrase Josep's comments: a car needs to be fixed routinely or they take it away), to which Javier responds either with reluctant and resigned loud sighs or with attempts at playful banter that address the car

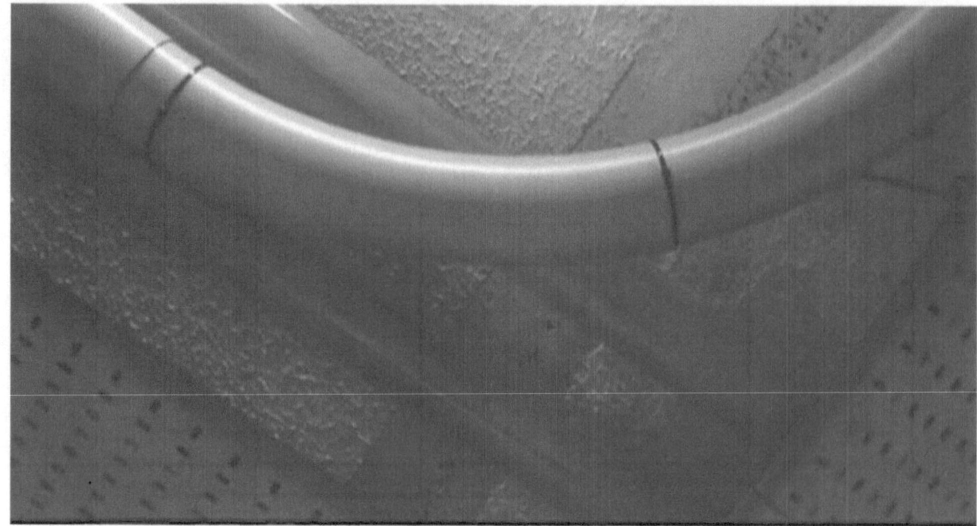

6.2: Tubing from *Una cierta verdad* (2008), Evohé Films, S.L., Corporació Catalana de Mitjans Àudiovisuals, S.A. y Vértice Cine, S.L.

metaphor but return to the issue of his quality of life. Javier puts it most accurately and lucidly when he admits there is a distance between the pair's divergent goals: "Tú tienes tu idea, yo tengo la mía [You have your idea, and I have mine]" (1:14:50). Josep's sole concern throughout seems to be to underscore the power the hospital has to intern Javier, not to address his concerns. The link between the hospital and the community liaison program ends up being characterized by control, not by communication.[35] The conversation between Javier and Josep is similar to those the former has with psychiatrists in the Taulí: he has the same concerns, the providers have the same answers, and he is not being heard. Whether inside or outside the hospital, the social battle is always tilted towards the side of clinical power.

Returning to the historical insights discussed by Foucault, it can be said that psychiatry perpetuates a much older clinical paradigm than does pathological anatomy, one that lacks precise instruments for diagnosis, treatment, and cure, and one in which the lack of meaningful dialogue between provider and patient recapitulates the irreconcilable gap between what is observed and what is known, between spoken and observed truths. The only middle ground that can be inhabited, one that García Roure's film presents for all to see, is clothed in the half-light of necessarily partial truths. Exploring this murky terrain, without the ability to establish and sustain effective resources for patients living in the community, contemporary psychiatry inevitably fails in its goal to cleanly isolate elements of schizophrenia and abstract them from the total person. The only options available to this confused and still primitive practice are clinical imprecision and the ever-present threat of violence.

Abel García Roure's documentary resolves the questions that originally drove the clinical paradigm's transition from audio and dialogic narrative towards visual and spatial observation as identified by Foucault (1994: 112). The film accomplishes this through the nuances of artistic form, expanding the concerns of the clinical paradigm to implicate the whole of social practice. We must keep in mind Foucault's suggestion that any balance between the visible and the legible, the spatial and the verbal, is more of a dream than a reality.[36] Facing the difficulty of observing psychiatric disability visually/spatially, and with little time and resources to put into language, narrative, and listening to patients on their own terms, the Taulí is forced into a poor solution. The result is a disproportionate emphasis on the quick fix of forced facility admission and of forced medication in imprecise doses. It may be a dream for clinical practice to balance the visible and the legible, but it seems that in a sense García Roure's cinematic essay has been able to make this an artistic reality.

The last words of the film – voiced by Javier, who in the final sequence becomes unquestioningly its central character – are a punctuating call to arms. A psychiatrist inquires more than once into the origins of Javier's schizophrenia – which he connects with a time during which he is beginning to think that his children are not his own – and when she suggests to him that this "es una inquietud, ¿no? [that is an anxiety]," he responds tellingly, "o, una cierta verdad [a certain truth]." The privileged positioning of this sequence as the very last dialogue in the film, which in fact unfolds on the screen after the first end titles and corresponding music have begun, is clearly intended to give Javier the last word. His statement is ultimately a condensation of both the clinical and the social approaches to disability: Javier simultaneously displays the cognitive impairment accompanying severe psychiatric disability and gives voice to the social autonomy that is still lacking in clinical dialogue. Remembering the "cathartic function" of many disability representations noted by Ato Quayson (2007: 25), it is important to recognize that here there is no such catharsis for the audience of *Una cierta verdad*. More than that, however, we see in this conversation the distilled kernel of conflict between providers and patients, or put another way, the distance between a clinical paradigm and a social paradigm of psychiatric disability.

Dialogue between two polarized social actors is propelled forward through time by the clinical view of schizophrenia as a problem to be solved, on one hand, and by the first-person acceptance of this perceived problem as a situation to be lived with, endured, and experienced, on the other. As staged by the director, this is a battle between forced medication and its effects on the body on one hand, and creativity, energy, and quality of life, on the other. Questions of individual autonomy and rights are brought into contact with social and discursive force, employed in the name of society against a disruption that can never be cured, only marginalized – all against the background where institutional and rhetorical claims to truth are inequitably distributed in society.

Conclusion

As a contribution to disability studies approaches in the humanities, *Cognitive Disability Aesthetics* has explored historical, theoretical, and cultural issues associated with cognitive disability representations in the introduction and chapters 1, 2, and 3. In chapters 4, 5, and 6, it has also analysed specific representations of intellectual, developmental, and psychiatric disabilities in examples taken from twenty-first-century cultural production in Spain. At a more basic level, it has asserted and reflected upon the relative invisibility of cognitive disabilities in both scholarship and society. In focusing on the nuances particular to specific visual texts, it has also corrected for that invisibility. In doing so it has reinvested in the hallmark elements of humanities scholarship – the value of close readings of visual texts, the acknowledgment of strong connections between cultural production and the larger social environment, and the relative autonomy and potentially radical relevance of art and aesthetics to political commitments.

As discussed in chapters 2 and 3, the iconic and indexical modes of signification so prominent in visual media have not been sufficiently explored in disability studies scholarship in the humanities. Scholarship in traditionally literary fields has launched a welcome and trenchant critique of how disability functions in literature as a foil for normative social relationships, exposing the way disability functions as a metaphorical and narrative device in prose. This tradition has since been transposed to the realm of cinema, delivering what are certainly valuable analyses. In the process, however, a literary mode of analysis has cast aside the material links that visual media offer for drawing connections between bodies and minds as represented aesthetically/culturally and the bodies and minds of real people who live, love, and work off-screen or off-page in ableist social environments. I have called for a disability studies criticism that attends to visual media precisely on account of their power to render the material experiences of cognitive disabilities visible in both art and society. I believe that this is particularly important when it comes to those cases of severe cognitive impairment that the able-minded public encounters most infrequently, whether as social or cultural representations. At present, visual media – and particularly the visual media circulated in marginal circuits of capital accumulation, such as the low-budget film in the style of the new disability documentary cinema that underscores the everydayness or non-spectacular nature of cognitive disability; and also the auteur graphic novel/comic intended for a niche market of consumers – arguably present an opportunity for viewers to do some important "visual work." This understands the connection between vision and knowledge outlined by Rosemarie Garland-Thomson, a connection that just does not operate in the same way in prose literature, given its reliance on arbitrary forms of signification and on the normative social convention that pervades linguistic signs, semiotically speaking. The iconic/indexical aspects of painting/photography, film, and graphic novels are more immediate links to an embodied material experience of disability, and to experience that does not exist as such in prose literary representations.

The focus on intellectual, developmental, and psychiatric disabilities changes how we view the relationship between text and world. This book has argued that it is particularly through visual culture that issues of cognition can be made more visible in society. This means attending to both concrete manifestations of cultural production and more diffuse cultural forces. In particular, the notion of the seam that I have borrowed from an essay by Mark Jeffreys and develop in relation to cognitive disabilities specifically proves to be an apt concept not just for negotiating the distance between biology and culture but also for noting how humanities approaches to visual disability representations negotiate the porous and friable border between text and world. If it was ever possible to talk about the existence of a purely literary humanities criticism, that moment has clearly passed. With the disciplinary rupture represented by cultural studies methods over the twentieth century, and with their spread to language and literature fields other than English, even the most traditional literary criticism now maintains a dialogue with the wider social world. Today only the most impoverished approach would seek to hermetically seal off the humanities text from the extra-textual reality in which it is immersed – in which it is created, published, distributed, and received. Attending to cognitive disability, whether in visual culture or in other cultural products, can further induce us to reconsider how representation operates to connect the aesthetic and social realms. It can allow us to see how the emphasis, in disability studies, on physical disability, has tended to reinforce mind/body dualism in the study of disability representations, even while simultaneously launching an effective critique of the normate.

Given the unresolved contradiction between the field's historical focus on physical bodies and its tendency to sidestep productive discussions regarding the issue of impairment – cognitive impairment in particular – I join disability theorists such as David Mitchell, Sharon Snyder, and Michael Bérubé in asking whether the time has come to reintroduce this issue to the academic field of disability studies. Doing so might create a more capacious approach that from the outset values issues of cognitive difference. In the end, humanities approaches focusing on individual visual cultural products could bring attention to the material experience of cognitive disability precisely because they have always been adept at bridging the dialectical distance between matter and theory, body and mind, and text and extra-textual world.

Specifically, I believe that the discussion of collaboration and community carried out in chapters 4, 5, and 6 of this book emphasizes the value of what humanities work does and the potential value of what it might still do. The case of the Trazos Singulares exhibit suggests the need for further – and more sustainable, more politically committed, more radical – large-scale attempts to correct for the social invisibility and urban marginalization of cognitive disabilities. The case of the comics text *María cumple 20 años* raises the question of how art, culture, and visual representation can be a prioritized area through which to encourage collaboration. The graphic novel *Arrugas* – and in particular the role of the necessarily collaborative practice of re-minding, taken in the context of Alzheimer's-related dementia – reaffirm the notion that interdependence is the foundation of human societies. The questions left unresolved in the documentary *Una cierta verdad* foreground the need for a more equal, collaborative solution to the problem of how to treat schizophrenia in the context of community-based care. These cultural products and these analyses articulate the mundane and pervasive everydayness of collaboration and interdependence, both as themes of artistic production and as social realities. They also necessarily pose somewhat provocative questions regarding the relationship of the health and medical sciences to the social sciences and the humanities in the wider context of the interdisciplinary field of disability studies.

Rather than trace these arguments as they have been made throughout the book, however, here I want to close by returning to the matters of scholarly discipline that reared their heads earlier. It is a commonplace that humanities scholars are trained to work, and are largely expected to work, in solitude. Our historical focus on individual literary authors, our traditional focus on the publication of single-authored monographs and articles, and the entrenched individualism of tenure and promotion at academic institutions all confirm the truth of this characterization. We can certainly provide more incentive for scholars to do collaborative work, and we have the responsibility to do so. But statements equating humanities scholars with intellectual loners – many of which I have heard from humanities scholars themselves – have always struck me as an overstatement, if not as inauthentic. However fragmented our disciplines may be, they are no less the product of academic communities. These communities are always created from granular relationships among individuals who share common interests. Academically speaking, these communities draw their enduring strength from the close collaborative professional relationships forged during graduate study and expanded in the academic department and wider field. Make no mistake: these communities are, from the smallest to the largest scale, riven through with more contradictions than consensus. Such is the nature of community, which is an abstraction that only holds meaning if we allow for it to ebb and flow, coalesce and disperse, fracture and reform.

No humanities scholar is an island, even if the popular imagination would encourage us to think so. Our programs, departments, associations, conferences, academic journals, and book series are academic communities of a sort. They also make such communities possible. In none of these contexts can it be said that humanities scholars work alone. It may be worth asking, why do we believe that humanities scholars are solitary workers when all the evidence points to the contrary? The myth of individualism that has proven so important for contemporary neoliberal capitalism – and that has been critiqued heavily by disability studies work focusing on interdependence – may play a role here. We must also consider the instrumentalizing and reifying vision that severs a single academic product – a lecture, an article, a book – from its wider context. We are all part of an interdependent network of other humanities scholars, though this is easily forgotten. Can we, as humanities scholars, assert that we are interdependent? And once we have done so, can we not also do even more to encourage further collaboration? I intend these questions as a transposition of the insights deployed in this book's chapters from the realm of cognitive disability aesthetics to the realm of disciplinary matters. Disability studies as an interdisciplinary field has demonstrated a remarkable ability to connect discourses that have traditionally been seen as separate. Here I am referencing not only the origin of the field in women's and gender studies programs but also its progressive fusion of humanities and social science, even health science perspectives. Humanities fields, in particular, and Hispanic studies among them, tend to be strongly interdisciplinary in approach and method. I assert that they derive their relevance, strength, and potentially transformative power from this fact.

Yet there is still much work to be done to recognize the relevance of disability studies in the Anglophone world to the study of disability experiences in non–English-speaking countries. Even having completed this book, I imagine a response similar to those I have received in the past. Speaking generally, I have frequently been asked to show what is "unique" about disability experiences in Spain. It has sometimes been suggested that I avoid analysing disability representations in Spain in light of Anglophone disability theory and debates. These responses ignore the historical and continuing influence of disability scholarship from the English-speaking world on Spanish scholarship; they also essentially tropicalize non-Anglophone contexts. Beyond this, one must consider the historical and global resonance of disability movements; the international precedent set by American legislation such as the 1990 Americans with Disabilities Act and the 2006 UN Convention on the Rights of Persons with Disabilities; the influence of Anglophone models of clinical disability practice on non-Anglophone contexts; and cross-cultural similarities regarding the social construction, definition, scope, and support of disability. I would read books on these subjects with interest, but I have not sought to write them.

This book is not a monad – no book is. It is necessarily incomplete and partial. Above all else it has been an attempt to engage disability studies across area studies disciplines – in the end, an attempt to fashion a liminal terrain. This terrain is located betwixt and between different scholarly traditions. Its advantage is that this cross-disciplinary landscape is the one in which it is most likely that a truly global disability studies community might take root. If some readers seek out this book only for the introduction and the first three chapters, or if others are only interested in the final three chapters focusing on Spanish cultural production, then so be it. Even this in itself would be the start of a wonderful conversation.

I began *Cognitive Disability Aesthetics* with the idea that a second-wave disability studies focused on cognitive difference is necessary if we are to move beyond a first-wave disability studies focused above all else on the physical body. Finding ways to incorporate the notions of impairment and biology – and even health and medicine – into disability studies practice is crucial if we are to address the material experiences of severe cognitive disability. This second wave of scholarship must simultaneously pursue both prose literature and visual culture. It must explore the differential textures of both what are arguably the Anglophone roots of disability studies and the experiences of disability in a full range of global contexts. The obstacles to sustaining these conversations were mentioned in the introduction to this book and built upon throughout its chapters. There may be working frictions between a social critique based on bodily difference and one grounded in cognitive difference; between the expectation for social groups in representational democracy to employ self-representation and self-narration and practical understandings of the material experiences of cognitive disability; between the short-term goal of increasing inclusion, access, and participation and the long-term goal of effecting a radical shift in ableist neoliberalism; between the potential gains of identity politics and the collective aspirations of intersectional approaches; and between the universality and the particularity of disability experience. The degree to which we can become more interdisciplinary and collaborative in our scholarly thinking will surely determine how effectively we navigate these choppy waters of disability studies' second wave.

Notes

Preface

1 The quotation continues: "The expectations for a disabled presenter talking about their own experiences are very different than what the audience expects from a nondisabled professional ally. Each location offers useful information and adds to the pool of disability community knowledge ... Contrast this approach with Disability Studies where disclosure of one's relationship to disability is often considered to be private information."

Introduction

1 Importantly, Michael Bérubé's book *The Secret Life of Stories* (2016) – which I read as I finalized this book for publication in fall 2016 – notes "the general reluctance, in disability studies as in the disability rights movement, to talk about disability in terms of function" (2016: 56). The quotation continues: "Inevitably it seems, any discussion of functionality with regard to disability will involve some normative ideas about how bodies and minds *should* function (eyes should see, ears should hear, legs should walk, brains should be able to decode facial expressions and distinguish reality from fantasy), and thus any admission that disability involves a reduction or loss of function threatens not only to return us to the idea of disability as lack, but to give up on the foundational distinction between disability (as a social phenomenon) and impairment (as a somatic phenomenon). All disability thereby becomes impairment, and the idea that disability studies examines disability as *the social organization and administration of impairment*."

2 Impairment is arguably more visible as an issue in the *Routledge Handbook of Disability Studies* (Watson, Roulstone, and Thomas 2014; first published in 2012) than it is in *The Disability Studies Reader* (Davis 2013; first published in 1997), a fact that may indicate a distinction between UK and North American trends in disability studies research as well as a gap between humanities and social science approaches to disability. The former text's Part Two features six essays under the heading "Disablement, Disablism, and Impairment Effects" (2014: vi), for instance, and Part Three features another six under the heading "Social Policy and Disability: Health, Personal Assistance, Employment, and Education" (Ibid.). My point is not that impairment is not discussed in the literature, but that impairment (and cognitive impairment more than physical impairment) tends not to be discussed in humanities approaches to disability and that it is particularly absent from the North American disability studies tradition in which I have written this book.

3 Mitchell and Snyder's introduction to their pioneering edited volume *The Body and Physical Difference: Discourses of Disability* uses this argument to call attention to physical disability in the humanities: "The predominance of disability in the biological, social, and cognitive sciences parallels an equally ominous silence within the humanities. Perhaps because disabilities are exclusively narrated as debilitating phenomena in need of medical intervention and correction, the humanities have not privileged disability as a foundational category of social experience or social investment" (1997: 1).

4 Indeed medical language is highly suspect in many strains of disability studies research in the humanities, as is language that is judged to recognize and thus purportedly essentialize impairment. Mitchell and Snyder share the interesting example of a new policy on impairment language adopted by the journal *Disability and Society* (2015: 158).

5 An example, as I mentioned in the preface of this book, concerns the case for a strong Deaf identity in the US context and elsewhere, which has been made through arguments for the capital-d Deaf as a linguistic and cultural minority.

6 Jasbir Puar's critique of minority model approaches, "homonormativity," is discussed in Mitchel and Snyder's book in terms of rights-based assimilation, where the authors define ablenationalism: "We refer to this tactic of integrating a privileged minority at the expense of the further abjection of the many as ablenationalism" (2015: 45).

7 Mitchell and Snyder write that "the social model is itself a creature of late liberalism's strategic embrace of devalued identities and its corrective

efforts to include rather than exclude what Nicole Markotić and Sally Chivers refer to as 'the problem body'" (2015: 37).

8 Mitchell and Snyder explore in detail the "weak strain of accommodation" (2015: 36) and the "weakened strain of inclusionism extant in neoliberalism" (2015: 38), and detail the hidden costs of what should be considered gains, for example when discussing the contradiction that support for community living may rise as the social services supporting that community living are eroded. "Neoliberalism continues to oversee greater and more pressing exclusions with respect to the terms undergirding opportunities for integration that then go unfunded or receive drastic cuts at a later point in time" (2015: 37). Chapter 6 of this book mentions the inadequate support for people living with schizophrenia by exploring the argument over institutional versus community living in a broad sense and by delving into case studies at the Taulí hospital in Sabadell (Barcelona, Spain). See also Prendergast (2013).

9 Mitchell and Snyder's wording in *The Biopolitics of Disability* is not always as inclusive of matters of cognition, as when they write that "the social and minority models stress revision of tangible barriers such as accessible architecture and the modification of public transportation systems, to name just two sites of political intervention identified as critical to disability integration. To revise the environment for greater accessibility for all bodies represents the most tangible pathway to disability inclusion" (2015: 62).

10 For their part, the authors of *The Biopolitics of Disability* ask a most pertinent question that reaffirms the need to attend to the specific material forms that the disability experience takes in an ableist society: "If we are all effectively 'disabled,' then what is to mark disability as a nuanced experiential condition?" (Mitchell with Snyder 2015: 30). I read this question as a call to recognize that not all experiences of disability are the same, even if they do share a common origin in ableist social environments. Through recognizing the reality of impairment, these works advocate a return to the specificity of individual experience that has either been ignored or else taken for granted in previous approaches.

11 On the concept of the "the terrain of the biocultural," Davis writes: "I use that term, coined by David Morris (with whom I cowrote chapter 9) and promulgated by a number of people including myself, to describe the intersection among the cultural, social, political, technological, medical and biological. The well of this book resides in issues around the body and the mind in the context of disability and disability studies. I explore sexuality, emotion, psychology, genetics, death, narrative, performance, and a host of other issues through a complex interdisciplinary lens" (2013: vii).

I am much less interested in exploring Davis's argument that diversity is the new normal, one that – while fundamental to his book – is somewhat more complex than my discussion here will allow. This is in part because I do not easily accept his argument – drawing on Georgio Agamben and distinguishing between *bios* and *zoe* – that some populations are "at base not consumers and most likely never will be" (2013: 5). My belief is that even understood as *zoe*, the group in which Davis would list "homeless people, impoverished people, end-stage cancer patients, the comatose, heroin, crack or methamphetamine addicts" (2013: 4) are in fact deeply connected to patterns of consumption in late capitalism involving not merely consumer goods but also consumer choices in health care treatment, rent, and so on – whether they are made autonomously or made for such populations by other providers, agencies, the conditioning of availability, and so on. Both FDA-approved pharmaceuticals in general and disease treatments specifically – as well as non-regulated drugs outside of treatment contexts – are a huge part of capital accumulation strategies and in fact depend upon the abject bodies that are never fully able to separate themselves from these strategies. Mitchell with Snyder here in fact also agree with Davis in the sense that they imply that disabled persons, as what they call non-workers, are not impacted by or implicit in the capital accumulation strategies of advanced capitalist states or their corresponding consumer cultures. "Many of the disabled people we know," they write, "prove to be some of the worst consumers on the planet because they have neither the means nor the interest of mistaking meaning with the market. For instance, disabled artists and activists in Chicago and London with whom we have worked live sparing, nonconsumptive lives and, yet, this is what we admire about them" (2015: 217). I assert that it is not possible, in Chicago or London, to fully separate from consumer markets that involve food, clothing, housing, health care, and so on. The implication in the text may be that consumption and consumerism are about leisure, but leisure is merely one aspect of the process of capitalist accumulation, not its totality.

12 One could say that in the process of underscoring materialist concerns he unfortunately turns performance and social constructedness into an arena that is purely immaterial. This goes against his own stated attempt, developed more fully in chapter 2 of his book, to move beyond the simplistic perspective he associates with post-positivist realists or PPRs. It is difficult to read the book's first two chapters from a perspective that does not get caught oscillating between the stark polarities of realism and idealism – the writing on his page 25 is an excellent example of this.

13 Although Davis addresses this issue directly in the text (see his chapters 1 and 2), *The End of Normal* is nevertheless, in part, a book pulled thin between the extremes of pure idealism and pure materiality. Catering to these extremes (or better said, these philosophical abstractions) does not, in my view, move us any closer to understanding the material experience of severe cognitive impairment in contemporary society.

14 Clearly, as Davis's argument illustrates, intellectual and developmental disabilities can be marketed to, just as can physical disabilities. Here Mitchell and Snyder's exploration of the uncomfortable, objectionable social reality that some health treatments for disabling conditions are not pursued because no market has been identified, while others are pursued specifically because there is a potential market, is also relevant (2015: 157).

15 The authors respond to the claim attributed to Davis – one he refutes directly, in fact – that he believes disability to be universally shared, a part of the human experience. "As explained earlier, we disagree with positions advanced by Davis, Watson, Shakespeare, and others that argue for a more general recognition that 'we are all disabled' as a substantive solution to the marginalization of people with disabilities" (Mitchell with Snyder 2015: 164). The full quotation from the body text reads: "If we all share inefficient, discordant, and non-normative bodies, then 'the end of normalcy' seems to result in a flattening of the social/biological playing field of difference (Davis, *End of Normal* 29–30). Isn't this a form of interpretation that ultimately 'negate(s) disability as meaning in its own right' … If we are all effectively 'disabled,' then what is to mark disability as a nuanced experiential condition?" (Mitchell with Snyder 2015: 30).

16 I regard the entire quotation as significant: "new materialist approaches offer an enrichment of the way alternative cognitions/corporealities allow us to inhabit the world as vulnerable, constrained, yet innovative embodied beings rather than merely as devalued social constructs or victims of oppression" (2015: 7).

17 Readers may be interested in the full quotations I have abbreviated in the body text: "Where contemporary scholarship discusses reappropriation of the terms of oppression, or trades in artful means for evading pervasive structures of stigma, some disability studies 'body talk' (including our own work in this mix) dares to name diagnoses or conditions as something other than forms of medical false consciousness. One key goal of critical materialist analyses is to research the histories and experiences that attend diagnostic etiologies in order to create pragmatic knowledge in methods that often arrive at one's bedside under emergency conditions, much akin to psychiatric survivor movements from the sixties" (Mitchell

with Snyder 2015: 160); "Perhaps it is time to return to the scholarly suppressed topic of impairment in parallel to what Robert McRuer pointedly asks of the limits of disability identity models" (2015: 160; see McRuer 2010: 172).

18 See Mitchell and Snyder 2015: 205, understanding that Davis treats disability somewhat apart from the matter of diversity. Also: "While rehabilitation often refers to a productive process of recovery leading to a return to approximations of normative embodiment (and, ultimately, employability), here the term suggests something less optimum. Cultural rehabilitation refers to normalization practices at work within the neoliberal era through which nonnormative (i.e., nonproductive) bodies become culturally docile. This process accomplishes its task of adjustment through a gradual ceding of democratic state power and the duty to govern on behalf of the people to corporate interests both benign and disciplinary. Such practices jettison the value of the commons (literally selling off the collectively held riches of the commonwealth) while enlisting nonnormative bodies in service of inclusionism as a further fetishization of the accomplishments of the neoliberal state's normalcy. Claims to neoliberal exceptionality rely on a largely rhetorical celebration of this accomplishment of inclusion long before any such utopian realizations could be justifiably demonstrated. Or, rather, such arrivals at inclusionist goals prove successful only because their application to marginalized lives is so meager. Throughout this book we have referenced this implementation of neoliberal diversity as the 'weakened stain' of inclusionism akin to inoculations from disease that introduce a small amount of virus into a system in order to ward off greater degrees of infection in the future" (2015: 205).

19 Michael Bérubé puts this in similar terms (2016: 57).

20 This slippage is implied and addressed by the work of Michael Bérubé, who focuses on intellectual disability and who notes "the hierarchy within disability studies itself, which has been challenged in recent years (chiefly by people working on autism and mental illness) but which remains very much in effect, whereby physical disability stands in for disability *in toto*" (2016: 27).

21 In addition, as I highlight in the introduction to *Cultures of Representation* (Fraser 2016a), and as evident in Olga María Alegre de la Rosa's *La discapacidad en el cine* (2003), Spanish-language work on disability in film within Spain has been itself very focused on anglophone products, even as social and cultural awareness of disability increases, as evident in the documentary *Capacitados*, for example.

22 A recent review of my book *Disability Studies and Spanish Culture* in *Journal of Literary and Cultural Disability Studies* 10(1) (2016), for example, does not mention at all the artistic dimensions of any of the texts I study, nor does it address the aesthetic dimensions of my analysis of those cultural texts.

1 On the (In)Visibility of Cognitive Disability

1 On the relationship of this philosophical question to intellectual disabilities see the work of feminist philosopher Licia Carlson, in particular her book *The Faces of Intellectual Disability: Philosophical Reflections* (2010). See also the volume edited by Licia Carlson and Eva Feder Kittay, *Cognitive Disability and Its Challenge to Moral Philosophy* (2010) and the chapter by Leslie Francis (2009).

2 See, for example, *Mad Matters: A Critical Reader in Canadian Mad Studies* [2013], edited by Brenda A. LeFrancois, Robert J. Menzies, and Geoffrey Reaume, as well as the contribution to *Disability and Society* 30(2) (2015) by Brigit McWade, Damian Milton and Peter Beresford titled "Mad Studies and Neurodiversity: A Dialogue." Félix Guattari's work is also a point of reference here, perhaps in particular the work *Chaosophy* (1995). This is not to say that the medical model is not itself being received ambivalently by those in health disciplines (see for example Brosco 2010).

3 Consider Charles A. Riley's comments: "Legislation defining disability rights began with deafness, blindness, and various mobility impairments such as spinal cord injury and amputation, the so-called physical disabilities, and rapidly expanded to include AIDS and 'mental' disabilities from the most serious, such as bipolar disorder, to such controversial conditions as recovery from drug and alcohol addiction, attention deficit disorder (ADD), and Asperger's syndrome, an autism-like condition that makes children react strongly to any change in their routine" (2005: 10) – one might ask why the word "mental" appears in quotes here. See also the emphasis on physical disability by disability rights activist Marsha Saxton (quoted extensively in Norden 1994: 11; on advocacy, human rights, and disability rights more generally see Carey 2009; Charlton 1998; Herr, Gostin, and Hongju Koh 2003; Pardeck 2005; Shapiro 1994; Sulmasy 2010; and Williams and Shoultz 1984).

4 See my review of Minich's *Accessible Citizenships* in *Arizona Journal of Hispanic Cultural Studies* for a closer look into this fascinating text (Fraser 2015).

5 The book follows from her chapter titled "The Politics of Staring: Visual Rhetorics of Disability in Popular Photography" in the MLA volume *Disability Studies: Enabling the Humanities* (Garland-Thomson 2002b).

6 In addition to Mitchell and Snyder, Murray here mentions work by Lennard J. Davis, Rosemarie Garland-Thomson, and Mairian Corker/ Tom Shakespeare.

7 Photography became commercially viable in 1839. Similarly, the freak show in its modern and popular form, as discussed below in this section, can be traced to the 1830s shows by P.T. Barnum. Significantly, disability photography features in Lee Fontanella's *La historia de la fotografía en España* (1981).

8 I draw here from Hevey's essay "The Enfreakment of Photography," reprinted from his 1992 book for the first edition of *The Disability Studies Reader*. The full quotation reads: "The social absence of disabled people creates a vacuum in which the visual meanings attributable (symbolically, metaphorically, psychically, etc.) to impairment and disablement appear free-floating and devoid of any actual people. In the absence of disabled people, the meaning in the disabled person and their body is made by those who survey. They attempt to shift the disablement on to the impairment, and the impairment into a flaw. The very absence of disabled people in positions of power and representation deepens the use of this 'flaw' in their images. The repression of disabled people makes it more likely that the symbolic use of disablement by non-disabled people is a sinister or mythologist one. Disablement re-enters the social world through photographic representation, but in the re-entry its meaning is tied not by the observed, disabled people, but by the non-disabled observers" (1997: 345; see also Millet-Gallant 2004; Garland-Thomson 2002b; Haller 2010).

9 What is most relevant about Stiker's book is the way he folds physical and developmental disabilities together even in the examples appearing in his introduction ("the Down's syndrome child, the woman without arms, the worker in a wheelchair," [1982]1997: 10; "the parents of autistic children [...] persons confined to a wheelchair or crippled by traumatic after-effects," [1982]1997: 2).

10 McDonagh's book includes a quite relevant quotation: "Of course, from the early decades of the twentieth century the physical separation and isolation in institutions of those people who wore the 'idiocy' label made the historical processes shaping the concept even more invisible. That the history of ideas of idiocy and its flip side, intelligence, has been ignored as an appropriate subject of investigations and analysis, and that the relations of this history to other streams of thought, other realms of discussion, suggests just how effectively the idea has been absorbed within frameworks that shape its meaning" (2008: 9).

11 See Norden (1994: ch. 1) for how associations between begging and disability were a staple of much early film.

12 Stiker's work ties into but diverges from that of Foucault, whose critique of prisons and hospitals remains relevant to the topic and in particular to the topic of mental illness as discussed in chapter 6 of this book. See also Mitchell with Snyder (2015: 215) on feeblemindedness, Foucault, and the nineteenth-century institution.

13 The issue of madness and its connection to more contemporary discussions of psychiatric disability is an interesting one in itself and is covered extensively in chapter 6 of this book ("Screening Schizophrenia"). Winzer writes that "before the advent of widespread literacy, when pushing the plow was more important than pushing the pen, mildly intellectually disabled people – those labelled today as learning disabled and those at the upper end of the spectrum of mental retardation, for example – would simply have merged into the general populace. In early times it seems probable that only the grossest examples of mental defect would have been considered remarkable … However, those far down the continuum, affected perhaps with multiple disabilities or medically fragile conditions, could not have been expected to survive" (1997: 80).

14 "Our ability to assess the scope of the problem in earlier societies is further obscured by the lack of a consistent, sound means of discriminating between people who had physical disabilities (i.e. were crippled, dwarfed, epileptic, or deaf) and those who were intellectually impaired or mentally ill. All were considered to form one, all-encompassing category. The lack of clear definitions means that the history of disability tends to focus on particular disabilities, those that were more clearly distinguished from the others" (Winzer 1997: 80). The lumping together of madness and physical disability in this account should not surprise, particularly given the historical view that madness and mental disorders were produced by physical causes (Winzer 1997: 85).

15 Accounts of specific physical disabilities are much easier to trace back into history than cognitive disabilities, as I found when editing and translating the anthology *Deaf History and Culture in Spain: A Reader of Primary Documents* (Gallaudet UP, 2009). See also Fraser (2007, 2009, 2010b, 2012; made possible by Plann 1997).

16 While not a book-length study, Paul K. Longmore's "Screening Stereotypes: Images of Disability" (1985), republished in *Screening Disability* (2001, eds. Enns and Smit), was an earlier forerunner of Norden's general approach, "claiming that Hollywood films were

essentially ableist in their depiction of people with disabilities" (Enns and Smit 2001b: xi).

17 Even late in the book he continues to emphasize this central point – for example, "the history of physical disability images in the movies has mostly been a history of distortion in the name of maintaining an ableist society" (Norden 1994: 314)

18 Norden here follows a line of thinking established by Paul K. Longmore in his 1985 essay "Screening Stereotypes" where the scholar noted: "Positive images in commercials and other programs reflect the growing socio-political perception of disabled people as a minority group and the increasing impact of the disability civil rights movement. Whether these new depictions will become an important trend depends partly on the response from the disability community itself" (Longmore 2001: 15).

19 This productively ambivalent perspective is conveyed also in Snyder and Mitchell (2010), for example, who comment on film as a critical arena in their book chapter. Mitchell and Snyder (2015, 2016) also address the potential of cinematic disability representations.

20 Even the volume's third section, "Disability as Trauma, Mental Illness, and Dysfunction in Post-Vietnam Cinema," emphasizes physical disability in all but a single essay, which deals with the representation of depression, family dysfunction, and suicide.

21 For example, their extremely brief reading of Peter Bogdonavich's film *Mask* (1985) illustrates how understanding the cinematic tradition of the melodrama genre potentially leads to a more robust understanding of the film's portrayal of disability (2001: 39).

22 See chapter three of Chivers's monograph *The Silvering Screen* (2011), titled "Grey Matters: Dementia, Cognitive Difference, and the 'Guilty Demographic' on Screen," for a discussion of cognitive disability.

23 By design, my own edited volume *Cultures of Representation: Disability in World Cinema Contexts* (2016) included discussion of representations of a mix of both physical and cognitive disabilities. But of course it should be noted that this collection was published more than twenty years after Norden's book, a fact that only reconfirms the pioneering value of that first-wave disability studies work (Fraser 2016a).

2 Signification and Staring

1 In a sense, this recapitulates the distinction between syntagmatic and paradigmatic relationships in structural linguistics, but this knowledge is not required for appreciation of its role in the present context.

2 I have explored Antonio López García's painting, its spatial context, and its related philosophy in the monographs *Encounters with Bergson(ism) in Spain* (2010c) and *Antonio López García's Everyday Urban Worlds* (2014).

3 For work on the ontological qualities of photography, see work by Roland Barthes and Susan Sontag; on the cinema's relationship to physical reality, see work by Béla Balázs and Siegfried Kracauer (1968).

4 Érice's debt to Japanese filmmakers makes this an appropriate comparison. See the work by Linda Ehrlich (1995, 2000).

5 Stephen Prince (1999) continues and updates Wollen's line of thought on the indexical and iconic modes of the filmic sign, which are also important for the geographical film criticism of Hopkins (1994). See also Fraser (2010c).

6 Note that these arguments bemoan the legacy of twentieth-century film theory that has been overly influenced by Saussure: "In its analysis of images, film theory since the 1970s has been deeply indebted to structuralist and Saussurean-derived linguistic models. Indeed, it would be difficult to overstate the depth and importance of this relationship"; "Film theory since the 1970s has tended to place great emphasis upon what is regarded as the arbitrary nature of the signifier-signified relationship, that is, upon the purely conventional and symbolic aspect of signs. What this focus has tended to displace is an appreciation of the iconic and mimetic aspect of certain categories of signs, namely pictorial signs, those most relevant to an understanding of the cinema. This stress upon the arbitrary nature of semiotic coding has had enormous consequences for the way film studies as a discipline has tended to frame questions about visual meaning and communication" (Prince 1999: 99).

7 A relevant example would be the Society for Cinema and Media Studies conference for work on film, or the American Association of Geographers for work using spatial approaches. In truth, and despite the overwhelming preponderance of Hispanic studies scholars in comparison to those in other language and culture areas, there is currently only a single journal in Hispanic studies expressly devoted to film scholarship (*Studies in Spanish and Latin American Cinemas*, formerly *Studies in Hispanic Cinemas*). Regarding disability studies in the humanities specifically, the publication of several important single-authored and edited volumes mentioned in previous chapters of this book stands as a challenge to such traditionally literary thinking (see texts by Norden 1994; Enns and Smit 2001a; Chivers and Markotić 2010; Mogk 2013; Marr 2013; and Fraser 2013a, 2016a).

8 Indeed of the contributions to that volume, only Darke's chapter, part of the first chapter (2010: 31–2), and brief moments of chapters by Cheu and Diehl, can be considered relevant to the present argument.

9 See also Snyder and Mitchell (2010: 202–3). As examples of what "many contend even in disability studies," the authors give the following brief list in parentheses in the text: "(Finkelstein 30–36; Shakespeare 293–300; Barnes 577–80)" (2015: 199).

10 Bérubé makes reference to "the Rob Spirko-induced insights that disability in literary texts need not be located in, or tied to, a specific character with an identifiable disability" and "the Phyllis Eisenson-induced insight that disability in the relation between text and reader *need not involve any character with disabilities at all.* It can involve *ideas about* disability, regardless of whether any specific character can be pegged with a specific diagnosis. This opens the field of criticism considerably; and I am going to suggest that this is a good thing, not least because I am determined to cure disability studies of its habit of diagnosing fictional characters" (2016: 19, original emphasis).

11 At the time of this book's publication, the film can also be viewed online at https://www.youtube.com/watch?v=cXz_TNZAVFk.

12 "Film spectators arrive at the screen prepared to glimpse the extraordinary body displayed for moments of uninterrupted visual access – a practice shared by clinical assessment rituals associated with the medical gaze" (Snyder and Mitchell 2006: 158).

13 On sexuality and disability see Robert McRuer and Anna Mollow's *Sex and Disability* (2012) as well as Michael Gill's *Already Doing It: Intellectual Disability and Sexual Agency* (2015). Many of the contributions to the book *Cultures of Representation: Disability in World Cinema Contexts* (Gill 2016), including Gill's own chapter therein, in fact deal with these very points, points that have shaped important strata of disability studies criticism.

14 Remember, too, the role arguably played by Down syndrome in Lennard J. Davis's discussion of the materiality of disability in his 2013 book, discussed in the introduction of the present book.

15 This is precisely to consider the uniqueness of visual representations when compared with prose narrative. Here Garland-Thomson writes: "Her likeness emerges from the sharp line her stately features form against the background; her nose and chin lift imperially; her eyes gaze impassively down on the world beneath her. Her head is turbaned with a richly colored and ornately patterned aristocratic headdress, and her shoulders reveal a simple but elegant gown. On first glance she looks like a modern Florentine lady. On second glance, however, we recognize a face we have never seen in a portrait. We see the distinct features of a person with Down syndrome, her hair wrapped in a bright beach towel, her face in a faraway reverie, and a simple heart tattooed on her shoulder below her bathing suit strap" (2009: 83).

16 See Prince (1999: 99), also: "But, as we will see, the spectator's understanding of cinematic images seems more immediately explicable in terms of mimetic, referential coding rather than via the chains of displaced, arbitrary, and relational meaning in prevailing theories. In other words, this is understanding is more of a matter of recognition than translation" (1999: 102); "Thus, with respect to pictures, film theory might ask if there is a nonlinguistic, even biological, basis on which visual communication might exist" (1999: 105).

17 To use semiotic terms developed in the study of naturally occurring language, the selection of the im-sign for a given film is equivalent to the paradigmatic relationship of the linguistic sign, while the embedding of that im-sign within a grammatical structure of film is equivalent to the syntagmatic relationship of the linguistic sign (see work by Saussure, Jakobson 1960). In this sense film possesses a two-layered structure that is complementary to the double articulation of natural languages. But in general film theory has traditionally privileged the syntagmatic relationships of the cinema over, and in isolation from, its paradigmatic relationships. The same can be said for disability studies scholarship involving the cinema, which has privileged the syntagmatic relationships of disability narrative over the paradigmatic relationships of the disability im-sign. The point is that through the layering of pre-grammatical and grammatical levels of disability representation, the temporal dimension of film allows viewers to see how disability representations are linked to a social context.

18 I have discussed Judith Scott and her representation in greater depth in an article in *Cultural Studies* (2010a) and also in *Disability Studies and Spanish Culture* (2013a). Here I refer to Scott as a way of making a much more general point.

19 Consider, for example, Norden 1994; Chivers and Markotić 2010; Mogk 2013; and Fraser 2016a.

20 In this respect see chapters by Victoria L. Garrett and Nicola Gavioli in the book edited by Antebi and Jörgensen (2016).

21 See essays on *Yo, también* in Fraser (2011a, 2013a) and especially Gill (2016).

22 This tradition is arguably alive and well in Hispanic studies. In *Disability Studies and Spanish Culture* (2013) I explored the value of representing disabled characters as embedded in relationships in analyses of disability representations in films such as *¿Qué tienes debajo del sombrero?* (What's under Your Hat?) (2006) and *Yo también* (Me, Too) (2009). I also explored director Joaquim Jordà's move to include himself in his documentary on agnosia/alexia titled *Más allá del espejo* (2006).

23 As a sidenote, it is interesting that Snyder and Mitchell use cerebral paralysis as an example where the boundary between cognitive and physical disability becomes significant as well as partly discursive in nature: "As a result, people with physical disabilities find themselves refuting cognitive 'involvements' (such as in the case of CP); and, in turn, people with cognitive disabilities find themselves having to charge those with physical disabilities with a further sedimenting of their own socially derived stigma. However, in either case the effort finds itself impossible because the fates of both groups are historically tethered to each other" (2010: 198–9).

3 Disability Sholarship at the Seam

1 See the Preface to the present book, where I disclose my relationship with disability as suggested by O'Toole (2013) and stress why my research focuses on severe cognitive disability.

2 As indicated in this book's introduction, a decade after Jeffreys (2002) published his insights, books by Davis (2013) and by Mitchell with Snyder (2015) have illustrated that disability studies has never fully resolved the matter of whether impairment is a defining aspect of disability constructions or if disability itself is just another manifestation of the more heterogeneous notion of social difference, defined by its opposition to the normate (Garland-Thomson 1997).

3 The authors continue: "he is the bearer of an entrenched identity (pathetic or vengeful); he is the literal embodiment of the evidence of the fall of man; he personifies the fiendish specter of war; he is singular and exceptional rather than common and ordinary; he can be viewed as the most interior to a social order (the most human in suffering) or the most exiled (lacking in natural human affections); his physical excesses provide a ready source material for caricature. Finally a scapegoat patterning to the play reiterates exile as a culturally sanctioned historical solution to the social disruption that disabled people are perceived to present" (Mitchell and Snyder 1997: 14).

4 In Spanish literature, one could look in a similar way at the spectacular representation of cognitive difference in Juan Benet's novel *Volverás a Región* (Return to Region, trans. Gregory Rabassa), in which disordered cognitive process serves as a metaphor for the destructive impact of the Spanish Civil War, a theme of warring brothers with biblical resonance that pervades Benet's work. Interestingly, Benet was heavily influenced by Faulkner. Readers can consult my book on Juan Benet for more information, though I do not engage a disability studies approach there.

5 She quotes Michael Bérubé's suggestion that "Faulkner based his portrait of Benjy Compson [in *The Sound and the Fury*] on a local Mississippi man with Down syndrome" (1996: xv; cited in Hall 2016: 109–10). Discussion there also addresses Mark Haddon's *The Curious Incident of the Dog in the Night-Time* and Naoki Higashida's *The Reason I Jump*. Hall brings up issues of self-representation in narrative art that are arguably more nuanced and perhaps even problematic for populations with cognitive disabilities than they are for able-minded populations with physical disabilities, citing Bérubé and Straus as I also do, following her lead. These issues are discussed later in this chapter. Bérubé comments on *The Curious Incident* and autism somewhat extensively in *The Secret Life of Stories* (2016).

6 Disability drag, as discussed by Tobin Siebers (2008: 114–19) is an interesting point in its own right that I do not discuss here.

7 See my discussion of this in Fraser (2010c).

8 Both genres of cultural production – prose narrative and film – are artistic or textual representations that are intimately connected to extra-textual worlds. They both mediate and restage experience, involving real-world referents. What is of interest, however, is that this process happens differently in prose literature disability representations than it does in the more expressly visual representations such as film, painting, and sculpture, or the graphic novel, for that matter.

9 This does not mean there can be no transgressive literary representations of disability, it only explains why ableist literary disability representations are so common. Similarly, as discussed in the later parts of this chapter, it is not that visual disability representations are by their nature transgressive, only that the visual materiality of their connections with disability constitutes a factor non-existent in literary disability representations, one whose potential can be harnessed by artistic creators and attended to by scholarship working "at the seam."

10 This model is also explainable in terms of Saussurean linguistics by the chain model of arbitrary signification whereby a sign (signifier/signified) relates to another sign, which relates to another, and another ... Due to the fact that Saussurean linguistics heavily weights arbitrary signification over iconic/indexical signification (both of which exist in spoken language), the chain of signifiers can be imagined to hover over reality. Another investigation might explore more substantially the impact of Saussurean linguistics on literary scholarship and on disability scholarship in particular, accomplishing what Peter Wollen and Stephen Prince, for example, have accomplished in film theory. The notion of form is equally intriguing. This is not the form of the novel, its structure or prose organization, nor

the form of a linguistic sign (the written word itself, whose connection to meaning is largely constituted through arbitrary signification and social convention), but rather the surface of a representation.

11 It is important to understand that although prose literature representations seem to deal with bodies, at a semiotic level they deal only with the symbolism of bodies. This is significant because in visual media it is possible to deal more directly – via icon/index – with bodies. And as we will see, the representation of bodies in visual narrative evades the routine literary presentation of disembodied cognition and is able to actually embody cognition, presenting it through movement and action in a way impossible in literary narrative.

12 For example, other attempts to bridge the literary text and the world include the various techniques of realism as well as metafictional techniques that turn the act of reading inside out and problematize the division between literature and non-literary life.

13 Also: "Literature does not merely reflect any already socially interpreted reality, but adds another tier of interpretation that is comprehensible within the terms set by the literary-aesthetic domain" (Quayson 2007: 14).

14 Readers might consider whether there are echoes here of the argument from Lennard J. Davis (2013) discussed in the introduction to this book (in the section titled The Universality / Specificity of Disability) and concisely expressed in his phrase "kicking the rock."

15 The quotation's last sentence may be of interest to comics scholars. It reads, in full: "It is only conspicuous when it is a matter of a story *in images*, spread over the multiframe in a situation of co-occurence" (Groensteen 2007: 115). I do not assume a readership conversant in comics theory in this book and thus prefer not to address the concept of the multiframe, although I do so in a work in progress about a graphic artist from Mallorca, Spain. At the level of the multiframe, iconic redundancy can be generalized to intersect with what Groensteen defines as the principle of iconic solidarity: "interdependent images that, participating in a series, present the double characteristic of being separated – this specification dismisses unique enclosed images within a profusion of patterns or anecdotes – and which are plastically and semantically over-determined by the fact of their coexistence *in praesentia*" (2007: 18). See also Postema (2013: 55) on the "co-presence of images," where her discussion cites Groensteen.

16 "It seems to me that comics (and the visual story in general) are not apt to produce, by itself, an equivalent of the operation known in the literary domain as a description" (Groensteen 2007: 124).

17 As Groensteen explains, "once the same motif is represented several times it transports all of its attributes (its predicates) along with it. If we want to provide recognition to the descriptive properties of the drawing, we must therefore admit that it is a description that is infinitely restarted, to which we cannot assign a particular site. Contrarily, in a text, the descriptions are generally given 'once and for all'; once described, a character, for example, can thereafter be designated simply by his name, by a pronoun or a deictic. The description cedes the place to the designation, where it can therefore be considered a form of extension" (2007: 124).

18 A reviewer of my work once commented that it was colonializing of me to be writing about disability as an able-bodied scholar, or even about disability in literary/filmic texts produced by ablebodied authors and that, citing Spivak's foundational essay directly, subalterns should speak for themselves, a statement that struck me as particularly indicative of how cognitive ableism cloaks itself in the identity politics of disability studies scholarship. That is, arguments that populations with severe cognitive disabilities need to engage in the self-narration and self-representation that inform identity politics at the national scale seem quite false to me in that they map a physical disability model of the requirements of engaging with representational democracy to a cognitive disability model for which this argument is naive at best and perhaps even inappropriate.

19 Bérubé writes of prose literature that "thus, be cause the textual representation of cognitive disability requires the depiction of minds that do not have this capacity for self-reflection, it can be read without too much difficulty as a device with which to explore and reflect on the cognitive capacities necessary for textual self-representation" (2005: 572–3).

20 The full quotation reads: "One of the tasks undertaken by disability studies so far has been to point out these tropes and these characters, and to critique them for their failure to do justice to the actual lived experiences of people with disabilities. That project is long overdue and still needed; yet it sometimes proceeds as if characters in literary texts could be read simply as representations of real people" (2005: 570). Also consider: "As for my emphasis on the 'fictional' nature of the intellectual disabilities I examine here: I am relying on the ancient – and yet always critical – insight that literary characters are not real people" (2016: 29).

21 In fact, a reader offering suggestions about the material that was eventually included in this book manuscript asserted that people with Alzheimer's were only frustrated when not receiving proper care ... I will only say that I think this perspective overapplies the social model of disability by ignoring the material experience of cognitive impairment.

4 Visualizing Down Syndrome and Autism

1 See the brief discussion of this point in chapter 2 related to the case of Judith Scott, and the article by Joseph N. Straus, "Autism as Culture" (2013), that I discuss both in the introduction and chapter 3.

2 Ann Millett-Gallant's comments on the installation of *Alison Lapper Pregnant* by British artist Marc Quinn in London's Trafalgar Square are also somewhat relevant to this topic: "Public art raises issues of social and artistic representation and the visibility and invisibility of certain members of society" (2013: 399).

3 This is thus quite a different endeavour when compared with the tradition of looking at canonical works of literature and culture in light of disability – as evidenced in Snyder's essay "Infinities of Forms: Disability Figures in Artistic Traditions" (2002).

4 *María y* yo (Gallardo and Gallardo 2007) as well as the eponymous film based on that graphic novel (Fernández de Castro 2010) were both analysed extensively in chapter 2 of my previous monograph *Disability Studies and Spanish Culture* (2013).

5 Brief clips of this appear in the online video "Inauguración." See also a previous version of the present argument in Fraser 2013b.

6 As he admits in *Disability Aesthetics*, "neither disabled artists nor disabled subjects are central to my argument" (2010: 3).

7 Here Johnston cites work by Barnes and Mercer; Barnes, Oliver, and Barton; and Riddell and Watson.

8 In addition, the recent Spanish feature-length film *Yo, también* (Me, Too) (2009), which includes key scenes filmed in Madrid, makes an effective case for these specific articles of the Convention; the lead role, played by Pablo Pineda, depicts a university-degree holding thirty-four-year-old man with Down syndrome who struggles to exercise autonomy in the spheres of work and love (see Fraser 2011a; Gill 2016).

9 In the DVD *Capacitados*, three well-known Spanish people (questionably/problematically) experience a full working day under conditions intended to replicate a physical/sensory disability experience – chef Ferran Adrià; the president of Coca-Cola Iberia, Marcos de Quinto; and María Garaña, the able-bodied president of Microsoft Ibérica (see the booklet accompanying *Capacitados*, 2010: 7). Journalist Amparo Mendo points out the lack of engagement with intellectual disability as an important flaw in the project (same booklet, 2010: 43).

10 On unemployment rates see Boeltzig, Sulewski, and Hasnain (2009: 753), also Titchkosky (2009: 76); on work integration in Spain specifically

see Vilà, Pallisera, and Fullana (2007); see also Pallisera, Vilà, and Valls (2003).

11 See Fraser (2011a, 2010a); see also Fraser (2013c, 2012, 2010b, ed. 2009, 2007).

12 Hevey continues (original emphases): "In addition, we could say that the general history of disability representation is one of oppressive or 'negative' forms. And this has happened precisely because disabled people are excluded from the production of *impairment-based* disability culture and excluded from the dominant 'disability' discourses" (1993: 423). Also, "disabled people have been the *subject* of various constructions and representations throughout history but disabled people have not controlled the *object* – that is, the means of producing or positioning our own constructions or representations" (1993: 423).

13 Among them are Don Mitchell (2003) and Kirsten Simonsen (2005), who has pointed to the relevance of Lefebvrian thought for feminist approaches.

14 See the discussion in Fraser (2011b: 9–14).

15 See Fraser (2008: 340).

16 See Lefebvre (1991b: 249; Fraser 2011b: 23–8).

17 Significantly, the notion of "access" might refer also to access to the discourse and production of art. Taylor (2005: 325) asks how some "disabled young people post 16" might gain better access to existing art curricula.

18 Although it is inappropriate to engage this idea in depth here, interested readers can turn to Peter Hall's *Cities of Tomorrow* and – highlighting planning history in (Barcelona) Spain – even my own "Ildefons Cerdà's Scalpel" (Fraser 2011c) as well as works by Tim Marshall and Joan Ramon Resina.

19 On the culture of the Movida in Spain, see the volume edited by Nichols and Song (2014).

20 On Gallardo, see Alary (2000: 56, 60), Beaty (2007: 116, 119), Cuadrado (2000: 510–12), Dopico (2005: 318–34), Fraser (2013a: 34–74), García (2010: 165), and Vilarós (1998: 211–13).

21 One of Miguel Gallardo's own characterizations of this shift appears in the 2010 documentary film by Fernández de Castro (2010: 24:26–25:12).

22 "I propose that the autobiographies are forging a language in which to talk about autism and in terms of which autistic people can think out their experiences. Biographies, in many cases written by a mother or father of an autistic child, are often of great interest in this respect. They tell us much about families with autistic children. Some of them are good representations of the child growing up. Some tell more about the parent and her attempts to make sense of what has happened" (Hacking 2010: 261).

23 Fraser (2013a). See also the chapter on the HBO film *Temple Grandin* authored by K. Lashley published in *Cultures of Representation* (2016).

24 Note that Grandin's book bylines testify to this form of collaborative authorship. As a sidenote, it should not be forgotten that there was a time when widespread autism narrative was virtually non-existent; nor should it be forgotten that the publishing industry as a rule only publishes what it believes is marketable. See also another publication by Hacking where he writes: "It does not matter for the present purposes who contributed what to the final print form of the text" (2009: 1468).

25 Beyond reading her books and following her rise to ever-greater celebrity, I was fortunate enough to hear Temple Grandin speak at the College of Charleston during my time as a faculty member there.

26 Ian Hacking brings up both Grandin and the question of whether autistic "autobiographers are speaking only for the high-functioning end of the spectrum" (2009: 1468), but he does not engage this issue at length. I argue that this issue deserves our close attention precisely because of the nuances given to experiences of severe disabilities where impairment is a factor.

27 The pages are unnumbered, but for practicality of analysis I use a numbering system that begins with page 1 corresponding to the dedication page. This page features an image of María walking away; the back of her shirt reads "Be water my friend" in English, and the Spanish dedication below the image reads "Dedicado a May [Dedicated to May]" – May is María's mother.

28 Andy Bondy and Lori Frost's book *A Picture's Worth: PCES and Other Visual Communication Strategies in Autism* (2002) charts how pictograms impact effective communication for people with autism (2002: 53–5). They also developed the Picture Exchange Communication System (PCES) (2002: 67–94). Note that other similar systems have been developed (2002: 131, 135; Boutot and Smith Myles 2011: 125–7).

29 See the prose description suggesting that María changes from song to song after hearing its first three seconds (2015: 20).

30 See also another page featuring a full-page panel illustrating María listening to music (2015: 24).

31 See Fraser (2013a: 70–1).

32 Remembering the thesis of Martin Norden's *Cinema of Isolation*, that disabled characters in film have tended to be portrayed as isolated loners, I point out that portraying María by herself listening to music or drawing is not the same thing as portraying her as isolated and alone – these are social activities that involve her in a social world: they bring a social world to her and prepare her for further social interactions. *María cumple 20 años* is, in fact, a consistent portrayal of the fact that María is embedded

in social relationships. Note too, that the previous graphic novel *María y yo* did include some metaphors of isolation – in particular the depiction of María on an island – whose impact was purposely heightened in the documentary film, I think, to its detriment.

33 I previously noted that the medical model of disability was much more prevalent in the documentary film than in the graphic novel version of *María y yo* (Fraser 2013a: 71).

34 This quality of the sequence can be explained by the qualities of background and comics composition analysed by McCloud (1994).

35 Frustrations with communication are also visible in the graphic novel's treatment of María's screaming (on 2015: 20, 25–6, 28; see also 51).

36 As a way of saying thank you to the people in this network, another page attempts a listing that runs from the top to the bottom margin of the page, with not a single image (2015: 57).

37 I was fortunate, while at the College of Charleston, to attend a lecture given by Michael Bérubé where his adult son with Down syndrome also gave a speech.

5 Sequencing Alzheimer's Dementia

1 See Dopico (2005: 317–34); Compitello 2014; Vilarós 1998. The second tome of Jesús Cuadrado's encyclopedia of Spanish comics and comics artists notes that he joined the "pornographic and Barcelonan" publication *Comix Kiss Comix* in 1994, and by 1995 was working alongside the scriptwriter and narrator Juan Miguel Aguilera (at times under the collective name Trazo) as well as in the alternative press (*BEM*) or guild publications (*Ganadería Trashumante*) (2000: 1083; the Paco Roca entry is of course relatively brief).

2 See Nichols and Song (2014), as well as volume 14 of the *Arizona Journal of Hispanic Cultural Studies*, and Triana Toribio.

3 On the recent attempt to move disability studies beyond the confines of Anglo-American contexts see the journal issues edited by Murray and Barker (2010) and Mitchell and Snyder (2010).

4 Disability in Spanish film has also been addressed by Conway (2000, 2001); Marr (2009, 2013); Minich (2010, 2014); and Prout (2008); see also *Discapacidades humanas* (2010); Ferreira (2008); Fraser (2013a); Gámez Fuentes (2005); and Hirtz (2009). See also the articles related to Spain in the special section of the *Arizona Journal of Hispanic Cultural Studies* edited by Encarnación Juárez-Almendros. The anglophone focus of Alegre de la Rosa's *La discapacidad en el cine* (2003) reveals how much work is still to be done in Spain on disability and film.

5 Given its melodramatic tenor, I regard the film *¿Y tú quién eres?* as a textbook example of the way in which this dependency anxiety tends to be screened. By contrast, *Arrugas* in both graphic novel and film form is a welcome correction to this trend. On the film, see Fraser 2016b.

6 Part of my reason for saying this has to do with the distinction between the audiences who consume graphic novels on one hand and those who consume films on the other. As the product of a very personal and individually produced artistic genre, sequential art – especially good sequential art – demands more of the reader than do most films, which are designed to appeal to wide audiences and whose production costs are wagered to bring a substantial economic return. But more than demonstrating this general principle, *Arrugas* is moreover a good example of how sophisticated even popular sequential art can be.

7 While the graphic novel in Europe has received some significant attention (e.g., Beaty's *Unpopular Culture: Transforming the European Comic Book in the 1990s*), graphic novels and comics on the Iberian peninsula have not enjoyed the attention in English publications that has been given to, for example, the French context. Nevertheless, comics and graphic novels published in Spain have figured into an increasing number of works published in Spanish (on the graphic novel in Spain see Alary 2000; Dopico 2005; Fraser 2013a; on adaptations of graphic novels to film see Hight 2007; Lefèvre 2007; on disability in the graphic novel outside of Spain see Alaniz 2014; Fink Berman 2010; and for relevant sources on the graphic novel in Europe see Beaty 2007; García 2010; Gasca and Gubern 2001; Merino 2002).

8 This trend is not unrelated to the social shifts prompted by a larger aging population that will see the total number of people living with AD in Spain rise to 1.5 million by 2050 (Medina 2013: 1689). Cultural scholar Raquel Medina writes of Alzheimer's that "in 2011, approximately 600,000 people in Spain had been diagnosed with AD, and another 200,000 were believed to be suffering from the disease without having had a medical diagnosis ... This staggering number, when taken in combination with the documented scarcity of nursing home places, diminishes the chances for a person with AD securing an adequate place to live in and to receive appropriate care. Apart from class and gender implications, what emerges from these figures is that the family replaces public health and social care as the main actor in providing care for older people and AD patients. Furthermore, the family can be left with the entire financial burden and responsibility for care regarding AD" (2013: 1689)

9 That is, whether we are speaking of senescent adults or younger persons with intellectual disabilities, of life inside of or outside of institutional

contexts, quality of life issues such as the lack of meaningful work and limitations to one's autonomy can take a toll (on disability and work see Chima 2005; Citron et al. 2008; Contardi 2002; Hartnett et al. 2008; Migliori et al. 2007; Morris 2002; Pardeck 2005; Parmenter 1991, 1996; Ping-Ying Li, Sing-Fai Tam, and Wai-Kwong Man 2006; Vilà, Pallisera, and Fullana 2007; Wehman, 1995, 2006; on autonomy and Spanish film see Fraser 2010a, 2011a, 2013a). Suzanne Abbott and Roy McConkey's article "The Barriers to Social Inclusion as Perceived by People with Intellectual Disabilities" is particularly relevant (see 2006: 276).

10 Similarly, the use of the subjective in *Arrugas* – both in graphic novel and film – squares with Naomi Feil's 1960s notion of Validation Therapy, discussed by Kitwood, which affirmed that "the experience of people with dementia should be taken with the utmost seriousness" (in Kitwood 2011: 56).

11 These citations are from Lucy Burke, who, while she does not work on Spanish cultural production, has produced analyses of textual explorations of Alzheimer's that are quite relevant here (see also Burke 2007, 2008b).

12 This notion is supplemented where advantageous to do so by published work on dementia by Annette Leibing and Lawrence Cohen, Tom Kitwood, Jaber Gubrium, Lucy Burke, Bruce Jennings, and Hilde Lindemann. Aagje Swinnen and Mark Schweda's volume *Popularizing Dementia* (2015) is another obligatory reference.

13 Jennings stresses that it is not a matter of coming to terms "with a diminished thing" and that instead "we should seek to attain a re-placed plenitude" (Jennings 2010: 171). "Moreover, it is not necessary to draw a sharp distinction between personal and social mind when dealing with dementia, just as it is not requisite to draw a sharp line between minding in the past and minding in the present (remembering and intending)" (2010: 173; see also the chapter in the same book by James Lindemann Nelson (2010) titled "Alzheimer's Disease and Socially Extended Mentation").

14 Generally speaking, this hedonic approach, rooted in a somewhat simplistic notion of satisfaction and of a necessarily social nature, is not yet the palliative care that might be carried out on the second floor of the facility. Opposed to a hedonic understanding of care that is linked to social satisfaction, palliative care is, of course, a practice rooted in comfort with necessarily social dimensions.

15 For a visual example of this linkage as seen in Spanish cinema see the documentary *Monos como Becky* (1999) by Joaquim Jordà, a director who is discussed in Fraser (2013a).

16 Jaber Gubrium (1986) looks at the importance of narrative and storytelling for the human experience in general and specifically at how significant these become for families and friends of loved ones with Alzheimer's disease (see also Gubrium 2003).

17 See Roy (2009: 41), who argues that individuals *are* narratives in a sense.

18 This intriguing article discusses a creative storytelling project carried out in multiple locations beginning in 1998 with Alzheimer's disease and related dementia (ADRD) patients (see also Basting 2001: 78; 2006).

19 This is explained well by Scott McCloud, whose important work *Understanding Comics* (1994) has been translated into Spanish by Astiberri in Bilbao.

20 At one moment Emilio repeats himself three times at dinner without realizing it (2008: 54). There is one character who seems unable to express himself but who repeats whatever he hears (2008: 12), and another who repeatedly shows off his bronze medal from 1953 (based on a real-life resident Roca met). Some of these behaviours are more serious or more emotionally heavy, such when Félix's roommate hits him on the head with a wrench out of frustration with his snoring, accidentally killing him; or when a woman who is no longer able to remember her husband takes up with another resident of the home, right in front of her husband during his visits (2008: 36–7). The closing scene at the end of the graphic novel depicts a story where an elderly man still allowed to live with family on the weekends, almost kills his leashed dog Milú in an elevator accident (2008: 100).

21 There is an incident Miguel finds humorous where Emilio defecates in the character Pellicer's collection bag of memories (2008: 88).

22 There is an extended depiction of motor skill exercises in the graphic novel, led by a younger woman who catches the eyes of the elderly men in the residence (2008: 25–31). Of great interest is that at a certain moment Emilio forgets the word that corresponds to the "pelota [ball]" that is being passed around (2008: 31). More than once the word is pronounced as "talope," a nonsense word that changes the syllable positioning within the word. It is not clear whether the physical trainer's repetition of this word is playing along or is on the other hand a semi-subjective portrayal of the fact that Emilio – or other Alzheimer's patients – are "losing" language (on motor skills and dementia see Masumoto et al. 2004).

23 The shock of sudden appearance at the beginning of the graphic novel will of course be replaced by the disappearance that tends to characterize ADRD toward the end of the *Arrugas* – most concretely the misplacement of Emilio's wallet and watch.

24 Kitwood mentions seven access routes through which "we can gain insight into the subjective world of dementia" (2011: 73–9). *Arrugas*, I argue here – which is based on some of the above, given the author's own experiences with people with dementia – would constitute a route 8 (or perhaps a modified route 6), in that there is value in approaching dementia through the poetic imagination of *another*. See also Burke (2007).

25 Research into Alzheimer's has looked into dissociation between proper name and common name production (Brennen et al. 1996: 96). A basic premise is that if you can name something you can give further information, but you may have further information without being able to recall the name: "Considerable evidence from many paradigms has shown that naming a person is more arduous than categorising them semantically" (1996: 94).

26 Consider what Ramanathan writes: "Thus, from this point of view, the Alzheimer patient's silences and broken speech are only degrees removed from what is in any case a vanishing spiral of smoke or vapour, with trace leading to trace" (2008: 15).

27 Hamilton recognizes the collective resonance of narratives in the context of Alzheimer's research specifically, noting "the multiple ways in which audience members contribute linguistically and non-linguistically to the emergence of the narrative" (2008: 54). She also allows for the fact that these narratives can be comprised of fragments: "In closing, short narratives told by individuals living with Alzheimer's disease may indeed not function well as 'self-portraits,' but even a narrative as 'snapshot' can provide clues that can help interlocutors reconstruct aspects of the individual's identity" (2008: 79–80). See also Ramanathan 2008.

28 See Peón Sánchez (2004) on caregiver syndrome as it relates to Alzheimer's.

6 Screening Schizophrenia

1 The last paragraph of the essay, which reflects I think a poor choice of words, ends with what the authors surely take to be a hopeful vision of the future, made possible by the ACA and by President Obama: "President Obama has recently made reducing prison populations a political priority … States that have declined to take federal funds for Medicaid expansion may recognize that their own expenditures on correctional institutions will remain high unless they find ways to reduce the number of mentally ill in jails and prisons. The community services that Medicaid helps to support would go a long way to accomplish this goal. The policies that

would emerge – such as expanded programs to integrate offenders back into the community – could also prove highly beneficial for the disabled. In the end, it is in everyone's interest – offenders, disabled and the general public – to have fewer people under lock and key" (2015: 72).

2 Certainly these are terms that have a legal resonance and that appear in Medicaid documents. Thus at the same time that I question their use in the *NYRB* essay, I also question their more popular and pervasive legalistic use. This is not the place, however, to engage this point more extensively. I merely want to draw attention to the inadequacy of such terms and their role in reaffirming a normative position on cognitive disability.

3 It is useful to know that just such a problematic distinction resonates through a Medicaid community handbook posted by the US Department of Health and Human Services, where the terms are similarly defined only vaguely. There, "mental illness" is itself considered a cause of disability and is presumed to be curable; "mental retardation" is contrasted with "mental disorder"; and somewhat paradoxically, "mental disorders include mental retardation, organic brain disorders and mental illnesses, among others." See "USING MEDICAID TO SUPPORT WORKING AGE ADULTS WITH SERIOUS MENTAL ILLNESSES IN THE COMMUNITY: A HANDBOOK" (https://aspe.hhs.gov/pdf-report/using-medicaid-support-working-age-adults-serious-mental-illnesses-community-handbook). "*We envision a future when everyone with a mental illness will recover, a future when mental illnesses can be prevented or cured, a future when mental illnesses are detected early, and a future when everyone with a mental illness at any stage of life has access to effective treatment and supports – essentials for living, working, learning, and participating fully in the community*"; "Mental illness is the leading cause of disability in the United States"; "Mental disorders include mental retardation, organic brain disorders and mental illnesses, among others."

4 There is also an interesting comment made regarding the developmentally disabled (Neier and Rothman 2015: 42).

5 In truth, this title is reserved for Foucault's second French edition of the book in 1972 (Foucault 2006: xxiii), the English translation of which was not available until 2006. See also Foucault (1973, 1994, 1995, and 2006).

6 "For clinical experience to become possible as a form of knowledge, a reorganization of the hospital field, a new definition of the status of the patient in society, and the establishment of a certain relationship between public assistance and medical experience, between help and knowledge, became necessary; the patient has to be enveloped in a collective, homogeneous space. It was also necessary to open up language to a whole new domain:

that of a perpetual and objectively based correlation of the visible and the expressible" (Foucault 1994: 196).

7 The relatively recent coining of the term Mad Studies, which arises out of the long history of anti-psychiatry movements, provides reason to connect Foucault's critique with present-day struggles. In their introduction, the editors of the volume *Mad Matters: A Critical Reader in Canadian Mad Studies* (2013) encourage "the radical reclaiming of psychic spaces of resistance against the psychiatric domination of Mad people as a collection of chemical imbalances needing to be corrected in a capitalist system that prizes bourgeois conformity and medical model 'fixes' above all" (LeFrancois, Menzies and Reaume 2013: 2). As I discuss it below, Abel García Roure's film cannot be said to fit neatly into the spirit of this newly forming academic discipline of Mad Studies. That is, by not dismissing the value of mental health supports wholesale and by instead acknowledging the potential life benefits of such support when provided to certain individuals, it poses a somewhat more complicated question. On one hand, the film affirms, in my view, that in some markedly severe cases where medication is desired, patients and providers may need to collaborate on plans of care. On the other, it affirms and critiques the fact that patients and providers do not enter into this collaboration with an equal degree of social power.

8 I have addressed this throughout the present book. While not the sole example of this trend, feminist philosopher Licia Carlson has been particularly important in this regard (see Carlson 2001, 2010; Carlson and Kittay 2010). In addition, a growing body of anglophone work has explored the representation of both physical and cognitive disabilities in film and media (see Chivers 2011; Chivers and Markotić 2010; Enns and Smit 2001a; Mogk 2013; Pointon and Davies 2008; Riley 2005), going beyond the primarily physical focus of Martin Norden's foundational title *The Cinema of Isolation: A History of Physical Disability in the Movies* (1994).

9 Important touchstone representations of schizophrenia in Iberian film and literature include Joaquim Jordà's *Monos como Becky* (1999) as well as the documentary *1% Esquizofrenia* (2006), directed by Ione Hernández and produced by the noted Spanish filmmaker Julio Medem, and the bestselling novel *Los renglones torcidos de Dios* (1979) published by Torcuato Luca de Tena. One must consider that Tobin Siebers's lucid remarks about the fundamental role of disability in modern aesthetics may warrant exploration in the medium of filmic representation specifically (2010: 4-5; see also Siebers 2008).

10 The film's producer, noted director Julio Medem, commented at a film festival where *1% esquizofrenia* was screened that "siempre me interesó

mucho el tema de la esquizofrenia … Me hice médico para ser psiquiatra, aunque no lo soy, por suerte; porque cuando descubrí la esquizofrenia, me di cuenta de que nunca sería capaz de ayudar a estas personas ... y mira, ni siquiera he sido capaz de dirigir esta película, una película que, aviso, remueve muchas cosas, y eso es fundamental" (The topic of schizophrenia has always interested me ... I pursued medicine to be a psychiatrist, even though I am not one, luckily; because when I discovered schizophrenia, I realized that I would never be able to help these people ... and look, I haven't even been able to direct this film, a film that, I warn you, changes many things, and this is fundamental) (Hermoso 2006: 37).

11 Regarding the issue of violence: "Las estadísticas demuestran que … tomados como muestra general, los enfermos con esquizofrenia son menos agresivos que la población general, curiosamente" (Statistics show that … taken as a general sample, those sick with schizophrenia are less aggressive than the general population, curiously) (35:53); "Es al revés, es decir que ellos son mucho más agredidos que agresores" (It is the opposite, that is, they are much more likely to be the victims of violence than the aggressors) (36:06). Regarding the theme of social marginalization, see 10:07.

12 The image of a crowd is a welcome shift, but occurs very late in the film (1:04:33, 1:05:19). We also see symbols of the pharmaceutical industry such as lab equipment and pills (respectively, 51:33, 52:53; 54:00, 54:44).

13 Another interview outlines the importance of social understanding and acceptance (11:20).

14 I am thinking here particularly of Torcuato Luca de Tena's bestselling Spanish novel *Los renglones torcidos de Dios* (The Twisted Lines of God) (1979), which presents themes restaged to a certain extent also in the more recent Hollywood film *Shutter Island* (2010).

15 In popular culture and discourse, schizophrenia is traditionally misunderstood as a split within a person's psyche, a point that the documentary itself attempts to correct (see discussion of "el mito de que eszuizofrénicos tienen dos personalidades o son dos personas diferentes en un solo cuerpo" (the myth that schizophrenics have two personalities, or are two different people in a single body) (0:48:56). See also de la Rosa (2007), where this splitting is appropriately framed as between the patient and reality. *Una cierta verdad* goes a step further by showing viewers that this split has a social as well as a clinical dimension, as discussed later on in this article.

16 Regarding "the particular characteristics of the Catalan context," this study noted that "in our country, no community-based psychiatric and social services were established after the deinstitutionalization national policy, and National Health Service resources for psychiatric patients

living in the community are limited to outpatient psychiatric visits for medication control. Only recently and very slowly are some additional psychological and social programs being provided" (Duñó et al. 2001: 688). Of great interest is the fact that Dr Roser Guillamat – who appears in *Una cierta verdad* – is a co-author of this study, whose authors are all based at the Parc Taulí in Sabadell (Barcelona). See also Pousa et al. (2008).

17 In that study, "fair agreement" was the lowest rating regarding items from the category of met needs, ranking below "almost perfect," "substantial," and "moderate" but above levels of agreement between staff and patients regarding unmet needs, which were lower still (Ochoa et al. 2003: 205).

18 "In conclusion, the CLAMORS study has shown that the prevalence of MS in Spanish patients with schizophrenic, schizophreniform and schizoaffective disorders receiving antipsychotic therapy, while lower than in North America or Scandinavia, seems considerably higher than in the reference general and clinical populations, presenting values that these latter populations reach only when 10 to 15 years older. This situation in an already excessively stigmatized patient population group should be a source of concern for public health care and society as a whole" (Bobes et al. 2007: 171). Note that Julio Bobes is one of those interviewed on screen during the *1% esquizofrenia* (2006) documentary film (see 1:08–1:09 for his image).

19 A reference to the Quijote appears in the film, spoken by Javier, who says that because he was acting like Cervantes's protagonist with the windmills, he took his medication (1:31:43). Notably a reference to the Quijote also appears in *1% esquizofrenia* (11:25).

20 At one moment, Javier, discussed below, tells a psychiatrist that now that he isn't on Risperdal he sleeps much better, approximately 7½ hours per night (0:53:00; also 1:01:53). Earlier in the film, he also complains that the medications he is taking at times leave him without strength to take care of himself: "Sí, si tengo ... un poquito de fuerza, porque ... las medicaciones te dejan demasiado chafado y no te da para hacer ... lavar la ropa por ejemplo" (Yes, if I have … a bit of energy, because … the medications leave you too flattened and don't leave you able … to wash your clothes for example) (0:32:25). Later on, Javier repeats that Risperdal leaves him in a coma-like state (1:31:49); and points directly to the consequences of how relaxing patients generally means rendering them inactive: "relaja pero mata los sistemas eléctricos; o los mata o los reduce" (it relaxes [a person], but it kills one's electrical systems: either it kills them or it reduces them) (1:27:15).

21 Importantly, two of the privileged psychiatrists portrayed in the documentary go on record explicitly about wanting the best for patients, and even about wanting to minimize the impact of side effects on patients (1:21:22).

22 To describe this non-spectacular aspect of the film in other terms, it is useful to gauge student reactions to the documentary. I included this film in a disability series for students interested in the Hispanic world, and a room packed with some one hundred students let out a collective groan when the credits started. Other films in the series were not met with such a clear collective reaction. After also teaching the film in another class featuring undergraduate students interested in health care careers and even to a select number of graduate students, I am tempted to explain the reaction as a comment on the way in which spectators are not prepared to consume non-spectacular (everyday, slow, careful, contemplative) visual narrative regarding psychiatric illness.

23 Olga Real-Najarro has written of narratives that relate the patient experience of schizophrenia as either "desde dentro [from within/emic]" or "desde fuera [from without/etic]" (2011: 171), neither of which fully applies in this case.

24 This reliance of psychiatry providers on narrative is thus potentially combatted by patient narrative itself, as when, in *Una cierta verdad*, Bernat shares the story that he successfully changed a judge's opinion in order to avoid being interned against the wishes of his doctor.

25 One film reviewer has gone so far as to say this explicitly – "Es quizás por esta ausencia de punto de vista que en la película de Roure es difícil saber quién es el protagonista o si tan siquiera lo hay. Aunque es probable que ésa no sea una cuestión importante en un film que en realidad pretende cuestionar los límites de la cordura y la locura así como los códigos sociales sobre los cuales se asienta la concepción contemporánea de la normalidad [It is perhaps because of this absence of viewpoint that in Roure's film it is difficult to know who is the protagonist or if there even is one. Even though it is possible that this isn't an important question in a film that in truth seeks to question the limits of sanity and madness just as it does the social codes upon which the contemporary conception of normality rests]" (Petrus 2009). The point of view, of course, is precisely one that views the limits between madness and reason with an appropriate scepticism, as the second statement above makes clear.

26 One in-depth review piece does well in suggesting that "al contrario de *Mones com la Becky*, aquí no se trata de cuestionar el uso institucional de la locura, sino que se encuadra en un compromiso ético al querer desterrar los prejuicios sociales que envuelven a estos pacientes" (in contrast to *Monos como Becky*, here it is not a matter of questioning the institutional idea of madness, but instead of framing it within an ethical commitment by seeking to get rid of the social prejudices that envelop these patients)

(Montoya 2009). Another scholar characterizes the film as "un ejemplo de cine comprometido y necesario" (an example of committed and necessary cinema) (Rodríguez Chico 2009).

27 Abel García Roure has said that "no hay percepción posible sobre el mundo que nos rodea que no esté siempre teñida de la subjetividad (con sus innumerables matices y facetas) de quien percibe; toda percepción de la realidad está siempre sujeta a una infinitud incalculable de interpretaciones y puntos de vista subjetivos, tantos como sujetos existen e, incluso, multiplicados por tantos como los instantes que se suceden uno detrás de otro, en cada momento" (there is no possible perception of the world surrounding us that is not shaped by the subjectivity [with its innumerable nuances and facets] of the person doing the perceiving: every perception of reality is always subject to an incalculable infinity of interpretations and subjective points of view, as many as there are people and, even, multiplied by the number of instants that each follow the others, in every moment) (quoted in Rodríguez Herrero 2012: no pag.).

28 Javier, for example, was originally interned for stabbing a young boy while having an episode, and more recently for wanting to attack someone with a hammer (1:14:29); Rosario admits to having previously attempted suicide, by trying to throw herself from a balcony.

29 During this effective sequence, the film's editing uses cross-cutting to contrast Alberto with another patient who is quite verbal but strapped to a gurney, thus portraying the range of experiences of those receiving help at the Taulí.

30 Neither do we have significant access to the faces of a number of other relatively minor characters in the film's narrative, including Jordi D.A., Rosa M.S., Xavier Piñol, and F.J.P., who are credited at the film's close.

31 To put it somewhat crudely, if there are three or four main patient characters on the side of madness, there are three or four doctor characters on the side of reason. Among those physicians listed in the film's credits are Dr Josep Moya, Dra Gabriela Severino, Dra Roser Guillamat, Dr Jesús Cobo, Dr Esteve Bonet, Dra Raise Agustín, Dra Isabel Parra, and Dr Isreal Álvarez.

32 In one effective example of cross-cutting, there is a schizophrenic patient talking to camera crew at his house, which is then cross-cut with the same patient delivering a lecture on his experience to a group of providers, presumably at the Taulí (0:16:31–0:17:51).

33 In the first case, the cut separates Javier's question of what happens if a doctor decides she wants to make people into hamburgers (0:59:07–0:59:13) and Dr Guillamat's explanation of what happens to a patient

when a crisis starts (0:59:14–0:59:49); in the second case, Javier first complains about not understanding why he is being interned – "no capto la razón (... de eso, ingresarme al Taulí ...), no he cometido ningún delito, no he hecho nada, ninguna cosa, no entiendo, no entiendo" (I don't get the reason [...for this, for being interned in the Taulí], I have committed no crime, I haven't done anything, nothing, I don't understand, I don't understand" (0:58:16) – and then points to the risks of the medication he is being forced to take, saying "no tiene efectos secundarios por el momento. Hace ya veinticinco años que medico, y yo creo que ya es demasiado tiempo largo, tanta medicación, oye" (there are no secondary effects [known] at this time. I've been on medicine for twenty-five years, and I think that this is too long, too much medication, you know) (0:58:32). Another example is when the editing cuts away after Javier expresses how meaningful it is to be able to be creative and draw, something he cannot do when on Risperdal (1:31:57).

34 In fact at a later moment in the film, Josep attempts to use cellular/neuronal vocabulary and other metaphors to explain the operation of schizophrenia to Javier in the latter's apartment (starting at 1:08:25).

35 When Javier speaks with a psychiatrist at the film's approximate midway point about the issue of medication (1:01:57–1:03:31), the camera switches from having the pair share the frame to framing each separately, thus illustrating their disagreement. Speaking with Josep in his apartment, Javier complains that the providers won't spend time talking with him anymore: "Bueno es que los psiquiatras no te dicen nada, ni hablas con ellos. Nada más la inyección ... te dicen pues 'te voy a internar.' Total que, yo, que ¿quién está más loco?" (Well it is that the psychiatrists don't tell you anything, nor do you talk to them. Just the injection ... They just tell you 'I'm going to intern you.' So that, I wonder who is more crazy) (1:11:26).

36 "A hearing gaze and a speaking gaze: clinical experience represents a moment of balance between speech and spectacle. A precarious balance, for it rests on a formidable postulate: that all that is *visible* is *expressible*, and that it is *wholly visible* because it is *wholly expressible*. A postulate of such scope could permit a coherent science only if it was developed in a logic that was its rigorous outcome. But the reversibility, without residue, of the visible in the expressible remained in the clinic a requirement and a limit rather than an original principle. Total *description* is a present and ever-withdrawing horizon; it is much more the dream of a thought than a basic conceptual structure" (1994: 115, original emphasis).

References

Abbott, S., and D. McConkey. 2006. "The Barriers to Social Inclusion as Perceived by People with Intellectual Disabilities." *Journal of Intellectual Disabilities* 10(3): 275–87. https://doi.org/10.1177/1744629506067618

Alaniz, José. 2014. *Death, Disability, and the Superhero: The Silver Age and Beyond*. Jackson: University Press of Mississippi. https://doi.org/10.14325/mississippi/9781628461176.001.0001

Alary, Viviane. 2000. "La historieta en España: entre el futuro y el pasado." In *Cuatro lecciones sobre el cómic*, ed. Antonio Ballesteros and Claude Duée, 35–66. Cuenca: Ediciones de la Universidad de Castilla-la Mancha.

Alegre de la Rosa, Olga María. 2003. *La discapacidad en el cine*. Tenerife: Octaedro.

Amanzio, Martina, Giuliano Geminiani, Daniela Leotta, and Stefano Cappa. 2008. "Metaphor Comprehension in Alzheimer's Disease: Novelty Matters." *Brain and Language* 107(1): 1–10. https://doi.org/10.1016/j.bandl.2007.08.003

Anon. 2011. "Familiares de enfermos piden una 'política de Estado' contra el Alzheimer" [Relatives of Alzheimers' Disease Patients Are Asking for a "State Policy" against Alzheimer's]. *El publico.es*, 21 September. http://www.publico.es/espana/397522/familiares-de-enfermos-piden-una-politica-de-estado-contra-el-alzheimer

Antebi, Susan. 2016. "Cripping the Camera: Disability and Filmic Interval in Carlos Reygadas's Japón." In *Libre Acceso: Latin American Literature and Film through Disability Studies*, ed. S. Antebi and B. Jörgensen, 103–20. Albany: SUNY Press.

– 2009. *Carnal Inscriptions: Spanish American Narratives of Corporeal Difference and Disability*. New York: Palgrave Macmillan.

Antebi, Susan, and Beth Jörgensen, eds. 2016. *Libre Acceso: Latin American Literature and Film through Disability Studies*. Albany: SUNY Press. Print

Attoh, Kafui A. 2011. "What *Kind* of Right Is the Right to the City." *Progress in Human Geography* 35(5): 669–85. https://doi.org/10.1177/0309132510394706

Balázs, Béla. 1970. *Theory of the Film: Character and Growth of a New Art*. Trans. Edith Bone. New York: Dover Publications.

Balota, David, Michael J. Cortese, Janet M. Duchek, David Adams, Henry L. Roediger, III, Kathleen B. McDermott, and Benjamin E. Yerys. 1999. "Veridical and False Memories in Healthy Older Adults and in Dementia of the Alzheimer's Type." *Cognitive Neuropsychology* 16(3–5): 361–84. https://doi.org/10.1080/026432999380834

Barrera, Lola, and Iñaki Peñafiel, dir. 2006. *¿Qué tienes debajo del sombrero?* Alicia Produce. Film.

Barthes, Roland. 1979. *The Eiffel Tower and Other Mythologies*. Trans. Richard Howard. New York: Hill and Wang.

Basting, Anne Davis. 2001. "'God Is a Talking Horse': Dementia and the Performance of Self." *Drama Review* 45(3): 78–94. https://doi.org/10.1162/10542040152587123

– 2006. "Creative Storytelling and Self-Expression among People with Dementia." In *Thinking about Dementia: Culture, Loss, and the Anthropology of Senility*, ed. Annette Leibing and Lawrence Cohen, 180–94. New Brunswick: Rutgers University Press.

Beaty, Bart. 2007. *Unpopular Culture: Transforming the European Comic Book in the 1990s*. Toronto: University of Toronto Press.

Ben-Moshe, Liat. 2013. "'The Institution Yet to Come': Analyzing Incarceration through a Disability Lens." *The Disability Studies Reader*, 4th ed., ed. L.J. Davis, 132–43. New York: Routledge.

Bérubé, Michael. 1996. *Life as We Know It: A Father, A Family, and an Exceptional Child*. New York: Pantheon Books.

– 2005. "Disability and Narrative." *PMLA* 120(2): 568–76.

– 2016. *The Secret Life of Stories: From Don Quixote to Harry Potter, How Understanding Intellectual Disability Transforms the Way We Read*. New York: NYU Press.

Bobes, Julio, Celso Arango, Pedro Aranda, Rafael Carmena, and Margarida García-García. Javier Rejas on behalf of the CLAMORS Study Collaborative Group. 2007. "Cardiovascular and metabolic risk in outpatients with schizophrenia treated with antipsychotics: Results of the CLAMORS Study." *Schizophrenia Research* 90: 162–73. http://www.elsevier.com/locate/schres; https://doi.org/10.1016/j.schres.2006.09.025

Boeltzig, Heike, Jennifer Sullivan Sulewski, and Rooshey Hasnain. 2009. "Career Development among Young Disabled Artists." *Disability and Society* 24(6): 753–69. https://doi.org/10.1080/09687590903160258

Bogdan, Robert. 1988. *Freak Show: Presenting Human Oddities for Amusement and Profit*. Chicago: University of Chicago Press.

– 2012. *Picturing Disability: Beggar, Freak, Citizen, and Other Photographic Rhetoric.* With Martin Elks and James A. Knoll. Syracuse: Syracuse University Press.

Bondy, Andy, and Lori Frost. 2002. *A Picture's Worth: PCES and Other Visual Communication Strategies in Autism*. Bethesda: Woodbine House.

Boutot, E. Amanda, and Brenda Smith Myles. 2011. *Autism Spectrum Disorders: Foundations, Characteristics, and Effective Strategies*. Upper Saddle River: Pearson.

Brennen, Tim, Danielle David, Isabelle Fluchaire, and Jacques Pellat. 1996. "Naming Faces and Objects without Comprehension – A Case Study." *Cognitive Neuropsychology* 13(1): 93–110. https://doi.org/10.1080/026432996382079

Brosco, Jeffrey P. 2010. "The Limits of the Medical Model: Historical Epidemiology of Intellectual Disability in the United States." In *Cognitive Disability and Its Challenge to Moral Philosophy*, ed. L. Carlson and E.F. Kittay, 27–54. Malden,: Wiley-Blackwell. https://doi.org/10.1002/9781444322781.ch2

Brown, Joan L. 2010. *Confronting Our Canons: Spanish and Latin American Studies in the Twenty-First Century*. Lewisburg: Bucknell University Press.

Brueggemann, Brenda Jo. 1999. *Lend Me Your Ear: Rhetorical Constructions of Deafness*. Washington, DC: Gallaudet University Press.

Burch, Susan, and Alison Kafer, eds. 2010. *Deaf and Disability Studies: Interdisciplinary Perspectives*. Washington, DC: Gallaudet University Press.

Burke, Lucy. 2007. "The Poetry of Dementia: Art, Ethics and Alzheimer's Disease in Tony Harrison's *Black Daisies for the Bride*." *Journal of Literary Disability* 1(1): 61–73. https://doi.org/10.3828/jlcds.1.1.7

– 2008a. "'The Country of My Disease': Genes and Genealogy in Alzheimer's Life-Writing." *Journal of Literary Disability* 2(1): 63–74. https://doi.org/10.3828/jlcds.2.1.8

– 2008b. "Introduction: Thinking of Cognitive Impairment." *Journal of Literary Disability* 2(1): i–iv. https://doi.org/10.3828/jlcds.2.1.1

Butler, Judith. 1993. *Bodies That Matter: On the Discursive Limits of Sex*. New York: Routledge.

"Campaña 'Derechos para personas con discapacidad intelectual.'" http://www.youtube.com/watch?v=NlObVO966Ic

"Campaña [2] 'Derechos para personas con discapacidad intelectual.'" http://www.youtube.com/watch?v=UKu832m-lBI&feature=related

"Campaña [3] 'Derechos para personas con discapacidad intelectual.'" http://www.youtube.com/watch?v=VQ5BSOUrx60&feature=related

Capacitados. 2010. Madrid: Fundación ONCE. DVD + 64-page booklet (the documentary is also available online at www.capacitados.org).

Carey, Alison C. 2009. *On the Margins of Citizenship: Intellectual Disability and Civil Rights in Twentieth-Century America*. Philadelphia: Temple University Press.

Carlson, Licia. 2001. "Cognitive Ableism and Disability Studies: Feminist Reflections on the History of Mental Retardation." *Hypatia* 16(4): 124–46. https://doi.org/10.1111/j.1527-2001.2001.tb00756.x

– 2010. *The Faces of Intellectual Disability: Philosophical Reflections*. Bloomington: Indiana University Press.

Carlson, Licia, and Eva Feder Kittay. 2010. "Introduction: Rethinking Philosophical Presumptions in Light of Cognitive Disability." In *Cognitive Disability and Its Challenge to Moral Philosophy*, ed. L. Carlson and E.F. Kittay, 1–26. Malden: Wiley-Blackwell. https://doi.org/10.1002/9781444322781.ch1

Charlton, J.I. 1998. *Nothing about Us without Us: Disability Oppression and Empowerment*. Berkeley: University of California Press. https://doi.org/10.1525/california/9780520207950.001.0001

Chima, Felix O. 2005. "Persons with Disabilities and Employment." *Journal of Social Work in Disability and Rehabilitation* 4(3): 39–60. https://doi.org/10.1300/J198v04n03_05

Chivers, Sally. 2011. *The Silvering Screen: Old Age and Disability in Cinema*. Toronto: University of Toronto Press.

– 2013. "Seeing the Apricot: A Disability Perspective on Alzheimer's in Lee Chang-dong's *Poetry*." In *Different Bodies*, ed. M.E. Mogk, 65–74. Jefferson: McFarland Press.

Chivers, Sally, and Nicole Markotić, eds. 2010. *The Problem Body: Projecting Disability on Film*. Columbus: Ohio State University Press.

Citron, T., N. Brooks-Lane, D. Crandell, K. Brady, M. Cooper, and G. Revell. 2008. "A Revolution in the Employment Process of Individuals with Disabilities: Customized Employment as the Catalyst for System Change." *Journal of Vocational Rehabilitation* 28: 169–79.

Cohen, Lawrence. 2006. "Introduction: Thinking about Dementia." In *Thinking about Dementia: Culture, Loss, and the Anthropology of Senility*, ed. A. Leibing and L. Cohen, 1–19. New Brunswick: Rutgers University Press.

Compitello, Malcolm Alan. 2014. "Sketching the Future Furiously: La Movida, Graphic Design, and the Urban Process in Madrid." In *Toward a Cultural*

Archive of La Movida: Back to the Future, ed. Ed. William J. Nichols and H. Rosi Song. Madison: Farleigh Dickinson University Press. 203–32.

Contardi, A. 2002. "From Autonomy to Work Placement." In <I have this book published byWiley in 2002> *Down Syndrome across the Life Span*, ed. Monica Cuskelly, Anne Jobling, and Susan Buckley, 139–46. London, Philadelphia: Whurr.

"Convención sobre los derechos de las personas con discapacidad." 2010. http://www.sindromedown.net/wp-content/uploads/2014/09/68L_convencion.pdf

Conway, Madeline. 2000. "The Politics and Representation of Disability in Contemporary Spain." In *Contemporary Spanish Cultural Studies*, ed. Barry Jordan and Rikki Morgan-Tamosunas, 251–59. London: Arnold.

– 2001. "Representing Difference: A Study of Physical Disability in Contemporary Spanish Cinema." PhD diss., Birkbeck College, University of London.

Counsell, Colin, and Peri Stanley. 2005. "Performing Impairment: The Cultural Enactment of Disability." *Atenea* 25(1): 77–93.

Cuadrado, Jesús. 2000. *De la historieta y su uso, 1873–2000*. Madrid: Ediciones Sinsentido; Fundación Germán Sánchex Ruipérez.

Davis, Lennard J. 1995. *Enforcing Normalcy: Disability, Deafness, and the Body*. London: Verso.

– 1997. "Introduction: The Need for Disability Studies." In *The Disability Studies Reader*, 1st ed., ed. L.J. Davis, 1–6. New York: Routledge.

– 2013. *The End of Normal: Identity in a Biocultural Era*. Ann Arbor: University of Michigan Press.

Davis, Lennard J., ed. [1997]2013. *The Disability Studies Reader*, [1st ed.]. 4th ed. New York: Routledge.

de la Rosa, Mercedes. 2007. "A veces oigo voces" [Review]. *El País*, 14 October. http://elpais.com/diario/2007/10/14/eps/1192342546_850215.html

Discapacidades humanas. 2010. 2 discs. Madrid: Fundación ONCE/Productora FARO. DVD.

Dopico, Pablo. 2005. *El cómic underground español, 1970–1980*. Madrid: Cátedra.

Duñó, Rosó, Esther Pousa, Cristina Domènech, Ainhoa Díez, Ada Ruiz, and Roser Guillamat. 2001. "Subjective Quality of Life in Schizophrenia Outpatients in a Catalan Urban Site." *Journal of Nervous and Mental Disease* 189(10): 685–90. https://doi.org/10.1097/00005053-200110000-00005

Ehrlich, Linda C. 1995. "Interior Gardens: Víctor Érice's 'Dream of Light' and the 'Bodegón' Tradition." *Cinema Journal* 34(2): 22–36. https://doi.org/10.2307/1225834

– 2000. *An Open Window: The Cinema of Víctor Érice*. Lanham: Scarecrow Press.

Enns, Anthony, and Christopher R. Smit, eds. 2001a. *Screening Disability: Essays on Cinema and Disability*. Lanham: University Press of America.
Enns, Anthony, and Christopher R. Smit. 2001b. "Introduction: The State of Cinema and Disability Studies."In *Screening Disability: Essays on Cinema and Disability*., ed. A. Enns and C.R. Smit, ix–xvii. Lanham: University Press of America. https://doi.org/10.1007/978-1-4613-0171-4_1
Erevelles, Nirmala, and Andrea Minear. 2013. "Unspeakable Offenses: Untangling Race and Disability in Discourses of Intersectionality." In *The Disability Studies Reader*, 4th ed, ed. Lennard J. Davis. <pages?> New York: Routledge.
Érice, Víctor. 1992. *El sol del membrillo*. Rosebud Films. Film.
Fernández de Castro, Félix. 2010. *María y yo*. Bausan Films and Pelis Chulas. Film.
Ferreira, Miguel A.V. 2008. "Una aproximación sociológica a la discapacidad desde el modelo social: apuntes caracteriológicos." *Revista Española de Investigaciones Sociológicas (REIS)* 124(124): 141–74. https://doi.org/10.2307/40184909
Ferreras, Ignacio, dir. 2011. *Arrugas*. Perro Verde. Film.
Fiedler, Leslie. 1978. *Freaks: Myths and Images of the Secret Self*. New York: Simon and Schuster.
Fink Berman, Margaret. 2010. "Imagining an Idiosyncratic Belonging: Representing Disability in Chris Ware's 'Building Stories.'" In *The Comics of Chris Ware: Drawing Is a Way of Thinking*, ed. David M. Ball and Martha B. Kuhlman,191–205. Jackson: University Press of Mississippi. https://doi.org/10.14325/mississippi/9781604734423.003.0014
Fontanella, Lee. 1981. *La historia de la fotografía en España: desde sus orígenes a 1900*. Madrid: El Viso.
Foss, Chris, Jonathan W. Gray, and Zach Whalen, eds. 2016. *Disability in Comic Books and Graphic Narratives*. New York: Palgrave Macmillan. https://doi.org/10.1057/9781137501110
Foucault, Michel. 1973. *Madness and Civilization: A History of Insanity in the Age of Reason*. Trans. Richard Howard. New York: Vintage. Print
– 1994. *The Birth of the Clinic: An Archaeology of Medical Perception*. Trans. A.M. Sheridan Smith. New York: Vintage.
– 1995. *Discipline and Punish: The Birth of the Prison*, 2nd ed. Trans. Alan Sheridan. New York: Vintage.
– 2006. *History of Madness*, ed. Jean Khalfa. Trans. J. Khalfa and Jonathan Murphy. London: Routledge.
Francis, Leslie P. 2009. "Understanding Autonomy in Light of Intellectual Disability." In *Disability and Disadvantage*, ed. Kimberley Brownlee and

Adam Cureton, 200–15. Oxford: Oxford University Press. https://doi.org/10.1093/acprof:osobl/9780199234509.003.0008

Fraser, Benjamin R. 2007. "Deaf Cultural Production in Twentieth-Century Madrid." *Sign Language Studies* 7(4): 431–57. https://doi.org/10.1353/sls.2007.0022

– 2008. "Toward a Philosophy of the Urban: Henri Lefebvre's Uncomfortable Appropriation of Bergsonism." *Environment and Planning. D: Society and Space* 26(2): 338–58. https://doi.org/10.1068/d5307

– 2010a. "The Work of (Creating) Art: Judith Scott's Fiber Art, Lola Barrera and Iñaki Peñafiel's *¿Qué tienes debajo del sombrero?* (2006), and the Challenges Faced by People with Developmental Disabilities." *Cultural Studies* 24(4): 508–32. https://doi.org/10.1080/09502380903406684

– 2010b. "Spain, 1795: A Reconsideration of Lorenzo Hervás y Panduro (1735–1809) and the Visual Language of the Deaf." *Dieciocho* 33(2): 259–77.

– 2010c. *Encounters with Bergson(ism) in Spain: Reconciling Philosophy, Literature, Film, and Urban Space.* Chapel Hill: North Carolina Studies in the Romance Languages and Literatures / University of North Carolina Press.

– 2011a. "Toward Autonomy in Love and Work: Situating the Film *Yo, también* (2009) within the Political Project of Disability Studies." *Hispania* 94(1): 1–12.

– 2011b. *Henri Lefebvre and the Spanish Urban Experience: Reading the Mobile City.* Lewisburg: Bucknell Univeristy Press.

– 2011c. "Ildefons Cerdà's Scalpel: A Lefebvrian Perspective on Nineteenth-Century Urban Planning." *Catalysis Reviews* 25: 181–200.

– 2012. "Visualizing Spain's Enlightenment: The Marginal Universality of Deafness." In *Sociability and Cosmopolitanism: Social Bonds on the Fringes of the Enlightenment*, ed. Scott Breuninger and David Burrow, 27–45. London: Pickering and Chatto.

– 2013a. *Disability Studies and Spanish Culture: Films, Novels, the Comic, and the Public Exhibition*. Liverpool: Liverpool University Press.

– 2013b. "Disability Art, Visibility, and the 'Right to the City': The 'Trazos Singulares' (2011) Exhibit at Madrid's Nuevos Ministerios Metro Station." *Arizona Journal of Hispanic Cultural Studies* 17(1): 245–62. https://doi.org/10.1353/hcs.2013.0014

– 2013c. "Salvador García Jiménez, 'autor de minorías': La novela *Angelicomio* (1981) y el modelo social de la discapacidad." *Bulletin of Spanish Studies* 90(8): 1339–56. https://doi.org/10.1080/14753820.2013.847160

– 2014. *Antonio López García's Everyday Urban Worlds*. Lanham: Bucknell University Press. Print

– 2015. "Review of *Accessible Citizenships: Disability, Nation, and the Cultural Politics of Greater Mexico* by Julie Avril Minich." *Arizona Journal of Hispanic Cultural Studies* 19: 291–3.

– 2016b. "Senescence, Alzheimer's Dementia, and the Semi-Subjective in Ignacio Ferreras's Film *Arrugas*." *Journal of Literary and Cultural Disability Studies* 10(1): 21–35. https://doi.org/10.3828/jlcds.2016.2

Fraser, Benjamin, ed. 2009. *Deaf History and Culture in Spain: A Reader of Primary Sources*. Washington, DC: Gallaudet University Press.

– 2016a. *Cultures of Representation: Disability in World Cinema Contexts*. New York: Wallflower Press, Columbia University Press. https://doi.org/10.7312/fras17748

Fraser, Benjamin, Susan Larson, and Malcolm Compitello. 2014. "Notes on the Renegotiation of a Hispanic Studies Canon: *Confronting Our Canons*." *ADFL Bulletin* 43(1): 77–90. https://doi.org/10.1632/adfl.43.1.77

Gallardo, María, and Miguel Gallardo. 2007. *María y yo*. Bilbao: Astiberri.

– 2015. *María cumple 20 años*. Bilbao: Astiberri.

Gámez Fuentes, María José. 2005. "Representing Disability in 90's Spain: The Case of ONCE." *Journal of Spanish Cultural Studies* 6(3): 305–18. https://doi.org/10.1080/14636200500312367

García, Santiago. 2010. *La novela gráfica*. Bilbao: Astiberri.

García Roure, Abel, dir. 2008. *Una cierta verdad*. Evohé Films. Film.

Garland-Thomson, Rosemarie. 1997. *Extraordinary Bodies: Figuring Physical Disability in American Culture and Literature*. New York: Columbia University Press.

– 2002a. "Integrating Disability, Transforming Feminist Theory." In *Feminisms Redux: An Anthology of Literary Theory and Criticism*, ed. Robyn Warhol-Down and Diane Price Herndl, 487–513. New Brunswick: Rutgers University Press.

– 2002b. "The Politics of Staring: Visual Rhetorics of Disability in Popular Photography." In *Disability Studies: Enabling the Humanities*, ed. Sharon Snyder, Brenda Jo Bruggemann, and Rosemarie Garland-Thomson, 56–75. New York: Modern Language Association.

– 2005. "Disability and Representation." *PMLA* 120(2): 522–7.

– 2009. *Staring: How We Look*. Oxford: Oxford University Press.

Garland-Thomson, Rosemarie, ed. 1996. *Freakery: Cultural Spectacles of the Extraordinary Body*. New York: NYU Press.

Garrett, Victoria L. 2016. "Violence, Injury, and Disability in Recent Latin American Film." In *Libre Acceso: Latin American Literature and Film through Disability Studies*, ed. S. Antebi and B. Jörgensen, 135–51. Albany: SUNY Press.

Gasca, Luis, and Román Gubern. 2001. *El discurso del comic*, 4th ed. Madrid: Cátedra (Signo e imagen).

Gavioli, Nicola. 2016. "Mythicizing Disability: The Life and Opinions of (*what is left of*) Estamira." In *Libre Acceso: Latin American Literature and Film through Disability Studies*, ed. S. Antebi and B. Jörgensen, 191–208. Albany: SUNY Press.

Gill, Michael. 2015. *Already Doing It: Intellectual Disability and Sexual Agency*. Minneapolis: University of Minnesota Press.

– 2016. "Refusing Chromosomal Pairing: Inclusion, Masculinity, Sexuality, and Intimacy in *Yo, también* (2009)." In *Cultures of Representation: Disability in World Cinema Contexts*, ed. B. Fraser, 47–62. New York: Wallflower Press. https://doi.org/10.7312/fras17748-006

Goffman, Erving. 1963. *Stigma: Notes on the Management of Spoiled Identity*. Englewood Cliffs: Prentice Hall.

Greimas, A.J. 1983. *Structural Semantics*. Lincoln: University of Nebraska Press.

Groensteen, Thierry. 2007. *The System of Comics*. Trans. Bart Beaty. Jackson: University of Mississippi Press.

Guattari, Félix. 1995. *Chaosophy*, ed. Sylvère Lotringer. New York: Semiotext(e).

Gubrium, Jaber F. 1986. *Oldtimers and Alzheimer's: The Descriptive Organization of Senility*. Greenwich and London: JAI Press.

– 2003. "What Is a Good Story?" *Generations* 27(3): 21–4.

Hacking, I. 2009. "Autistic Autobiography." *Philosophical Transactions of the Royal Society of London, Series B, Biological Sciences* 364(1522): 1467–73. https://doi.org/10.1098/rstb.2008.0329

– 2010. "How We Have Been Learning to Talk about Autism: A Role for Stories." In *Cognitive Disability and Its Challenge to Moral Philosophy*, ed. L. Carlson and E.F. Kittay, 261–78. Malden: Wiley-Blackwell. https://doi.org/10.1002/9781444322781.ch15

Hall, Alice. 2016. *Literature and Disability*. New York: Routledge.

Hall, Peter. [1988]2002. *Cities of Tomorrow*, 3rd ed. Oxford: Blackwell.

Haller, Beth. 2010. *Representing Disability in an Ableist World*. Louisville: Advocado Press.

Hamilton, Heidi E. 2008. "Narrative as Snapshot: Glimpses into the Past in Alzheimer's Discourse." *Narrative Inquiry* 18(1): 53–82. https://doi.org/10.1075/ni.18.1.04ham

Hartnett, E., P. Gallager, G. Kiernan, C. Poulsen, E. Gilligan, and M. Reynolds. 2008. "Day Service Programmes for People with a Severe Intellectual Disability and Quality of Life." *Journal of Intellectual Disabilities* 12(2): 153–72. https://doi.org/10.1177/1744629508091340

Harvey, David. 1990. *The Condition of Postmodernity*. Cambridge, MA, and Oxford: Blackwell.

Hermoso, Borja. 2006. "Un escalofriante documental se adentra en los infiernos de la esquizofrenia." *El Mundo*, 6 November, 37. http://www.juliomedem.org/filmografia/archivos/Esquizofrenia_FestSevilla.pdf

Hernández, Ione, dir. 2007. *1% esquizofrenia*. Prod. Julio Medem. Alicia Produce. DVD.

Herr, Stanley S., Lawrence O. Gostin, and Harold Hongju Koh, eds. 2003. *The Human Rights of Persons with Intellectual Disabilities: Different but Equal*. Oxford: Oxford University Press.

Hevey, David. 1997. "The Enfreakment of Photography." In *The Disability Studies Reader*, 1st ed., ed. Lennard J. Davis. New York and London: Routledge. 332–47.

– 1992. *The Creatures Time Forgot: Photography and Disability Imagery*. London and New York: Routledge. Print

– 1993. "From Self-Love to the Picket Line: Strategies for Change in Disability Representation." *Disability, Handicap, and Society* 8(4): 423–9. https://doi.org/10.1080/02674649366780391

Hight, Craig. 2007. "American Splendor: Translating Comic Autobiography into Drama-Documentary." In *Film and Comic Books*, ed. Ian Gordon, Mark Jancovich, and Matthew P. McAllister, 180–98. Jackson: University Press of Mississippi.

Hirtz, Bárbara. 2009. "Más del 60% de los discapacitados intelectuales están en paro." www.buscarempleo.es, 18 December.

Hoeksema, Thomas B., and Christopher R. Smit. 2001. "The Fusion of Film Studies and Disability Studies." In *Screening Disability: Essays on Cinema and Disability*, ed. A. Enns and C.R. Smit, 33–43. Lanham: University Press of America.

Hopkins, Jeff. 1994. "Mapping of Cinematic Places: Icons, Ideology, and the Power of (Mis)representation." In *Place, Power, Situation, and Spectacle: A Geography of Film*, ed. S. Aitken and L. Zonn, 47–65. Lanham: Rowman and Littlefield.

"Inauguración de la exposición 'Trazos Singulares.'" 2011. Speech by José Ignacio Echeverría, 12 April. Videoclip on www.madrid.org 'Prensa' page. Web.

Jakobson, Roman. 1960. "Linguistics and Poetics." In *Style in Language*, ed. T. Sebeok, 350–77. Cambridge, MA: MIT Press. Print

Jeffreys, Mark. 2002. "The Visible Cripple (Scars and Other Disfiguring Displays Included)." In *Disability Studies: Enabling the Humanities*, ed.

Sharon L. Snyder, Brenda Jo Brueggemann, and Rosemarie Garland-Thomson, 31–9. New York: MLA Publications.

Jennings, Bruce. 2010. "Agency and Moral Relationship in Dementia." In *Cognitive Disability and Its Challenge to Moral Philosophy*, ed. L. Carlson and E.F. Kittay, 171–82. Malden: Wiley-Blackwell. https://doi.org/10.1002/9781444322781.ch10

Johnston, Kirsty. 2009. "Building a Canadian Disability Arts Network: An Intercultural Approach." *TRiC/RTaC* 30(1–2): 152–74. Web.

Jordà, Joaquim, dir. 1999. *Monos como Becky*. Canal+ España. DVD.

– 2007. *Más allá del espejo*. Alicia Produce. Film.

Juárez-Almendros, Encarnación. 2010. "Aging Women and Disability in Early Modern Spanish Literature." In *Disability in the Middle Ages: Reconsiderations and Reverberations*, ed. Joshua R. Eyler, 197–208. Farnham: Ashgate.

Juárez-Almendros, Encarnación, ed. 2013. "Disability Studies in the Hispanic World: Proposals and Methodologies." Special section of the *Arizona Journal of Hispanic Cultural Studies* 18: 151–261.

Kafer, Alison. 2013. *Feminist Queer Crip*. Bloomington: Indiana University Press.

Kittay, Eva Feder. 1999. *Love's Labor: Essays on Equality, Dependence, and Care*. New York: Routledge.

– 2001. "When Caring Is Just and Justice Is Caring: Justice and Mental Retardation." Print *Public Culture* 13(3): 557–79. https://doi.org/10.1215/08992363-13-3-557

Kittay, Eva Feder, and Licia Carlson, eds. 2010. *Cognitive Disability and Its Challenge to Moral Philosophy*. Malden: Wiley-Blackwell. https://doi.org/10.1002/9781444322781

Kittay, E.F., Bruce Jennings, and Angela A. Wasunna. 2005. "Dependency, Difference, and the Global Ethic of Longterm Care." *Journal of Political Philosophy* 13(4): 443–69. https://doi.org/10.1111/j.1467-9760.2005.00232.x

Kitwood, Tom. 2011. *Dementia Reconsidered: The Person Comes First*. Berkshire: Open University Press.

Kracauer, Siegfried. 1968. *Theory of Film: The Redemption of Physical Reality*. New York and Oxford: Oxford University Press.

Lane, Harlan. 1993. *The Mask of Benevolence: Disabling the Deaf Community*. New York: Vintage.

Lashley, Katherine. 2016. "Displaying Autism: The Thinking and Images of *Temple Grandin* (2010)." In *Cultures of Representation: Disability in World Cinema Contexts*, ed. B. Fraser, 126–40. New York: Wallflower Press. https://doi.org/10.7312/fras17748-011

Lefebvre, Henri. 1991a. *The Production of Space*. Trans. Donald Nicholson-Smith. Oxford: Blackwell.

– 1991b. *Critique of Everyday Life*, vol. 1. Trans. John Moore. London and New York: Verso.

– 1996. "The Right to the City." In *Writings on Cities*, ed. and trans. E. Kofman and E. Lebas, 63–181. Oxford: Blackwell.

– 2003. *The Urban Revolution*. Trans. Robert Bononno. Minneapolis: University of Minnesota Press.

Lefèvre, Pascal. 2007. "Incompatible Visual Ontologies? The Problematic Adaptation of Drawn Images." In *Film and Comic Books*, ed. Ian Gordon, Mark Jancovich, and Matthew P. McAllister, 1–12. Jackson: University Press of Mississippi.

LeFrancois, Brenda A., Robert J. Menzies, and Geoffrey Reaume, eds. 2013. *Mad Matters: A Critical Reader in Canadian Mad Studies*. Toronto: Canadian Scholars' Press.

Leibing, Annette, and Lawrence Cohen, eds. 2006. *Thinking about Dementia: Culture, Loss, and the Anthropology of Senility*. New Brunswick: Rutgers University Press.

Lewis, Bradley. 2013. "A Mad Fight: Psychiatry and Disability Activism." In *The Disability Studies Reader*, 4th ed., ed. L.J. Davis, 115–31. New York: Routledge.

Lige, Sara. 2011. "Adults with Intellectual Disabilities and the Visual Arts: 'It's NOT Art Therapy.'" MA thesis, Interdisciplinary Studies, University of British Columbia, Okanagan.

Lindemann, Hilda. 2010. "Holding One Another (Well, Wrongly, Clumsily) in a Time of Dementia." In *Cognitive Disability and Its Challenge to Moral Philosophy*, ed. L. Carlson and E.F. Kittay, 161–70. Malden: Wiley-Blackwell. https://doi.org/10.1002/9781444322781.ch9

Longmore, Paul K. 1985. "Screening Stereotypes: Images of Disability." *Social Policy* 16(1): 31–7.

– 2001. "Screening Stereotypes: Images of Disability." In *Screening Disability: Essays on Cinema and Disability*, ed. A. Enns and C.R. Smit, 1–18. Lanham: University Press of America.

Luca de Tena, Torcuato. [1979]2009. *Los renglones torcidos de Dios*. Madrid: Planeta.

Malick, Terrence. 1998. *The Thin Red Line*. Twentieth Century Fox. Film.

Marr, Matthew J. 2009. "Representation and the Cultural Politics of Aging in *Justino, un asesino de la tercera edad* (La Cuadrilla, 1994)." *Studies in Hispanic Cinemas* 6(2): 139–52. https://doi.org/10.1386/shci.6.2.139/1

– 2013. *The Politics of Age and Disability in Contemporary Spanish Film*. New York: Routledge.
Marshall, Tim. 2004. "Introduction." In *Transforming Barcelona*, ed. Tim Marshall, 1–24. London and New York: Routledge.
Masumoto, Kouhei, Tsuneo Takai, Satory Tsuneto, and Tetsuo Kashiwagi. 2004. "Influence of Motoric Encoding on Forgetting Function of Memory for Action Sentences in Patients with Alzheimer's Disease." *Perceptual and Motor Skills* 98(1): 299–306. https://doi.org/10.2466/pms.98.1.299-306
McCloud, Scott. 1994. *Understanding Comics: The Invisible Art*. New York: Harper Collins.
McDonagh, Patrick. 2008. *Idiocy: A Cultural History*. Liverpool: Liverpool University Press.
McRuer, Robert. 2006. *Crip Theory: Cultural Signs of Queerness and Disability*. New York: NYU Press.
– 2010. "Disability Nationalism in Crip Times." *Journal of Literary and Cultural Disability Studies* 4(2): 163–78. https://doi.org/10.3828/jlcds.2010.13
McRuer, Robert, and Anna Mollow, eds. 2012. *Sex and Disability*. Durham: Duke University Press. https://doi.org/10.1215/9780822394877
McWade, Brigit, Damian Milton, and Peter Beresford. 2015. "Mad Studies and Neurodiversity: A Dialogue." *Disability and Society* 30(2): 305-9. https://doi.org/10.1080/09687599.2014.1000512
Medina, Raquel. 2013. "From the Medicalization of Dementia to the Politics of Memory and Identity in Three Spanish Documentary Films: *Bicicleta, cullera, poma, Las voces de la memoria*, and *Bucarest: la memòria perduda*." *Ageing and Society* •••: 1688–710.
Meeuf, Russell. 2013. "*Chocolate*'s Ass-Kicking Autistic Savant: Disability, Globalization, and the Action Cinema." In *Different Bodies*, ed. M.E. Mogk, 101–8. Jefferson: McFarland Press.
Merino, Ana. 2002. *El cómic hispánico*. Madrid: Cátedra.
Merlo, Claudia. 2009. "Esquizofrenia hoy: superando el estigma." Máster de Psicología Clínica y de la Salud/Instituto Superior de Estudios Psicológicos (ISEP). http://www.isep.es/tesina/esquizofrenia-hoy-superando-el-estigma
Migliori, A., D. Mank, T. Grossi, and P. Rogan. 2007. "Integrated Employment or Sheltered Workshops: Preferences of Adults with Intellectual Disabilities, Their Families, and Staff." *Journal of Vocational Rehabilitation* 26: 5–19.
Millet-Gallant, Ann. 2013. "Sculpting Body Ideals: *Alison Lapper Pregnant* and the Public Display of Disability." In *The Disability Studies Reader*, 4th ed., ed. L.J. Davis, 398–410. New York: Routledge.

– 2004. "Exceeding the Frame: The Photography of Diane Arbus." *Disability Studies Quarterly* 24(4): no pag. http://dsq-sds.org/article/view/881/1056

Minich, Julie. 2010. "Life on Wheels: Disability, Democracy, and Political Inclusion in *Live Flesh* and *The Sea Inside*." *Journal of Literary and Cultural Disability Studies* 4(1): 17–32. https://doi.org/10.1353/jlc.0.0040

– 2014. *Accessible Citizenships: Disability, Nation, and the Cultural Politics of Greater Mexico*. Philadelphia: Temple University Press.

Mirón Canelo, José Antonio, Montserrat Alonso Sardón, Alberto Serrano López de las Hazas, and María del Carmen Sáenz González. 2008. "Calidad de vida relacionada con la salud en personas con discapacidad intelectual en España." *Rev Panam Salud Pública/Pan Am J Public Health* 24(5): 336–44. https://doi.org/10.1590/S1020-49892008001100006

Mitchell, David T., and Sharon L. Snyder. 2000. *Narrative Prosthesis: Disability and the Dependencies of Discourse*. Ann Arbor: University of Michigan Press.

– 2015. *The Biopolitics of Disability: Neoliberalism, Ablenationalism, and Peripheral Embodiment*. Ann Arbor: University of Michigan Press.

– 2016. "Global In(ter)dependent Disability Cinema: Targeting Ephemeral Domains of Belief and Cultivating Aficionados of the Body." In *Cultures of Representation: Disability in World Cinema Contexts*, ed. B. Fraser, 1–17. New York: Wallflower Press. https://doi.org/10.7312/fras17748-004

Mitchell, David T., and Sharon L. Snyder, eds. 1997. *The Body and Physical Difference: Discourses of Disability*. Ann Arbor: University of Michigan Press.

– 2010. "The Geo-Politics of Ablenationalism." Special issue of the *Journal of Literary and Cultural Disability Studies* 4(2). Web.

Mitchell, Don. 2003. *The Right to the City: Social Justice and the Fight for Public Space*. New York and London: Guilford.

Mogk, Marja Evelyn. 2013. *Different Bodies*. Jefferson: McFarland Press.

Montoya, Daniela T. 2009. "*Una cierta verdad*" [Review]. *Encadenados: Revista de Cine*, 14 May. http://www.encadenados.org/rdc/sin-perdon/1340-una-cierta-verdad-3

Morris, Errol, dir. 1988. *The Thin Blue Line*. American Playhouse. Film.

Morris, M. 2002. "Economic Independence and Inclusion." In *Down Syndrome: Visions for the 21st Century*, ed. W.I. Cohen, L. Nadel, and M.E. Madnick, 17–81. New York: Wiley-Liss.

Mulvey, Laura. [1975]1999. "Visual Pleasure and Narrative Cinema." In *Film Theory and Criticism: Introductory Readings*, ed. Leo Braudy and Marshall Cohen, 833–44. New York: Oxford University Press.

Murray, Stuart. 2008. *Representing Autism: Culture, Narrative, Fascination*. Liverpool: Liverpool University Press.

Murray, Stuart, and Clare Barker, eds. 2010. "Disability Postcolonialism." Special issue of *Journal of Literary and Cultural Disability Studies* 4(3). Web.

Nichols, William J., and H. Rosi Song, eds. 2014. *Toward a Cultural Archive of La Movida: Back to the Future*. Madison: Farleigh Dickinson University Press.

Neier, Aryeh, and David J. Rothman. 2015. "Under Lock and Key: How Long?" *New York Review of Books*,17 December, 5, 70–2.

Nelson, James Lindemann. 2010. "Alzheimer's Disease and Socially Extended Mentation." In *Cognitive Disability and Its Challenge to Moral Philosophy*, ed. L. Carlson and E.F. Kittay, 225–36. Malden: Wiley-Blackwell. https://doi.org/10.1002/9781444322781.ch13

Nielsen, Niels Peter, Elisabeth H. Wiig, Siegbert Warkentin, and Lennart Minthon. 2004. "Clinical Utility of Color-Form Naming in Alzheimer's Disease: Preliminary Evidence." *Perceptual and Motor Skills* 99: 1201–4. Web.

Norden, Martin F. 1994. *Cinema of Isolation: A History of Physical Disability in the Movies*. New Brunswick: Rutgers University Press.

Ochoa, S., J.M. Haro, J. Autonell, A. Pendàs, F. Teba, and M. Márquez, and the NEDES Group. 2003. "Met and Unmet Needs of Schizophrenia Patients in a Spanish Sample." *Schizophrenia Bulletin* 29(2): 201–10. http://schizophreniabulletin.oxfordjournals.org/content/29/2/201.full.pdf; https://doi.org/10.1093/oxfordjournals.schbul.a006998.

Orsini, A., L. Trojano, L. Chiacchio, and D. Grossi. 1988. "Immediate Memory Spans in Dementia." *Perceptual and Motor Skills* 67(1): 267–72. https://doi.org/10.2466/pms.1988.67.1.267

O'Toole, Corbett. 2013. "Disclosing Our Relationships to Disabilities: An Invitation for Disability Studies Scholars." *Disability Studies Quarterly* 33(2): no pag. Web.

Pallisera, M., M. Vilà, and M. Josep Valls. 2003. "The Current Situation of Supported Employment in Spain: Analysis and Perspectives Based on the Perception of Professionals." *Disability and Society* 18(6): 797–810. https://doi.org/10.1080/0968759032000119523

Palmer-Mehta, Valerie. 2013. "Refracting Mental Illness through Disability: Towards a New Politic of Cultural Locations." *Journal of American Culture* 36(4): 353–63. https://doi.org/10.1111/jacc.12055

Pardeck, J.T. 2005. "An Analysis of the Americans With Disabilities Act in the Twenty-First Century." *Journal of Social Work in Disability and Rehabilitation* 4(1): 121–51. https://doi.org/10.1300/J198v04n01_08

Parmenter, T. 1991. "Quality of Life for People with Developmental Disabilities." *International Review of Research in Mental Retardation* 18: 247–87. Web.

– 1996. "Living in the Community." In *New Approaches to Down Syndrome*, ed. Brian Stratford and Pat Gunn, 421–23. London: Cassell.

Pasolini, Pier Paolo. 1988. *Heretical Empiricism*, ed. Louise K. Barnett. Trans. Nem Lawton and Louise K. Barnett. Bloomington: Indiana University Press.

Pastor, Álvaro and Antonio Naharro, dirs. 2009. *Yo, también*. Golem. Film

Peón Sánchez, M. J. 2004. "Atención de enfermería hacia el cuidador principal del paciente con enfermedad de Alzheimer. Prevención y cuidados en el 'síndrome del cuidador'" [Nursing care for the primary caregiver of the Alzheimer's patient. Prevention of and care for the 'caregiver syndrome']. *Enfermería Científica*, 264–5: 16–22. Web.

Petrus, Anna. 2009. "Una cierta verdad" [Review]. Blogs&docs, 4 May. http://www.blogsandocs.com/?p=384

Ping-Ying Li, E., A. Sing-Fai Tam, and D. Wai-Kwong Man. 2006. "Exploring the Self-Concepts of Persons with Intellectual Disabilities." *Journal of Intellectual Disabilities* 10(1): 19–34. https://doi.org/10.1177/1744629506062270

Plann, Susan. 1997. *A Silent Minority: Deaf Education in Spain 1550–1835.* Berkeley: University of California Press.

Pointon, Anne, and Chris Davies, eds. 2008. *Framed: Interrogating Disability in the Media*. London: British Film Institute.

Postema, Barbara. 2013. *Narrative Structure in Comics: Making Sense of Fragments*. Rochester: RIT Press.

Pousa, Esther, Rosó Duñó, Gildas Brébion, Anthony S. David, Ada I. Ruiz, and Jordi E. Obiols. 2008. "Theory of Mind Deficits in Chronic Schizophrenia: Evidence for State Dependence." *Psychiatry Research* 158(1): 1–10. http://www.elsevier.com/locate/psychres; https://doi.org/10.1016/j.psychres.2006.05.018

Prendergast, Catherine. 2013. "The Unexceptional Schizophrenic: A Post-Postmodern Introduction." In *The Disability Studies Reader*, 4th ed., ed. L.J. Davis, 236–45. New York: Routledge.

Price, Margaret. 2013. "Defining Mental Disability." In *The Disability Studies Reader*, 4th ed., ed. L.J. Davis, 298–307. New York: Routledge.

Prince, Stephen. 1999. "The Discourse of Pictures: Iconicity and Film Studies." In *Film Theory and Criticism*, 5th ed., ed. Leo Braudy and Marshall Cohen, 99–117. Oxford: Oxford University Press.

Propp, Vladimir. 1968. *Morphology of the Folk Tale*. Austin: University of Texas Press.

– 2016. "Otras competencias: Ethnobotany, the *Badianus codex*, and Metaphors of Mexican Memory Loss and Disability in *Las buenas hierbas* (2010)." In

Libre Acceso: Latin American Literature and Film through Disability Studies, ed. S. Antebi and B. Jörgensen, 83–101. Albany: SUNY Press.
Prout, Ryan. 2008. "Cryptic Triptych: (Re)Reading Disability in Spanish Film 1960-2003: *El cochecito, El jardín de las delicias*, and *Planta cuarta*." *Arizona Journal of Hispanic Cultural Studies* 12: 165–87.
Puar, Jasbir. 2007. *Terrorist Assemblages: Homonationalism in Queer Times*. Durham: Duke University Press. https://doi.org/10.1215/9780822390442
Quayson, Ato. 2007. *Aesthetic Nervousness: Disability and the Crisis of Representation*. New York: Columbia University Press.
Quintanilla, Alberto. 2007. "Ione Hernández: 'A un esquizofrénico se le ayuda queriéndole y aceptándole.'" *El País*, 22 March. http://cultura.elpais.com/cultura/2007/03/22/actualidad/1174518003_850215.html
Ramanathan, Vaidehi. 2008. "Applied Linguistics Redux: A Derridean Exploration of Alzheimer Lifehistories." *Applied Linguistics* 29(1): 1–23. https://doi.org/10.1093/applin/amm013
Rapley, Mark. 2004. *The Social Construction of Intellectual Disability*. Cambridge: Cambridge University Press. https://doi.org/10.1017/CBO9780511489884
Real-Najarro, Olga. 2011. "En salud mental: revision de algunos antecedents literarios." *Frenia* 11: 171–92. Web.
Reilly, Jamie, Amy D. Rodriguez, Martine Lamy, and Jean Neils-Strunjas. 2010. "Cognition, Language, and Clinical Pathological Features of Non-Alzheimer's Dementias: An Overview." *Journal of Communication Disorders* 43(5): 438–52. https://doi.org/10.1016/j.jcomdis.2010.04.011
Resina, Joan Ramon. 2008. *Barcelona's Vocation of Modernity: Rise and Decline of an Urban Image*. Stanford: Stanford University Press. https://doi.org/10.11126/stanford/9780804758321.001.0001
Ridge, Stanley G.M., Sinfree Makoni, and Elaine Ridge. 2003. "'I Want to Be Like a Human Again': Morbidity and Retained Ability in an Alzheimer Sufferer." *AILA Review* 16: 149–69. https://doi.org/10.1075/aila.16.13rid
Riley, Charles A. 2005. *Disability and the Media: Prescriptions for Change*. Hanover: University Press of New England.
Rivera-Cordero, Victoria. 2009. "Spatializing Illness: Embodied Deafness in Teresa de Cartagena's *Arboleda de los enfermos*." *La coronica* 37(2): 61–77.
– 2013a. "Rebuilding the Wounded Self: Impairment and Trauma in Isabel Coixet's *The Secret Life of Words* and Pedro Almodóvar's *Los abrazos rotos*." *Arizona Journal of Hispanic Cultural Studies* 17(1): 227–44. https://doi.org/10.1353/hcs.2013.0010
– 2013b. "The Self Inside and Out: Authenticity and Disability in *Mar adentro* and *Yo, también*." *Hispania* 96(1): 62–70. https://doi.org/10.1353/hpn.2013.0011

Roca, Paco. 2008. *Arrugas*. Bilbao: Astiberri.
– 2000. *Gog*. Barcelona: La Cúpula.
– 2004. *El Faro*. Bilbao: Astiberri.
– 2007. *Hijos de la Alhambra*. Madrid: Planeta.
– 2009. *Las calles de arena*. Bilbao: Astiberri.
– 2010. *El invierno del dibujante*. Bilbao: Astiberri.
– 2011. *Memorias de un hombre en pajama*. Bilbao: Astiberri.
– 2011. *La metamorphosis*. Bilbao: Astiberri.
– 2012. *El juego lúgubre*. Bilbao: Astiberri.
Roca, Paco, and Miguel Gallardo. 2009. *Emotional World Tour*. Bilbao: Astiberri.
Rodríguez Chico, Julio. 2009. "Seminci'53: Javier Angulo busca su Espiga entre lo hispano." *Film Historia* 19(1): no pag. http://revistes.ub.edu/index.php/filmhistoria/article/view/13678.
Rodríguez Herrero, Virginia. 2012. "Cine sociología y antropología. La construcción social de la ficción cinematográfica." *Gazeta de Antropología* 28(1): article 13. http://hdl.handle.net/10481/20643
Roman, Leslie G. 2009a. "The Unruly Salon: Unfasten Your Seatbelts, Take No Prisoners, Make No Apologies." *International Journal of Qualitative Studies in Education: QSE* 22(1): 1–16. https://doi.org/10.1080/09518390802581901
– 2009b. "Disability Arts and Culture as Public Pedagogy." *International Journal of Inclusive Education* 13(7): 667–75. https://doi.org/10.1080/13603110903041912
Roy, Wendy. 2009. "The Word Is Colander: Language Loss and Narrative Voice in Fictional Canadian Alzheimer's Narratives." *Canadian Literature* 203: 41–61.
Saffran, Eleanor M., and H. Branch Coslett. 1996. "'Attentional Dyslexia' in Alzheimer's Disease: A Case Study." *Cognitive Neuropsychology* 13(2): 205–28. https://doi.org/10.1080/026432996382006
Saussure, Ferdinand. 1983. *Course in General Linguistics*. London: Duckworth.
Scully, Jackie Leach. 2014. "Deaf Identities in Disability Studies: With Us or Without Us?" In *Routledge Handbook of Disability Studies*, ed. N. Watson, A. Roulstone, and C. Thomas, 109–21. London and New York: Routledge.
Sedgwick, E.K. 2002. *Touching Feeling: Affect, Pedagogy, Performativity*. Durham: Duke University Press. https://doi.org/10.1215/9780822384786
Sennett, Richard. 1992. *The Conscience of the Eye: The Design and Social Life of Cities*. New York: W.W. Norton.
Shapiro, J.P. 1994. *No Pity*. New York: Three Rivers.
Siebers, Tobin. 1998. *The Subject and Other Subjects*. Ann Arbor: University of Michigan Press.
– 2008. *Disability Theory*. Ann Arbor: University of Michigan Press.

– 2010. *Disability Aesthetics*. Ann Arbor: University of Michigan Press.
– 2013. "Disability and the Theory of Complex Embodiment." In *The Disability Studies Reader*, 4th ed., ed. L. Davis, 275–82. New York: Routledge.
Siebers, Tobin, ed. 2000. *The Body Aesthetic: From Fine Art to Body Modification*. Ann Arbor: University of Michigan Press. https://doi.org/10.3998/mpub.23061
Simmel, Georg. 2000. "The Metropolis and Mental Life." In *Readings in Social Theory: The Classic Tradition to Post-Modernism*, 3rd ed., ed. James Farganis, 149–57. New York: McGraw-Hill.
Simonsen, Kirsten. 2005. "Bodies, Sensations, Space, and Time: The Contribution from Henri Lefebvre." *Geografiska Annaler: Series B* 87(1)1: 1–14. https://doi.org/10.1111/j.0435-3684.2005.00174.x
Sisti, Dominic, and Emanuel Ezekiel. 2016. "A Better Cure for Mental Illness [Letter to the Editor]." *New York Review of Books*, 25 February, 41–2.
Smith, Angela M. 2011. *Hideous Progeny: Disability, Eugenics, and Classic Horror Cinema*. New York: Columbia University Press.
Snyder, Sharon L. 2002. "Infinities of Forms: Disability Figures in Artistic Traditions." In *Disability Studies: Enabling the Humanities*, ed. Sharon L. Snyder, Brenda Jo Brueggemann, and Rosemarie Garland-Thomson, 173–96. New York: MLA Publications.
Snyder, S.L., B.J. Brueggemann, and R. Garland-Thomson, eds. 2002. *Disability Studies: Enabling the Humanities*. New York: Modern Language Association.
Snyder, Sharon L., and David T. Mitchell. 2010. "Body Genres: An Anatomy of Disability in Film." In *The Problem Body: Projecting Disability on Film*, ed. S. Chivers and N. Markotić, 179–204. Columbus: Ohio State University Press.
– 2006. *Cultural Locations of Disability*. Chicago: University of Chicago Press.
Soja, Edward. 1989. *Postmodern Geographies: The Reassertion of Space in Critical Social Theory*. London: Verso.
Sontag, Susan. 1977. *On Photography*. New York: Farrar, Straus and Giroux.
Stephens, Elizabeth. 2011. *Anatomy as Spectacle: Public Exhibitions of the Body from 1700 to the Present*. Liverpool: Liverpool University Press.
Stiker, Henri-Jacques. [1982]1997. *A History of Disability*. Trans. William Sayers. Foreword by David T. Mitchell. Ann Arbor: University of Michigan Press.
Straus, Joseph N. 2013. "Autism as Culture." In *The Disability Studies Reader*, 4th ed., ed. L.J. Davis, 460–84. New York: Routledge.
Sulmasy, David. 2010. "Dignity, Disability, Difference, and Rights." In *Philosophical Reflections on Disability*, ed. D.C. Ralston and J. Ho,183–98. Dordrecht: Springer Verlag. Web.
Swinnen, Aagje, and Mark Schweda, eds. 2015. *Popularizing Dementia: Public Expressions and Representations of Forgetfulness*. Bielefeld: Transcript-Verlag.

Taylor, Margaret. 2005. "Access and Support in the Development of a Visual Language: Arts Education and Disabled Students." *International Journal of Art and Design Education* 24(3): 325–33. https://doi.org/10.1111/j.1476-8070.2005.00456.x

Titchkosky, Tanya. 2009. "Disability Images and the Art of Theorizing Normality." *International Journal of Qualitative Studies in Education: QSE* 22(1): 75–84. https://doi.org/10.1080/09518390802581893

– 2011. *The Question of Access: Disability, Space, Meaning*. Toronto: University of Toronto Press.

Triana Toribio, Núria. 2000. "A Punk Called Pedro: *La Movida* in the films of Pedro Almodóvar." In *Contemporary Spanish Cultural Studies*, ed. Barry Jordan and Rikki Morgan-Tamosunas, 274–82. London: Arnold.

Valverde, Miguel A. 2010. "Un dilemma bioético a propósito de los antipsicóticos." *Revista de Bioética y Derecho* 20: 4–10. http://www.bioeticayderecho.ub.es

Van Dormael, Jaco. 1995. *The Kiss*. Included on *Lumière et compagnie*. Cinétévé/Fox Lorber. Belgium: Film.

Vázquez, Asier. 2009. "Abel García Roure: Director del documental 'Una cierta verdad'" [Interview]. *Punto de Encuentro* 22: 18–20. https://consaludmental.org/publicaciones/PuntodeEncuentro22.pdf

Venneri, Annalena, Simon J. Pestell, and Paolo Caffarra. 2002. "Independent Representations for Cursive and Print Style: Evidence from Dysgraphia in Alzheimer's Disease." *Cognitive Neuropsychology* 19(5): 387–400. https://doi.org/10.1080/02643290143000204

Vilarós, Teresa M. 1998. *El mono del desencanto. Una crítica cultural de la transición española (1972–1993)*. Madrid: Siglo XXI.

Vilà, Montserrat, María Pallisera, and Judit Fullana. 2007. "Work Integration of People with Disabilities in the Regular Labour Market: What Can We Do to Improve These Processes?" *Journal of Intellectual & Developmental Disability* 32(1): 10–18. https://doi.org/10.1080/13668250701196807

Ware, Linda. 2008. "Worlds Remade: Inclusion through Engagement with Disability Art." *International Journal of Inclusive Education* 12(5–6): 563–83. https://doi.org/10.1080/13603110802377615

Watson, Nick, Alan Roulstone, and Carol Thomas, eds. 2014. *Routledge Handbook of Disability Studies*. London and New York: Routledge.

Wehman, P. 1995. "Supported Employment for People with Disabilities: What Progress Has Been Made?" In *Down Syndrome: Living and Learning in the Community*, ed. L. Nadel and D. Rosenthal, 263–75. New York: Wiley-Liss.

– 2006. "Integrated Employment: If Not Now, When? If Not Us, Who?" *Research and Practice for Persons with Severe Disabilities* 31(2): 122–6. https://doi.org/10.1177/154079690603100203

Wendell, Susan. 1996. *The Rejected Body: Feminist Philosophical Reflections on Disability*. New York: Routledge.

Westmacott, Robyn, Morris Freedman, Sandra E. Black, Kathryn A. Stokes, and Morris Moscovitch. 2004. "Temporally Graded Semantic Memory Loss in Alzheimer's Disease: Cross-Sectional and Longitudinal Studies." *Cognitive Neuropsychology* 21(2–4): 353–78. https://doi.org/10.1080/02643290342000375

Wijdicks, Eelco F.M. 2015. *Neurocinema: When Film Meets Neurology*. Boca Raton: CRC Press.

Williams, Katherine Schaap. 2009. "Enabling Richard: The Rhetoric of Disability in *Richard III*." *Disability Studies Quarterly* 29(4): no pag. http://www.dsq-sds.org/article/view/997/1181; https://doi.org/10.18061/dsq.v29i4.997

Williams, Paul, and Bonnie Shoultz. 1984. *We Can Speak for Ourselves: Self-Advocacy by Mentally Handicapped People*. Bloomington: Indiana University Press.

Williams, Raymond. [1986]2007. "The Future of Cultural Studies." In *Politics of Modernism: Against the New Conformists*, 151–162. London: Verso.

Winzer, Margaret A. 1997. "Disability and Society before the Eighteenth Century: Dread and Despair." *The Disability Studies Reader*, 1st ed., ed. Lennard J. Davis, 75–109. New York: Routledge.

Wollen, Peter. 1972. *Signs and Meaning in the Cinema*, 3rd ed. Bloomington: Indiana University Press.

Index

Toronto Iberic

1 Anthony J. Cascardi, *Cervantes, Literature, and the Discourse of Politics*
2 Jessica A. Boon, *The Mystical Science of the Soul: Medieval Cognition in Bernardino de Laredo's Recollection Method*
3 Susan Byrne, *Law and History in Cervantes' Don Quixote*
4 Mary E. Barnard and Frederick A. de Armas (eds), *Objects of Culture in the Literature of Imperial Spain*
5 Nil Santiáñez, *Topographies of Fascism: Habitus, Space, and Writing in Twentieth-Century Spain*
6 Nelson Orringer, *Lorca in Tune with Falla: Literary and Musical Interludes*
7 Ana M. Gómez-Bravo, *Textual Agency: Writing Culture and Social Networks in Fifteenth-Century Spain*
8 Javier Irigoyen-García, *The Spanish Arcadia: Sheep Herding, Pastoral Discourse, and Ethnicity in Early Modern Spain*
9 Stephanie Sieburth, *Survival Songs: Conchita Piquer's* Coplas *and Franco's Regime of Terror*
10 Christine Arkinstall, *Spanish Female Writers and the Freethinking Press, 1879-1926*

11 Margaret Boyle, *Unruly Women: Performance, Penitence, and Punishment in Early Modern Spain*
12 Evelina Gužauskytė, *Christopher Columbus's Naming in the* diarios *of the Four Voyages (1492-1504): A Discourse of Negotiation*
13 Mary E. Barnard, *Garcilaso de la Vega and the Material Culture of Renaissance Europe*
14 William Viestenz, *By the Grace of God: Francoist Spain and the Sacred Roots of Political Imagination*
15 Michael Scham, Lector Ludens*: The Representation of Games and Play in* Cervantes
16 Stephen Rupp, *Heroic Forms: Cervantes and the Literature of War*
17 Enrique Fernandez, *Anxieties of Interiority and Dissection in Early Modern Spain*
18 Susan Byrne, *Ficino in Spain*
19 Patricia M. Keller, *Ghostly Landscapes: Film, Photography, and the Aesthetics of Haunting in Contemporary Spanish Culture*
20 Carolyn A. Nadeau, *Food Matters: Alonso Quijano's Diet and the Discourse of Food in Early Modern Spain*
21 Cristian Berco, *From Body to Community: Venereal Disease and Society in Baroque Spain*
22 Elizabeth R. Wright, *The Epic of Juan Latino: Dilemmas of Race and Religion in Renaissance Spain*
23 Ryan D. Giles, *Inscribed Power: Amulets and Magic in Early Spanish Literature*
24 Jorge Pérez, *Confessional Cinema: Religion, Film, and Modernity in Spain's Development Years (1960-1975)*
25 Joan Ramon Resina, *Josep Pla: Seeing the World in the Form of Articles*
26 Javier Irigoyen-García, *"Moors Dressed as Moors": Clothing, Social Distinction, and Ethnicity in Early Modern Iberia*
27 Jean Dangler, *Edging Toward Iberia*
28 Ryan D. Giles and Steven Wagschal (eds): *Beyond Sight: Engaging the Senses in Iberian Literatures and Cultures, 1200-1750*
29 Silvia Bermúdez, *Rocking the Boat: Migration and Race in Contemporary Spanish Music*
30 Hilaire Kallendorf, *Ambiguous Antidotes: Virtue as Vaccine for Vice in Early Modern Spain*
31 Leslie Harkema, *Spanish Modernism and the Poetics of Youth: From Miguel de Unamuno to* La Joven Literatura
32 Benjamin Fraser, *Cognitive Disability Aesthetics: Visual Culture, Disability Representations, and the (In)Visibility of Cognitive Difference*

www.ingramcontent.com/pod-product-compliance
Lightning Source LLC
La Vergne TN
LVHW040151080826
844660LV00014B/920/J

* 9 7 8 1 4 8 7 5 0 2 3 3 1 *